THE CINEMA OF MALCOLM LOWRY

To a remarkable extent the filmscript of *Tender Is the Night*, which Malcolm Lowry wrote in 1949-50 with the help of Margerie Bonner Lowry, is less an adaptation of F. Scott Fitzgerald's novel than an extension of Lowry's own fiction. As Miguel Mota and Paul Tiessen show, Malcolm Lowry's script contains important passages which are really "cinematic" restatements of parts of Lowry's novel *Lunar Caustic*, and of short stories such as "Through the Panama" and "Strange Comfort Afforded by the Profession."

The editors note also the many direct and indirect allusions to elements from Lowry's master-work, *Under the Volcano* (1947), a novel regarded by many critics as one of the most "cinematic" prose works of the twentieth century. A close study of the text reveals that Lowry took on the *Tender Is the Night* project partly as a means of reopening his *Under the Volcano* narrative, of re-exploring its plot and problems and its characters and themes, and of carrying as far as possible the "cinematic" style he had begun to examine in that work.

Lowry's *Tender Is the Night* manuscript is important, then, not only as a completed, 455-page text in its own right but also as a text having a direct bearing on Lowry's own reading of *Under the Volcano* and of his sense of artistic direction after that work. Indeed, the editors consider the significance of the filmscript as a key—hitherto almost entirely overlooked—to understanding his projected multi-volume work, *The Voyage That Never Ends*.

This scholarly edition of Lowry's script presents 38 passages of varying length—from less than one page to over 100 pages—in which Lowry writes with a freedom and creativity that lead to a text narratively and stylistically quite separate and distinct from Fitzgerald's original. It excludes passages where Lowry adheres more or less slavishly, at 37 intervals, to Fitzgerald's novel, though it provides brief narrative summaries of and comments on those omitted sections.

Lowry's achievement in his filmscript demonstrates the nature of his life-long commitment to and extensive knowledge of the international cinema from the 1910s to the 1950s and also the nature of his view of the novelist's responsibility to participate in the development of film as an art.

The script also illustrates Lowry's relationship with F. Scott Fitzgerald as one in a series of literary kinships and, as the editors point out, the work becomes a criticism and analysis of both Fitzgerald's novel and of Fitzgerald himself.

MIGUEL MOTA is a doctoral candidate in the Department of English at Queen's University and co-editor, with Paul Tiessen, of a series of manuscripts by Lowry's friend, novelist, and radio-dramatist, Gerald Noxon.
PAUL TIESSEN is a professor in the Department of English and co-ordinator of communication studies at Wilfrid Laurier University. He is also editor of *The Malcolm Lowry Review*.

The Cinema of Malcolm Lowry

A Scholarly Edition of Lowry's "Tender Is the Night"

Edited with an Introduction by
MIGUEL MOTA AND PAUL TIESSEN

University of British Columbia Press
Vancouver 1990

© 1990 The Estate of Malcolm Lowry
Reprinted by permission of Literistic, Ltd.

Quotations from *Tender Is the Night* by F. Scott Fitzgerald (copyright 1933, 1934 by Charles Scribner's Sons), reprinted by permission of the publishers

Introduction and other editorial material
© 1990 Miguel Mota and Paul Tiessen

ISBN 0-7748-0345-2
Printed in Canada on acid-free paper

∞

Canadian Cataloguing in Publication Data

Lowry, Malcolm, 1909-1957
The cinema of Malcolm Lowry

Includes bibliographical references.
ISBN 0-7748-0345-2

1. Lowry, Malcolm, 1909-1957 – Motion picture plays. I. Mota, Miguel. II. Tiessen, Paul, 1944-   . III. Fitzgerald, F. Scott (Francis Scott), 1896-1940. Tender is the night. IV. Lowry, Malcolm, 1909-1957. Tender is the night. V. Title.
PN1997.T393L69 1990   822'912   c89-091652-7

This book has been published with the help of grants from the Canadian Federation for the Humanities, using funds provided by the Social Sciences and Humanities Research Council of Canada, and from the Research Office of Wilfrid Laurier University, Waterloo, Ontario, Canada.

Contents

Preface and Acknowledgements vii

Introduction 3

Works Cited in Preface and Introduction 39

A Note on the Text 43

A Scholarly Edition of Lowry's "Tender Is the Night" 45

Notes 243

Index 257

Preface and Acknowledgements

In 1965 Stephen Spender struck a note that helped to establish one of the scholarly and critical contexts for this edition of Malcolm Lowry's filmscript "Tender Is the Night." In his introduction to a reissue of Lowry's masterwork, *Under the Volcano* (1947), Spender pointed to Russian films of the mid-1920s to locate the roots of Lowry's narrative style, a style Spender called "essentially cinematic." "[T]he most direct influence on this extraordinary book is not ... from other novelists," he announced, "but from films, most of all perhaps those of Eisenstein. The movies—that is, the old, silent, caption-accompanied movies—are felt throughout the novel." Lowry scholar Sherrill Grace has developed an argument parallel to Spender's, though it is not in the Russian but in the German cinema of the 1920s, especially the silent Expressionistic films of Germany, that she has found the roots of Lowry's "cinematic" prose style. In their respective book-length studies—each entitled *Malcolm Lowry*—American scholars Daniel Dodson, Douglas Day, and Richard Hauer Costa also argued that a film aesthetic was prominent in much of Lowry's writing, and Canadian critic Anthony Kilgallin summed up the general scholarly view when he called Lowry's major work one of the "most cinematographic" novels of the century. Muriel Bradbrook, who studied with Lowry at Cambridge University in the late 1920s and early 1930s and who remembers something of the impact of cinema on the writers and literary critics—whether fellow undergraduates or faculty—there at that time, has suggested that Lowry "learnt from the cinema the art of suggestion, of collocation without comment, and transposed it into his own medium."

Of course, these critics are adding to the substantial sum of English-language literary analysis which, since 1919 or 1920, has found in cinema a model or metaphor—notwithstanding the variation of its definition from critic to critic or the variation of its application from writer to writer—for their analysis of literary style. In Lowry's case the model happens to be unusually apt, for it is persuasively argued not only by scholars analysing his novels but also by Lowry himself. In fact, Lowry insisted on having *Under the Volcano* read in terms of specific cinematic roots and, in what we have identified as the "Lowry-text" in his "Tender Is the Night" filmscript, he illustrated ways in which that might be done. Lowry always regarded cinema as a narrative medium closely allied to the novel, and in the "Lowry-text" presented in this volume, he demonstrates in a broad and general sense just what he had "learnt from the cinema." Thus, it is a text which not only illuminates Lowry's own literary aesthetic but also offers an outstanding demonstration and defence of the very idea and potential of cinema as an international art. It is a text which is a historically and conceptually rich, graphic enlargement of any of the cultural and intellectual definitions of the idea of cinema which filmmakers and theoreticians have already tested or conceptualized in this century.

In preparing this filmscript for publication we have been interested not only in the problems which arise in editing an outstanding literary manuscript, but also in questions about the development of historical and aesthetic relationships between cinema and literature. We accord Lowry the double role of artist and theoretician with respect to questions of literature and film; for all the critical emphasis on the presence of a cinema technique in his novels, so far he has been largely overlooked as a rewarding and challenging thinker and stylist in regard to these questions. Lowry's idea of cinema has so far remained obscure, preserved mainly in unpublished manuscript form in a university's archive and often distorted by scholars' largely false expectations that its expression, even when practised in its most explicitly "cinematic" manner, might, narrowly speaking, have more to do with literature and novelists and the problems of adaptation than with film and film history and creativity in their own right.

In a way it was Lowry's peculiar search for his identity as a *literary* figure and his own and many scholars' efforts to confirm and clarify such an identity that have militated against scholars giving him a place as a contributor to the practice and theory of cinema and as an original thinker with respect to understanding cinema as well as literature-and-film relationships. Lowry's life in the literary world— from 1929 to 1932 at Cambridge University as well as in Rye and on Cape Cod; from 1932 to 1934 in London and on the continent; from 1934 to 1939 in New York, Los Angeles, Mexico, and again Los Angeles; from 1939 to 1954 mainly in Canada; from 1954 to 1957 in

Europe and England—was lived mainly along its margins, though he struggled to make connections with the centre. In an important sense (and while it might even have contributed to that marginality in the literary world), Lowry's lifelong involvement as an emotionally passionate and intellectually sophisticated spectator of film and, ultimately, as a writer committed to revising and enlarging the definition of the international cinema is—despite the centrality of its place in his life and thought—even more marginal. He even took pains at certain intervals to render it invisible. It seems he felt he had to be wary of cultural prejudice throughout his career; from the late 1920s on, though he could openly indulge here and there for brief periods in imbibing fashionable mid- and late-1920s films such as those offered by the Cambridge Film Guild, it simply became less and less respectable for a literary figure to identify openly with the cinema, which in most circles had come to be identified with the popular and generally vulgar Hollywood "talkie."

In this volume we offer the substance and demonstrate the significance of Lowry's best writing for and about cinema. Readers of the Introduction will recognize our general indebtedness on the theoretical side to various studies of literature and film, such as Seymour Chatman's *Story and Discourse: Narrative Structure in Fiction and Film* (1978), Keith Cohen's *Film and Fiction: The Dynamics of Exchange* (1979), Edward Branigan's *Point of View in the Cinema: A Theory of Narration and Subjectivity in Classical Film* (1984), Colin MacCabe's *Theoretical Essays: Film, Linguistics, Literature* (1985), David Bordwell's *Narration in the Fiction Film* (1985), Bruce Morrissette's *Novel and Film: Essays in Two Genres* (1985), George M. Wilson's *Narration in Light: Studies in Cinematic Point of View* (1986), and Eisenstein's *Nonindifferent Nature* (1987).

We are indebted, too, to many scholars and filmmakers (especially those with literary roots at Cambridge University) and other people who, in response to our myriad questions, offered specific information about Lowry's own development as a writer who was as sensitive to the possibilities of film as of literature or about the immediate context in which Lowry lived and worked in different countries. To come to a full understanding of the milieux in which Lowry moved from the 1910s to the period in which he wrote the "Tender Is the Night" filmscript in 1949-50, we investigated at length and in detail the circumstances in which he found himself during these decades in England, Europe, the United States, Mexico, and Canada. We are deeply obliged to the many people around the world who have helped us to understand the forces that shaped Lowry, that most "cinematic" of twentieth-century literary artists.

In particular, we gratefully acknowledge the permission and encouragement of the late Margerie Lowry (1905-88) in the publication of this edition. Like the novelist Christopher Isherwood, who in 1950 urged Lowry to get the filmscript into print, Mrs. Lowry—who was Lowry's collaborator on the script, as on much of his work from 1939 on—was eager to see it published. With respect to our basic understanding of the structure of the filmscript, she agreed from the beginning of our discussions that the filmscript comprised two separate and alternating texts: one, an original, richly cinematic text essentially of Lowry's own making (what we here call the "Lowry-text"), which is a declaration of the power of Lowry's imagination, a manifesto of his aesthetic sensibility; the other, a text interspersed between parts of the "Lowry-text" and adhering more or less slavishly to the narrative structure and prose style of Fitzgerald's novel *Tender Is the Night*. Mrs. Lowry reinforced our interest, an interest not in any apparent adaptation of Fitzgerald which Lowry had ostensibly undertaken, but in Lowry's enactment of his own profound commitment to and extensive knowledge of cinema. In our 1960s and 1970s correspondence about Lowry and the filmscript, Margerie Lowry provided us with otherwise unknown details concerning Lowry's opportunity to fulfil as literally as possible his appetite for creation in terms of his cinematic imagination. As a culmination to our correspondence, in 1978 in Los Angeles Mrs. Lowry generously gave six consecutive days of her time to an intensive discussion of our questions concerning the filmscript.

Because Lowry expressed much of his passion for cinema only in private and because virtually no published material systematically documents aspects of most of the film worlds he entered, over the past two decades we have sought out scholars and those of his friends and other family members who either shared or had knowledge of his love. We sought out also those film society organizers and film practitioners and other professionals whose worlds he visited. Through their correspondence, sometimes augmented by conversation, they assisted us in clarifying some of the details and interpretations in our Introduction.

Not least among those to whom we owe our gratitude is Russell Lowry, Lowry's senior by only a few years; in extensive correspondence and conversation over a period of years, he generously gave us detailed portraits of his brother's encounters with the cinema during the mid- and late 1910s, when Lowry was a child growing up in Arthur Osborne Lowry's upper-middle-class family near Liverpool, and on into the mid-1920s, when Lowry would come home for holidays from the Leys School in Cambridge and ride on a motorbike with Russell to a movie in some nearby town.

Heribert Hoven of Munich, author of the 1988 German biography of Lowry, and Michael Doyé of Bonn provided us with information about Lowry's possible activities related to film in Germany when he studied there in 1928.

British filmmakers, scholars, and archivists, including Leonard Amey, Brian Baile, C. E. Baron of St. Catharine's College at Cambridge, Lowry biographer and critic Muriel Bradbrook, T. E. B. Clarke, Alistair Cooke, Ian Dalrymple, Thorold Dickson, Anthony Hodgkinson, the film historian Rachael Low, Bill Mason, R. McCarthy of the Bodleian Library, Jean Mossop of Jonathan Cape Limited, Peter Seward of the British Film Institute, and Basil Wright, shared with us a great deal of valuable information, especially about film activities at Cambridge University when Lowry was there as a student. Canadians Kenneth Blackwell of Mills Memorial Library at McMaster University and Peter McCubbin (while he was at Oxford) also helped gather information on those activities.

British novelist Arthur Calder-Marshall gave us his impressions of those same years in England when he first met Lowry. Calder-Marshall (who had been at Oxford) followed his and Lowry's mutual Cambridge University friend John Davenport to Hollywood as a scriptwriter in the mid-1930s; he helped us better understand Lowry's days in Hollywood in the fall of 1936 and also Lowry's possible associations with film personnel in Mexico from 1936 to 1938, during which time Calder-Marshall visited Lowry there.

Gerald Noxon, through nearly a decade of correspondence and conversation about European and Soviet cinema (about which his knowledge is first-hand and profound) and about Lowry (whom he, more than most of Lowry's friends, knew and understood and, at intervals, worked with intimately from the 1920s to the 1940s), provided us with many details central to an understanding of Lowry's life and thought and creative method. He also helped us to understand the situation involving the availability of serious films in London and on the continent in the late 1920s and early 1930s and at Cambridge University, where Noxon—during the first stage of his friendship with Lowry—established the Film Guild which he ran from 1929 to 1931. Noxon gave us also many details about the 1940–47 period of Lowry's life in Canada, when he, more than anyone else, was in close contact with the Lowrys and about the opportunities for filmmakers and serious filmgoers during those years in Canada. Indeed (as we read in *The Letters of Malcolm Lowry and Gerald Noxon, 1940–1952)*, it was to Noxon—then working for his friend, John Grierson, at the National Film Board of Canada—that Lowry wrote in 1940, nine years before he thrust himself upon another literary friend, Frank Taylor, with an actual script: "such great films have stormed in me day and night! One day I would like to assist you make one."

In extensive correspondence, Moira Amour, poet Earle Birney, Esther Birney, Len Chatwin, Catherine Firth, film producer Stanley Fox, film critic Clyde Gilmour, film producer Gene Lawrence, poet Dorothy Livesay, Fraser Macdonald, film producer George Robertson, artist Jack Shadbolt, Pearl Williams, and Douglas S. Wilson generously offered us their knowledge about Lowry's and others' film activities in Canada, especially in connection with the Vancouver Film Society in the late 1940s and early 1950s, during which time Lowry was writing his "Tender Is the Night" filmscript.

Frank Taylor, who, Lowry hoped, would produce that filmscript, and Jay Leyda and Christopher Isherwood (all of whom read it in 1950) generously provided us with a sense of the immediate historical context in which Lowry wrote the filmscript and in which they first reacted to it. Novelist David Markson and playwright/producer Fletcher Markle described to us some of Lowry's personal interests in film and related media in the 1940s and 1950s.

Anne Yandle, Head of the Special Collections Division of the University of British Columbia Library, where a copy of the filmscript is housed, began in 1968 to offer practical help and advice to us. The Lowry archive at the University of British Columbia is a storehouse of valuable information on Lowry and the cinema; not only better-known manuscripts but also versos of typed or holographic drafts, marginalia in prose manuscripts, unpublished letters, and even the charred remains of pages rescued after a fire destroyed the Lowrys' Dollarton cabin in British Columbia in June 1944 abound with Lowry's references to and discussions of film; we have been informed often by these, as well as by Lowry's lengthy correspondence about cinema with friends such as Clemens ten Holder of Germany and Frank Taylor.

Ellen S. Dunlap at the Humanities Research Center in Austin, Lilace Hatayama at the Library of the University of California in Los Angeles, Sara S. Hodson at the Huntington Library in San Marino, and Paula M. Larrabure of the Script Department of the Metro-Goldwyn-Mayer Film Co. helped us with several of the stages in our archival research, especially with respect to unpublished correspondence.

Preface and Acknowledgements

New Zealand scholar Chris Ackerley, Clarissa Aiken, British scholar Ronald Binns, Priscilla Bonner Woolfan (Margerie Lowry's sister), Lowry biographer Gordon Bowker, Belgian scholar Victor Doyen, Dennis J. Duffy and David Mattison of the Sound and Moving Image Division of the Provincial Archives of British Columbia, Canadian scholars Seth Feldman, Sherrill Grace, and Tony Kilgallin, the Conrad Aiken biographer Joseph Killorin, Betty Moss (a Lowry scholar who was also Margerie Lowry's close friend), British scholar Brian O'Kill, philosopher and film producer Wieland Schulz-Keil, and Canadian and British documentary filmmaker Evelyn Spice Cherry provided stimulation and encouragement in their many letters to us and, in most cases, in conversations with us.

Sheila Watson of the University of Alberta gave this project its first impetus over two decades ago. Joanne Buchan and Sheila Moore helped us with practical matters of typing, proofreading, and setting up the index. Finally, we gratefully acknowledge the permission and support of Peter Matson and of Scribner's. They joined the many others who helped us get this edition of "an amazing film" (as Jay Leyda once put it to Lowry) into print.

The Cinema of Malcolm Lowry

Introduction

Malcolm Lowry (1909-57) absorbed the best of both the European and the American cinemas; he learned equally from Griffith and Welles, Murnau and Pudovkin, Eisenstein and Lang. In the formal experiments of his fiction, in the allusions to film throughout his published letters and stories, in his notes and essays on his own forays into filmscript writing, he has enlarged and enlivened our sense of cinema, our understanding of its achievement and its potential. Lowry's is one of the supreme instances of the twentieth-century literary artist who registered the impact of cinema on the arts and on western culture in general. And more than most serious writers, he was also determined to contribute in an enlightened way to the artistic development of the new medium. The scenes from Lowry's "Tender Is the Night" filmscript, written in 1949-50 and published here for the first time, along with his simultaneous commentary reveal anew his grasp of the narrative possibilities he saw in cinema.

In his fiction and in his correspondence, Lowry insisted that it was the European art film of the 1920s that set the standard for serious cinema. In the early 1950s he often thought of his own widely acclaimed novel *Under the Volcano* (1947) as an extension of the forms of the European silent cinema, whether German or Russian or French. For example, in defining Chapters Two to Twelve as Laruelle's movie, he said of his novel, "it was my way of paying devout tribute to the French film" (*Selected Letters*, p. 192). It was the tradition of the European—especially the German—cinema he had most in mind, too, when the prospect of adapting *Under the Volcano* arose in the early 1950s. To Clemens ten Holder, the German translator of *Under the Volcano*, he wrote in October 1951:

Nothing could make us happier—happy is not the word, in fact—and what an opportunity it is!—than for a film to be made of the *Volcano* in Germany, providing it were done in the best tradition of your great films. . . . I would myself very much wish to make a treatment of the *Volcano* for the film, and I would be very anxious to work on that and the scenario with my wife, who not only was a movie actress for years, but has collaborated on one film ["Tender Is the Night"] with me . . . and who . . . knows the *Volcano* backwards. . . . [S]o, incidentally, do I, though I say it myself, and we are a first class team, the like of which is scarcely to be found, I dare say, even in Germany or anywhere else." (Tiessen, p. 135)

"[T]he *Volcano* has been a smash hit in Germany and there was even talk of making a movie of it there con Peter Lorre," he wrote gleefully in the spring of 1952 to his close friend Gerald Noxon, with whom he had long wanted to make a movie: "they sent me a contract months ago offering me fifty-fifty; I refused (even though broke) unless I— we [Lowry and his wife, Margerie] . . . (& even, the faint hope persisted, perhaps you?) . . . could have a say in the script" (*Lowry and Noxon Letters*, p. 158). Within *Under the Volcano* Lowry pays explicit homage to the films of the "Ufa days," the "days of the *Student of Prague*, and Wiene and Werner Krauss and Karl Grune . . . when a defeated Germany was winning the respect of the cultured world by the pictures she was making" (*UV*, p. 30). In letters of the early 1950s to ten Holder, he even testified that it was specifically the German cinema that had first led him, in the late 1920s, to a strong self-consciousness about his own artistic stirrings and talents, and in an October 1951 letter, he echoed the words of his novel:

I think I have seen nearly all the great German films, since the days of *Caligari*, some of them many times . . . [including] Conrad Veidt in *The Student of Prague*, and Murnau's wonderful things, all the films of the great Ufa days, and other later masterpieces. . . . [I]t is an enthusiasm that has not deserted me. . . . [O]nly recently we . . . [saw] Murnau's *Last Laugh*, Fritz Lang's *Destiny* (a pioneer piece if there ever was one) and other contemporary films and Klangfilms at the local Vancouver Film Society. (Tiessen, p. 133)

But Lowry—though he could be derisive, too—was also attracted to the Hollywood tradition with its populist strategies and successes rooted in D. W. Griffith's work of the 1910s. In 1950 he wrote with a moral and prophetic voice in response to the privileged position held by Hollywood in the lives of its mass audience; he argued that this production centre should feel some obligation to renew its commitment to the best aesthetic standards it had set years ago and take up a responsible ethical and spiritual role within society. He based his concerns on his own experience: it had been the Hollywood film that had made the strongest impact on him, when he was a child growing up in fairly prosperous middle-class circumstances outside Liverpool:

what Hollywood does is of importance in the world, especially now. . . . [T]here has never been any hesitation on Hollywood's part in infiltrating her values wherever she could reach in the world, even as far as New Brighton, England, where [I] was born. In fact for years as a boy I Malcolm . . . never saw a single British newsreel (let alone as it happened thank God a British film) only American. . . . The formative power, for better or worse, of Hollywood on the youth of the world has been colossal: and we shall never know how much our own character has been moulded by it. And it is the same in Canada. . . . To most people it's the only Sunday school, college, or military to say nothing of sexual training they ever get. ("Preface," p. 7)

Lowry felt that for all its tainted reputation, for all its pretentious artistic vulgarity, the Hollywood dream factory might still offer an artist a base flexible and resilient enough for important creative work. Mickey Mouse might still find a place somewhere alongside Pudovkin's *The End of St. Petersburg* (to take the side-by-side references still visible in charred remains of Lowry's manuscript for a proposed novel, *In Ballast to the White Sea*).

By the late 1940s, with over two decades of close observation of both film traditions behind him, Lowry felt ready to make a major statement in film himself. Through the practical use to which he decided he could put Hollywood, through the impact he felt he might make in actually reviving and transforming not only a slumping American but also a post-war international cinema, Lowry believed he could create a filmscript "intended as a director's inspiration . . . or a producer's inspiration" (*Selected Letters*, p. 205) for a Hollywood film which would have as great an effect on filmgoers as *Under the Volcano* had had on readers in the two or three preceding years.

Lowry foresaw a worldwide audience which would follow him through a visual/aural universe toward a sense of inner meaning and spiritual purpose. His film would work "nobly . . . and even greatly, even within such limitations as Hollywood provides, even those of the Catholic church," he said. "Man *wants* to be drawn upwards. (Even should the protagonist go downwards)" ("Preface," p. 10). While hoping to avoid temptations by the "ridiculous and sentimental side" ("Preface," p. 8) of such a project, he thought he would produce through it an audience that would leave the theatre "exultant and hopeful rather than depressed" ("Preface," p. 20) though the work itself might well be a tragedy. Its great artistry alone would inspire its audience: "in the sound movie as yet there is no filmic equivalent of *Antigone*, no filmic *Peer Gynt*, no *King Lear*, and so forth. ... [S]hould the film attempt seriously to reach the highest—by which we do not mean trying to portray Shakespeare which in our estimation is quite on the wrong tack—but to achieve something in its own cinematic terms, perhaps other limitations would fall away" ("Preface," p. 10):

when people say they want better films, one thing they long for is some sort of powerful reflection of the true dignity of man. ... This is not something we are just making up but something we have heard implied thousands of times. Nor is the yearning for the excellent satisfied, we suggest, whatever the financial returns, or their merits, by most of the great pseudo-serious hits that immediately come to mind: there is a sense of frustration one has seen expressed in a thousand gestures of impatience in cinema lobbies, a thousand exclamations of "after all" or "well, you know it's Hollywood" or that it's "just another movie," a thousand interruptions by people—vastly, even, to our annoyance—with no train to catch, and who have not seen the film through, but yet who go out before the end. ("Preface," pp. 10-11)

Though it has never been produced as a film, Lowry's 1949-50 filmscript is an energetic and elegant fulfilment of his intentions. It is also a complex essay on F. Scott Fitzgerald (1896-1940) and his work. And, even more significantly, it is a kind of essay and variation on *Under the Volcano*; it recasts and re-examines some of the forces and relationships explored there. It is, too, or rather, it incorporates a series of essays on the sea, on Jung, on America, on tragedy, on the human soul, and on the creative process.

As he wrote, Lowry time and again took leave of his source and followed interests of his own quite independent of Fitzgerald. The resulting "Lowry-text" within the overall filmscript, a text that is mainly the record of Lowry's own voice (a text within which is registered only here and there a smattering of Fitzgerald's words) is what is published in this volume. This "Lowry-text" lays bare the essential Lowry, extensively reflecting his published and other unpublished writing and at the same time playing upon the films he loved and upon film in general. Even as autobiography it is a rewardingly open text, inviting and revealing, in which the inner life of Lowry as artist, as critic, and as man is exposed with astonishing brilliance and candour and optimism. It is a self-portrait showing

Lowry in the act of creating not only art (while simultaneously validating that very act by comparing it with the best stages in his writing of *Under the Volcano* from 1936 to 1945) but also audience (as he speaks intimately and fully to and for the reader/viewer). It is a text the aesthetic of which is a critique and restatement, an illustration and enlargement, of his literary practice. It is a text which invites us not only to savour its own riches but also to read all of Lowry's fiction anew.

In 1909, the year Malcolm Lowry was born, James Joyce helped to establish the first movie house—though it had an uninspired opening program—in Dublin. About twenty years later, when Lowry was enjoying the screenings of the film society which Gerald Noxon had just announced at Cambridge, Joyce met Eisenstein in Paris and discussed the kinship between his *Ulysses* (1922) and Eisenstein's 1925 film *The Battleship Potemkin*. In helping to shape a new literature, Joyce and some of his co-modernists, such as Dorothy Richardson, revealed through parodic mimicry of cinema something of the impact of that new medium on high and low culture alike. But in registering the influence of cinema on the twentieth-century literary imagination, Joyce and his contemporaries were never as explicit or far-reaching as the much younger Lowry. In demonstrating in life as in art the importance of individual films and of the institutions of cinema for literary art and artist alike, Lowry went materially further than Joyce. Lowry's life in cinema—though it was often a secret life—and his thought about that world are paradigmatic within the twentieth-century literary milieu. His insights provide a way of newly experiencing and assessing literature and film alike.

Lowry started, like Joyce, with a simple enough interest in the movies. At first he saw films such as *Intolerance* on special family outings. Russell Lowry, his older brother, recalls that a little later, in summers from 1919 to 1921 and in 1926, he and Malcolm were together and often went by themselves to the movies—and to the music-hall and vaudeville—with (as he says in still remembering the pleasures of Mack Sennett, Harold Lloyd, and Tom Mix) only one aim firmly in mind: "Fun. Fun."

Lowry, however, soon began to develop an altogether new and sophisticated sense of film as art, a sense that remained with him. He became stimulated by the German films he saw during his studies in Bonn in 1928 and by films (like Paul Fejos' *The Last Moment* and Pudovkin's *The End of St. Petersburg*) he saw alone at the often empty "home of unusual films" in Liverpool (where, as he said in 1950 to Jay Leyda, he practically lived for a period in 1928). He was impressed also by the German, Russian, and French films screened at the Cambridge film society and at London's Shaftesbury Avenue Pavilion in the late 1920s and early 1930s.

With Gerald Noxon, whom Lowry in the 1940s praised as his first literary editor (for he had published Lowry's "Port Swettenham" in a 1930 issue of *Experiment*), he discussed developments in both film and literature. From 1926 to 1928 Noxon had experienced at first hand the avant-garde films on the continent. During his and Lowry's overlapping years at Cambridge (1929-31), he wrote informed essays on the Russian film; co-directed (with Stuart Legg) the 1931 documentary film called *Cambridge*; enjoyed the friendship of Humphrey Jennings, Basil Wright, and (though not a student) Len Lye; served as full-time film review editor of the weekly *Granta*; and was for Lowry a sensitive interpreter of the international film scene, which they would discuss in Noxon's rooms at Trinity College. Later—in the 1930s and early 1940s—Noxon became involved in the documentary film movement organized by John Grierson in England and then Canada. (Noxon recalls that although the hard-living Lowry sometimes went to movies in their Cambridge days simply to "sleep it off" during most of the show, Lowry would still be moved immensely by the beauty of a shot or the action of a sequence. Lowry distinguished himself as an astute re-creator even of films he did not watch in their entirety, often brilliantly rewriting the film in later conversation, not usually crudely following the baser reactions of the sort of fellow undergraduates who became the stamping, roaring, spitting, and belching mob at the Central Cinema, Hobson Street, Cambridge, he describes in his *Ultramarine* [1933].) Lowry's and Noxon's conversations about films of the last decade of the "silent" period and, simultaneously, about (as Noxon describes it in a 1964 essay on Lowry) the style Lowry might explore as a writer contributed to the effect cinema had on Lowry's literary experiments. In 1951 Lowry testified to that effect: nothing he had ever read, he said, had influenced "[his] own writing personally more than the first twenty minutes of Murnau's *Sonnenaufgang* [*Sunrise*, 1927, German director Murnau's first American film] or the first and last shots of Karl Grune's *The Street* [Germany, 1923]" (Tiessen, p. 133). And again: "the influences that have formed the *Volcano* are in a profound degree and largely German, though it may be hard to see where they come from. (It was in Bonn [in 1928] I saw Murnau's *Sonnenaufgang*; 70 minutes of this wonderful movie—though it falls to pieces later, doubtless due to the exigencies of Hollywood—have influenced me almost as much as any book I ever read, even though I've never seen it since" (*Selected Letters*, p. 239).

Hollywood films, too, remained ever present in Lowry's life. His literary mentor from 1929 to the mid-1930s, the much older American novelist, poet, and literary critic Conrad Aiken, must have kept alive for Lowry (as for Noxon, also one of Aiken's friends) the pleasures of the Hollywood cinema, which was Aiken's primary form of public entertainment; by the 1920s cinema had become the substitute, according to biographer Joseph Killorin, for Aiken's earlier interest in vaudeville and burlesque. Later in the 1930s, Lowry sporadically maintained a few contacts with Hollywood. Most notably, Lowry followed John Davenport (who, like Noxon, had been one of his Cambridge literary editors) to Hollywood in 1936. Davenport, who counted actor Michael Redgrave as a former co-editor of *Cambridge Poetry* magazine, had, with dozens of Cambridge and Oxford graduates, gone to work in the American and British cinemas. (In 1947 Lowry asked his publisher to send a review copy of *Under the Volcano* to Redgrave in Hollywood.) Many such graduates had been enticed by a film industry seeking educated writers who, it was commonly thought, would somehow cope with the sudden new demands of the "talkies." Davenport, yet another close friend of Aiken, had gone to Hollywood to work on a script for the actor Robert Donat. His presence there seemed to represent some hope for other of his friends who needed to make some money during those depression years: for Aiken, who wanted his novels made as movies; for Lowry, who wanted to work as a writer there. But no work materialized for Lowry, and he moved with his first wife, Jan Gabrial, to Mexico in November 1936.

Even in Mexico Lowry's visitors must have kept some thought of Hollywood before him. Aiken (who in 1941 tried to convince Stuart Legg, by then with the National Film Board of Canada as Grierson's main assistant, to get Lowry a job there) came in 1937, bringing along not only his new wife, Mary Hoover, but also the British surrealist painter Ed Burra, who knew Lowry from the early 1930s in England and Spain. Burra (to judge from his letters to Aiken and others) even more than Aiken seemed to live in commercial movie houses and would dwell deliciously if not deliriously on the cinema's carnivalesque charades, its visual spectacle, and even the on-screen and off-screen antics of its stars. The Oxford graduate and novelist Arthur Calder-Marshall came too, with his wife Ara. Quick to express himself sarcastically about Hollywood, Calder-Marshall was just then on leave from a kind of writing assignment there. Though Calder-Marshall must have been full of complaints about Hollywood's disdain toward creative talent—he felt he was being paid not to write—Lowry could still say to Davenport in August 1937 how much he wanted to rejoin him: "I would have liked, would like, to land some sort of job in Hollywood: who wouldn't? . . . If you had been able to help in that way it would have been swell" (JD, p. 21).

When Lowry did return to Hollywood in 1938-39, after Jan had left him in Mexico late in 1937, he was too busy with attempts to write a draft of *Under the Volcano*, and with the tumultuous vicissitudes of his chaotic life, to think much about the movies. But in the summer of 1939 he met Margerie Bonner, a former movie actress, and so Hollywood again became a topic of discussion. In September she left her job as a secretarial assistant to actress Penny Singleton to join him in Vancouver, where he had been placed by his father's legal representative when war broke out.

From 1939 to 1945 in Canada Lowry worked primarily on *Under the Volcano*, with encouragement and help mainly from Margerie, whom he married in December 1940. From his wilderness shack at Dollarton, outside Vancouver, he also maintained important contact with Gerald Noxon, who from 1940 to 1945 offered advice and prodding in getting Lowry to finish *Under the Volcano* and who also talked with Lowry about movies. In 1940, when Noxon held out some hope that Lowry might join him in a film job at the National Film Board in Ottawa, Lowry replied quickly and excitedly. He claimed status as a Canadian "Pudovkin of the Outhouse" eager to help Noxon even in some such "meek capacity as writing the least important part of the dialogue for a film about icebreakers" (*Lowry and Noxon Letters*, pp. 32-33). Lowry's joke, begun with serious references to the nature of the documentary and concluding with a punning reference to Eisenstein in his comic toast to Noxon's "Thunder over Canada," included a selective self-portrait—a gently mocking caricature of his own deeper feelings—of his life as a member of the film audience:

when I read your suggestion that there was a possibility of work . . . upon films, and at that, possibly, with yourself [in Toronto], I rubbed my eyes. It is, of course, probably some kind of joke—too good to be true. However, in case it is not a joke it has occurred to me that I might really be able to lend some useful assistance. . . . I am assuming that, if that work is upon documentary films, that you have to struggle against the form but at the same time accept it much as a poet no fool for iambic pentametres but committed to them has to struggle with them and against them: I have seen a great film about a duck, about an African lung fish, about Latter Day Saints in Utah. As for propaganda, good propaganda, I take it, is good art. (e.g. *The River*.) I have not seen the Hemingway film about Spain, but I did see one in Mexico called *España in Llames* [sic], which made me go straight out and land in gaol. That similar results were expected from such films as *Storm over Asia*—I will never forget how [in Cambridge] you made the gramophone play, in the silver fox scene, Joe Venuti's bamboozling the bassoon—is presumably why they were not more widely distributed. Knowing nothing even though I had been a fireman at sea and through a Chinese Revolution at the time I first saw *The End of St. Petersburg*, I did not recognize it as propaganda at all. I merely thought, responding to it emotionally, that it was marvellous, the best I had ever seen (etc.) up to that point: the opening sequence of windmills on the steppes made me weep, as it were "from the sheer beauty of it." In the same way, I was moved—or misled—by Alexander Room's *The Ghost That Never Returns*, of which I can, though I saw it only once and that eleven years ago, remember every detail. Anyhow, good propaganda, for whatever cause, is good art. *The Lion has Wings* would have done, I should have thought, damage to any cause, however noble. How many times and in how many English films do I have to see that bloody toy Spanish Armada, shot in a bathtub? There are a thousand things on this subject I would like to discuss with you: Paul Strand's *Redes*, Dovjenkho's *Frontier*. I will keep them for another letter or occasion. . . . As for films about regiments [brought to mind by Noxon's current work on *Un du 22ième*, a short film about the French-Canadian regiment at Valcartier, Quebec], the best one I ever did see was a French one about the Foreign Legion—not by Renoir, Duvivier, or Feyder, the director had some triple-barrelled name which I have forgotten. The music was by Eisler, and it was called simply, in Mexican, *Una Aventura en Moroc* [sic]. *An Adventure in Morocco*. Have you ever seen such a film, and if so, who made it? (*Lowry and Noxon Letters*, pp. 32-33)

"Que viva—life!" he concluded joyously, again thinking of Eisenstein and of his own recent past in Mexico. He continued the conversation—and puns—in his next letter, inviting Noxon to come to Dollarton "to visit the Cabinet of Dr. Caliglowry," thanking Noxon for mentioning him to John Grierson (whose 1929 film, *Drifters*, Lowry had seen at Cambridge), asking Noxon about Len Lye's whereabouts, and wondering if Noxon knew Karl Grune's *The Street* or *Abdul the Damned*: "Neither of those films are good looked at as a whole: both had genius, I thought" (*Lowry and Noxon Letters*, p. 34). Noxon lost his film job with the National Film Board in 1941, and it was not until 1944-45 that he was able to involve Lowry in a challenge partly anticipating Lowry's later filmscript writing; he opened for Lowry, and especially Margerie, the opportunity to write radio dramas for the Canadian Broadcasting Corporation in Toronto when Lowry was finishing the final draft of *Under the Volcano* and the Lowrys were living for about seven months with or near Noxon, first at Oakville, then at Niagara-on-the-Lake.

From 1945 (having mailed his *Under the Volcano* manuscript to his

New York agent, Harold Matson, in June) to 1954, Lowry continued to make Canada his home, but he travelled abroad frequently. It was during these years that Lowry held high his hopes of contributing to the world of cinema which had fallen, he felt, on hard times from a creative point of view. (In his view, even Rossellini's neo-realism was on the wane by 1949-50.) It was during these years that he wrote the "Tender Is the Night" filmscript and talked often of writing one based on *Under the Volcano*.

Even before *Under the Volcano* was published, and some years before he ever saw the possibility of writing a filmscript of *Tender Is the Night*, Lowry had considered the question of his own novel's potential as a film. He had, of course, corresponded about the legal question of film rights in May 1946 with Harold Matson in New York and Jonathan Cape in London. But Noxon in particular kept the subject alive with him. When he heard from Lowry in April 1946 that *Under the Volcano* had been accepted for publication, Noxon wrote back immediately: "every time I re-read it and I have done so often I become more enthusiastic. And what a movie it would make!" (*Lowry and Noxon Letters*, p. 121). A few months later: "Malc, how I'm looking forward to seeing that book in print. What's happening about movie rights, by the way? I think of it all the time in terms of screen values. It could make such a tremendous film. But who could make it?" (*Lowry and Noxon Letters*, p. 130).

The impact of Billy Wilder's immensely successful 1945 film, *The Lost Weekend*, which (together with the original novel in 1944 by Charles Jackson) raised for Lowry the spectre of his own novel about an alcoholic seeming derivative, laid the awesome power of Hollywood before him. The descriptions of the film *Drunkard's Rigadoon* that reach Sigbjørn Wilderness in *Dark as the Grave Wherein My Friend Is Laid* (*Dark*, pp. 21-26, 142, 188) convey a sense of Lowry's reaction to *The Lost Weekend*, particularly to the unsettling news of it spelled out to him during a visit to his wife's family in Hollywood in December 1945 when he met the film's cameraman.

Although even in the early 1940s Lowry had kept up with the few international films that were available in wartime Vancouver—he saw Eisenstein's *Alexander Nevsky*, for example, in 1942—it was only after *Under the Volcano* was in the publishers' hands that the great classics, many of which he had known over fifteen years before, again entered his life. In the fall of 1946 Lowry, along with Margerie, who had not seen many of the films, enthusiastically accepted the invitation to join the activities of the newly organized Vancouver Film Society. By 1947, after Earle Birney drew the attention of his writing students to the presence of the then-published author of

Under the Volcano living so near to Vancouver, Lowry and Margerie were often special guests at private screenings arranged by students such as Stanley Fox and George Robertson, who were also film society organizers. Or, in 1947 and again from 1949 to the early 1950s, the Lowrys would attend screenings at one of the theatres or halls used by the society, often after a lunch with Earle and Esther Birney at their home on the University of British Columbia campus. "I'm off to the movies to see Murnau's *Last Laugh*—true, it's taken rather a long time to get here—to be closely followed next week by *The Fall of the House of Usher*," Lowry wrote gaily to Maxwell Perkins in September 1946 (*Selected Letters*, p. 128). To Noxon he wrote in October 1946 for help for Vernon Van Sickle, "a very good fellow who is by way of carrying on bravely here in Vancouver certain works bravely started by yourself [in 1929] in Cambridge with the Film Society, etc." (*Lowry and Noxon Letters*, p. 127). Van Sickle's problems arose from his difficulty in acquiring the best films:

So far he has done very well: *Sunrise, The Baker's Wife, Crime and Punishment, Fall of the House of Usher, The Last Laugh, Cyprus is an Island, Night Mail* and so on: and such things as *Greed, The Loves of Jeanne Ney, Joan of Arc, The Italian Straw Hat*, and *M* are being shown during the winter. He shows the silent classics for the most part at a studio on Saturday, and has the Paradise theatre on Sunday nights every fortnight, much as you had the Tivoli [in Cambridge in 1929-31], for the others.

It is with the others curiously that he chiefly gets let down: he will have been promised, say, *La Bête Humaine*, but then at the last moment will be sent something dull like *Veille d'Armes* that no one would much want to see. Or *The Song of Ceylon* simply vanishes in transit. . . . Naturally he wants to get hold of as many of the finer French modern films as he can. . . . At all events I hope you will write him as this kind of work is important and can only lead to a Better Thing. (*Lowry and Noxon Letters*, p. 127)

Films such as these restored something of the visual and artistic environment that had first helped to form Lowry as an artist.

By 1947, then, while enjoying the world acclaim that accompanied the publication of *Under the Volcano*, Lowry was thinking often of adapting his novel as a film. He claimed he would advance the state of cinema by ten years if he were given a free hand at writing a treatment or script of it. Noxon continued to nudge him; he informed Lowry in May 1947 that a representative of MGM had been trying to reach him concerning *Under the Volcano* and also that he and Fletcher Markle (while they were working on the Studio One radio adaptation of *Under the Volcano* in New York in April) were, as he put it, "limp with sorrow that it wasn't a movie version [they] were working on" (*Lowry and Noxon Letters*, p. 146). A writer of the *Vancouver News-Herald* (maybe prompted by Lowry, who was spending a few days in Vancouver alone drinking) ran a March 15, 1947, news item citing Orson Welles' interest in *Under the Volcano* and anticipating Hollywood film companies arriving in Vancouver to get rights to "the year's most dramatic and dynamic novel."

But it was "family" that finally determined the course of the most direct contribution that Lowry was ever to make to the world of film—a contribution based on a text other than *Under the Volcano*. Frank Taylor, the Reynal and Hitchcock co-editor of *Under the Volcano*, had left his literary position in New York in 1948 to become a film producer for MGM in Hollywood. Like other friends whom Lowry turned into collaborating readers/audiences when creative projects beckoned (interlocutors such as Conrad Aiken and Gerald Noxon—not to mention Margerie Lowry—are notable examples), Lowry now insisted on treating Taylor as "family." He would write a filmscript for Taylor and thereby extend the relation he had established with him a few years before. Taylor would provide Lowry with the necessary point of reference, someone upon whom Lowry could rely, to whom he could report, to whom he could make promises. In Taylor Lowry felt he had found someone for whom he could produce a script responsive to world film yet innovative in its own right. Such a film would lend success to Taylor's new career in Hollywood, he thought. Furthermore, through Hollywood's however faulty machinery, it would offer the world a work that would revitalize film as art. It would be a sign, too, of spiritual rebirth within world culture.

So for nine months in 1949–50, in his waterfront cabin at Dollarton, Lowry set aside his other work and wrote what became his 455-page "eminently publishable" (to use his words) filmscript: "being writers ourselves," he said simply, "perhaps the best thing we could do was to try to write a good film ourselves" ("Preface," p. 6).

Though Frank Taylor's presence in Hollywood gave Lowry a specific context within which he felt he could accept the challenge of the Hollywood system, Lowry was still aware of the risk he was taking. He had just satirized Hollywood in *Under the Volcano*, contrasting its tendencies toward crude sentiment with the artistry of the 1920s European classics. Further, when he was undertaking his correspondence with Taylor, the critical tone he was about to take drew some words of caution from Margerie. He had kept abreast of the fate of novelists and playwrights from around the world who had accepted work as screenwriters and then warned others that there were few territories as treacherous for the serious and talented writer. Critics and intellectuals in America and Britain were quick to chastise not only the studio philistines but the writers themselves; they questioned the integrity of authors (like Fitzgerald himself, as Lowry well knew) who had succumbed to the insidious temptations of Hollywood. Working in Hollywood, the literary cognoscenti would say categorically, dried up a writer's creativity and absorbed it for an end not worthy of an artist's sensibility or talent. It must have been sentiments such as these that at least contributed to Lowry's reasons for keeping his filmscript a secret even from such close friends as Gerald Noxon. (And, of course, he did not want his publishers in New York to know that he was flying in the face of his contractual obligations to produce prose fiction, so he could say nothing at first to Matson or New York editor Albert Erskine.)

However wary he may have been of the widely publicized dangers of Hollywood to a serious novelist, Lowry at the same time abhorred the self-righteous and patronizing attitudes of such fashionable sentiments. Remembering the milieu of the 1920s when serious artists moved back and forth from one medium (including film) to another without any of the self-conscious feelings of awkwardness and embarrassment about film that set in after 1930, it was natural for Lowry to move from literature to film and back again. To Taylor he said vehemently that he had little sympathy for the condescending critics, especially writers, who condemned Hollywood out of hand. Firmly stating his surprise that "so many great writers, given, it would seem, every opportunity [in Hollywood], turn in something shoddy," Lowry refused to join them in "add[ing] their tithe to all the other obvious things that have been said in that great American pastime, the criticism and abuse of Hollywood" ("Preface," p. 6). Legitimate criticism was, of course, essential, he said: "when Chaplin or somebody lets forth a blast one listens indeed" ("Preface," p. 7). Some of his own comments to Taylor had been stimulated by a movie conference reported in the June 27, 1949, issue of *Life*, where Lowry's former fellow student Alistair Cooke, MGM production head Doré Schary, and writer/directors Joseph Mankiewicz and John Huston were among the participants considering the responsibilities of Hollywood. What Lowry deplored was "that so much other intelligent critical breath seem[ed] to be wasted by being directed at the wrong quarter" ("Preface," p. 7). Writers should stop posturing and look to themselves for their failures in film: "it is callous to abuse or discourage Hollywood for what may be indirectly one's own shortcomings" ("Preface," p. 7). It was the public responsibility of writers to write, to do "what individuals can do in their own bailiwicks" ("Preface," p. 6), that struck Lowry as important. "[W]riters who professed a love of the movies," he said, "but did little but criticize it, might best show their friendship by trying to write something good themselves" (*Selected Letters*, p. 202):

> it is precisely so many of our finest writers who consistently complain about the quality of films, sometimes one can't help wondering why they don't *do* something about it. Or more about it. There are, of course, certain recent brilliant and obvious exceptions to this in which there has been successful cooperation between writers and directors and producers, and you must assume we're bearing these exceptions in mind, and that doubtless more are being exemplified as we write; but most of the writers we have known personally whose works have been, say, bought by Hollywood, or have gone there themselves, seem to have failed, and then blamed the failure on Hollywood. Or even when they have succeeded, they have blamed the success on Hollywood. Very often—in fact above all—they blame it on the ethics of Hollywood. . . . They say a good many complicated things, but what it all boils down to is (1) the ethics of Hollywood are vile, because they wish to sell only sex; (2) the ethics of Hollywood are vile because it is impossible to write of sex, ergo, to tell the truth. You may substitute "aesthetics," "artistic standards" or even "politics" for ethics—but it seems to amount to much the same thing in the end. Yet should one look at the scripts responsible for these failures there is often only one reaction possible: they love not the film. Mysteriously, despite their protests, they love it not. They may have learned from it, they may even be able to tell you what a good film is, and write intelligently about it, but at bottom they feel superior to it—or to everything except the money to be made by it. ("Preface," p. 6)

Lowry argued that many such writers "cannot think visually and aurally"; if they could, he stated sharply, "the sacrifice of words would not seem so great. These writers cannot make you see and hear in their novels either" ("Preface," p. 6). In an earlier draft of the same statement, he wrote: "An enormous number of writers have learned, though not half enough, from the film: comparatively few have given anything back. It may be that there are some writers who have learned absolutely everything that they know about writing from the film but who if given a film to do would still turn in a stereotyped job. . . . Should their works be bought by the movies, they continue to complain: should they be given a free hand they very often make a mess of it" ("Preface," p. 4). He boldly claimed that a writer should even be willing to sacrifice language to visual imagery in a film adapted from that writer's novel.

Lowry's words seem excessive and strident; his image as one impervious to Hollywood's wiles, naive; his enthusiasm as film theorist and writer, cockily and impossibly herculean. It is tempting to observe that the ardour of his love for Hollywood was intact in 1949 simply because he had been barred from Hollywood earlier and, for that matter, from the practical exigencies of filmmaking of any kind. It was, after all, only as a member of the audience and as a contributor now at some distance from Hollywood that he demonstrated his love. But he was intuitively revelling in the thought of expanding upon what he had always loved as a writer and as a filmgoer—the visual and aural idioms available to the narrative artist and audience. The primacy of these idioms—his interest in making his readers see and hear—is apparent in all his fiction. Manuscript drafts in his handwriting include sections in which he seems to have tested the audio-visual precision of his fiction; parts of *Dark as the Grave Wherein My Friend Is Laid*, *October Ferry to Gabriola*, "The Bravest Boat," and "The Forest Path to the Spring," for example, are explored by means of tiny filmscripts which suggest a kind of scaffolding for certain scenes.

Frank Taylor, who (as Lowry crowed to his brother, Stuart) had become an MGM producer "on the strength of [*Under the Volcano*]" in October 1948 (*Selected Letters*, p. 220), had written the Lowrys in February 1949 (just after their return to Canada from a hectic and disconcerting fourteen-month sojourn in Europe) about his move from New York and about his working on a possible film of *Tender Is the Night*. In April 1949 Margerie gave Lowry a copy of *Tender Is the Night* (in *The Portable F. Scott Fitzgerald* edition published by Viking in 1945). That summer Lowry contrived to do some work on the film project himself. On July 1 he wrote Taylor that Margerie, who would be spending the second week of July in Los Angeles, would contact Taylor (still presumably occupied with "the divers responsibilities of the Ferris wheel," Lowry wrote in a punning letter, not overtly hinting at his own interest in "making a film of *Tender Is the Night* without taking an option also upon *Omar Khayyam*" (*Selected Letters*, pp. 179-80)). After all, she had been in "pixbiz" herself, he said. Taylor, having found himself in difficulty with the project, with his executive producer in fact having suspended it, let Margerie take along the treatment he had so that Lowry might get a chance to see it and perhaps even offer suggestions for renewing progress on it. Taylor must have rejoiced at having a writer of Lowry's stature and capacity to draw on for ideas just then.

Inspiration came immediately. Lowry's early letters to Taylor reveal his quick absorption in the challenge and the development of a vision for what might be done. In August Lowry wrote: "In a large intervallo so far as other work in progress [notably *Dark as the Grave Wherein My Friend Is Laid*] was concerned we started to devote ourselves whole heartedly to your Fitzgerald problem in *Tender Is the Night*, rereading the book several times, as well as the treatment, as well as all the other Fitzgerald books and Fitzgeraldiana we could scare up." In his judgement Taylor's earlier treatment was entirely inadequate, at best "a rationalization of . . . a misconception of the movie in the book" (*Notes*, p. xi).

Lowry at first thought he (with help from Margerie—whose background as a published novelist and as a Hollywood "ex movie (child, silent) star" (*Lowry and Noxon Letters*, p. 27) he frequently cited) would also write only a "précis" or treatment of the story: "even if it helps not and comes to nothing, [we thought] to send you a treatment of it ourselves. I cannot see how it can help but be better than the one you have though we say it who ought not," he wrote Taylor (*Notes*, p. xi). He offered a rough outline of points; some of these blossomed into the central themes, images, and sounds of the full-blown script:

While not insisting of course on the obvious Catholic League of Decency impossibilities such as the incest motif, it has occurred to us—having got right under the skin of the thing—to attempt a treatment such as Fitzgerald might have made himself. Actually the incest motif can go by the board without any great detriment to Fitzgerald's conception. For as I and we see it—and I think Fitzgerald, himself vastly influenced by the cinema by the way, would agree—what the thing is really about is the dividing line between sanity and madness. I have put this badly; what I should say rather is the action takes place for the most part on the window between those two things. Tender Is the Night . . . but there is no light. Well, there is the light of the moon. The moon is madness. Even the Divers' villa is the Villa Diana—and Diana is the moon, in case one forgot. The song about Au Claire de la lune mon ami Pierrot etc. is not just a charming song put there only as a contrast to ensuing horror, or merely as an additional medium of showing the Divers family at their best: it is, far more importantly, directly thematic and as sinister as could be, and refers precisely to the same thing. The same way with the mention of the shark at the beginning, suddenly cropping up in relation to the safe blue water, the shark that swims just below the "surface." This is almost a Melvillean shark—"The shark glides white through the phosphorus sea." (*Notes*, p. xii)

In savouring a movie made up of "continuously beautiful" camera work, Lowry exclaimed that "all these things could be as marvelous as could be cinematically. In fact the beginning of the book is largely cinematic—Fitzgerald's descriptive passages being scarcely more than a quid pro quo of first rate camera work." Lowry's reading of Fitzgerald had led him to recognize the "implicit cinema," the "drama in terms of cinema," at work within Fitzgerald's novel (*Notes*, p. xii).

In September Lowry reported: "We have become possessed by *Tender Is the Night*. . . . Something . . . seems to have made us do it" (*Notes*, p. vii). Further: "I believe as we are distilling [*Tender Is the Night*], it offers a general and sometimes particular architectonic of a great film. . . . I myself have never felt so creatively exhilarated since writing the better parts of the *Volcano* so that by this I mean that what we are doing is essentially creative" (*Notes*, p. xiii). (The process of Lowry's composition of *Under the Volcano* provides yet another parallel with "Tender Is the Night"; he filed a barrage of progress reports with a close friend and former editor in both cases, then with Noxon, now with Taylor.) As they worked, not only he but also Margerie filled the margins of successive drafts of the filmscript, changing their emphases as draft followed draft, each writer inviting help from the other here and there, she sometimes softening his extravagances, he sometimes lauding, sometimes questioning her "Margie Version." Generally, he spoke to her in the margins of the early drafts with the authority of a master cinematographer or director, giving advice to an apprentice, she to him as an everyman with connections to practical life, whether the internal politics of Hollywood or the routines of everyday living.

Although Lowry took note in the script of antecedents he found in directors such as the early Murnau and Lang, he also positioned the script firmly within its American tradition: "I see it as one of the greatest and most moving films of all time, one that is also a return to a great tradition of the movies, something that should combine the emotional impact of Griffith's *Broken Blossoms* and *Isn't Life Wonderful?* with *Citizen Kane*." Margerie's comments amplified the tone of Lowry's: "We have had what we think is a real inspiration and a new angle on *Tender Is the Night*. Malc's genius is working on all sixty cylinders, and, I may say, he is thoroughly enjoying himself" (*Notes*, p. xiii). Taylor expressed delight at Lowry's feeling of inspiration and at the prospect that a new approach just might—though he could not be too optimistic here—alter studio thinking.

In shielding news of his project from his agent and publisher as they awaited prose manuscripts in New York, Lowry coyly admitted (as, in November, to Albert Erskine, who had been Taylor's co-editor of *Under the Volcano*): "We are working on a kind of enthusiastic deviation from usual work—will tell you when finished, otherwise am withheld by superstition" (*Selected Letters*, p. 183). And in a slyly veiled message to him at Christmas: "We are working hard, having a good time" (*Selected Letters*, p. 184). It is tempting to wonder whether Lowry actually enjoyed the risk in his venture, just as he had (though on other planes altogether) enjoyed the risk in cinema before, "risking [his] neck even when at school (where movies were forbidden)" to see the masterpieces of European cinema in the 1920s or, in late 1940s and early 1950s visits to the Vancouver Film Society, risking his neck because of the ice "to keep up with the times" (Tiessen, p. 133). Then, too, perhaps Lowry liked the secrecy in this phase of his career simply because here he could dictate and act on his own terms, could write (within the context of his lifelong love) without pressure or obligation or external expectation except as he himself helped to determine these in the conditions of his self-defined relationship with Taylor.

Undeterred by a warning from Taylor that at MGM the project had been put officially on the shelf, Lowry reported to him in January 1950: "We're a gettin' there—and how!" He felt they were "almost at the end of the track—hard work now is in revising, cutting and typing chiefly." His description—a vivid sketch of Canada as a northern wilderness—of their working conditions during that winter period provides a gauge of his and Margerie's commitment and enthusiasm: "we have Arctic storms, then follow floods and have been almost frozen in. Temperature north of us in B.C. descended to 73 below zero. We have had 10 below in the house, the very ink in the inkpot has frozen and Margie's typewriter also has frozen. Some of the while, we have had to work in gloves and we have not taken our clothes off for three weeks." Embodying Lowry's inimitable restraint and grace, his words now remind us of many projects delayed in the last ten years of his life: "The above will delay the m.s. a little, but not much, but some way into February" (*Notes*, pp. xiii-xiv).

In mid-February Lowry wrote that while they had "more or less finished the opus," they still needed some time, "a month more in final typing and correcting." He again explained that Arctic weather—"the worst in all history here, much worse than I said, and myself with a frozen hand to boot"—still prevailed. But he also reminded Taylor of how much he and Margerie had "fallen in love with the thing" (*Notes*, p. xiv). (Taylor replied that he could hardly wait the extra month, that he and Christopher Isherwood were just enjoying reading *Under the Volcano* aloud to each other, that Fletcher Markle had just dropped in to introduce himself to Taylor.)

Introduction

From Lowry in March: "Don't reply. Don't even breathe. We're on the home stretch, though not quite on the home beach, but it will still be a few weeks yet." On April 6: "We have it gedone.... We are putting on a few final touches" (*Notes*, p. xiv). (Taylor wrote back that he and Isherwood had just hosted Lowry's friend Dylan Thomas on April 10, had in fact introduced him to Chaplin and Shelley Winters. It happened that Thomas had visited Lowry in Vancouver just a few days before.) Then, on April 12, 1950, Lowry sent a comprehensive covering letter with the finished script:

this [script] is sent to you in the earnest hope that it might in itself offer a challenge and help to start something or carry things along. Also it should be clear that it is intended as a practical basis for a film, though the grammar of the film has been scarcely used—scarcely words more complicated than cut, dissolve, or lap dissolve—and we don't always mean that of course, and any good or bad writing in it [is] either habit or incidental. The idea, however, was threefold, to try and give a vivid impression of a film actually in progress, a film that one had actually seen, and at the same time a film that, since it had not been made, left every scope for you or a director's imagination to work in. Since, perhaps understandably, there is no accepted form for this sort of thing we know of, we simply made one up. It is not meant entirely to be taken literally, not that it would be, but you might think we were naive enough to think so. There are some tentatively suggested shots in the sanitarium sequence. And there are two sections, one in New York, and another at sea, that may be in part unnegotiable, particularly, or as we have written it, the latter. Nonetheless, even if so, we felt strongly that a suggestion of the poetic and visual and aural *drang* in these two parts involved would relate the film enormously and add meaning to it: so they have been written in full.... [W]e have, so to speak, seen the film, and you are supposed to see it in a minute or two. But what you may see to cut, to put in, to improve, to take out, etc., etc., is equally part of the intention, while you are reading it.... [W]e have left enough out for an opera by Puccini.... But we strongly feel its basic structure to be sound.... Perhaps you might say that one has to start off by being unfair to [Fitzgerald] by depriving his book of the incest motif, but there is much greatness in the book that is only implied in it—take away the incest and what do you have left? ... The answer is everything: you have, for one thing, a great and unusual love story, on the other a sort of protagonist of the American soul, or of the soul of man himself, whose application to today is also patent. (*Selected Letters*, pp. 203-5)

Though the script was out of Lowry's hands, the thought of it never left him through the remaining years of his life. At first, simple anxieties about its being rejected mingled with his strong hope that it would find favour in Hollywood. But his comically expressed worries about its "falling into puddles, opened by the claws of the wind, being rewritten by the guard in the baggage car" (*Notes*, p. xiv) prefigured his later more grievous concerns about its fate. Reservation and self-doubt mingled with confidence and euphoria:

much dialogue would have to be rewritten, other parts slashed, reversed, stove in—that depends, depends on what sir, that again depends—so on and so forth. The idea was to present a structure that would be extremely hard to sink. . . . But if it's *all* wrong, a hopeless misconception, a swaggle-tailed bravura, a bearded what-not, a cornuted nonentity, and in short no damn good at all, the chagrin would be ours indeed, but it would be ours for having wasted your time in erroneously having given you to think we could do something about it. But I'd have to revise all my notions as to how far self-delusion can go in the case of artists to feel we've wasted ours, whatever the result. We've never had so much terrible fun doing anything. (*Notes*, pp. xiv–xv)

Lowry received outstanding reviews of the filmscript not only from Taylor but also from three other readers sensitive to both its literary and its cinematic nuances and depths, subtleties and implications: James Agee, Jay Leyda, and Christopher Isherwood. Agee, just then co-scripting *The African Queen* with John Huston (who, Taylor had informed Lowry in 1948, was thrilled by *Under the Volcano* and who in 1984 directed a film adaptation of it), wrote on April 18: "I . . . loved what little I got a chance to read of your great job on *Tender Is the Night*—because besides every accomplishment of insight and atmosphere, you're of course one of the maybe dozen really original, inventive minds that have ever hit movies" (*Selected Letters*, p. 444). A week later Taylor, busy on another project, dashed off a brief note of astonishment and appreciation; on May 19 he provided a fuller statement of his feelings:

I have not felt this way since my first reading of *Volcano*. On those rare occasions when I read something as brilliant, original and artful as your script, I am so humbled and awed that written words come only with the greatest difficulty. . . . I have read many scripts and seen many pictures, but never before have I seen writing so purely cinematic. . . . It goes devastatingly deep, and its direct filmic evocation of life's complexities is magic and miraculous. (*Selected Letters*, p. 441)

Leyda (whose interest in both literature and film, Melville and

Eisenstein, of course interested Lowry) congratulated Lowry for "putting an amazing film on paper" and hoped that it would get "off the paper onto film" (*Selected Letters*, p. 442). Isherwood put the filmscript into its literary tradition: "Quite simply said, it is a masterpiece—a new sort. I wait to see it filmed, of course—but equally I want to see your full script published with all your notes and comments.... It ought to be printed as well as played, because much of it is for a mental theatre like Hardy's *Dynasts*" (*Selected Letters*, p. 292). To his brother Stuart, Lowry wrote with elation that the reaction to his "projected film" from "two of the greatest authorities on the cinema and a now famous Metro-Goldwyn-Mayer producer, was in brief that 'it was obviously the greatest achievement in movies, what movies had been all adding up to, and that even to read, that it was comparable with the power of Theodore Dreiser and the titanic mental drama of Thomas Hardy's *The Dynasts*.' (I see no reason to be sparing of adjectives; they were not.) The producer is one of my ex-publishers of the *Volcano*" (*Selected Letters*, pp. 219, 223).

Now it was up to Taylor (whose first film, *Mystery Street*, was to be released by MGM that May) to interest Hollywood in this formidable *tour de force*. Though he wanted to show it to Joseph Mankiewicz at Twentieth Century-Fox, he was obligated to show it to MGM, who owned the screen rights to the novel, but who, he thought, would be least interested in Lowry's achievement. His letter that May was a mixture of caution and hope: "In the queer Hollywood scheme of things for me [having made only one film] to presume that Metro would now permit me to do a film of this proportion is doubtless ludicrous. It is also difficult to imagine a studio such as this understanding such a project. However if you will give me a little more time to think it out and consult with others more professionally experienced, I shall attempt to work out a plan of presentation. ... [B]elieve me, I will do everything I can from this day forward to realize our hopes" (*Selected Letters*, pp. 441–42). A few days later he went so far as to suggest that, along with a flat fee, the Lowrys might be interested in receiving weekly remuneration for undertaking future revision of the script.

By July 1950 the Lowrys were impatiently asking Taylor for "a bulletin ... a little news" (*Notes*, p. xvi). They were in some financial difficulty, had, in fact, asked Matson for an advance of a small sum of money. They tried cautiously to speak to Matson of their commercial worth, giving oblique hints about their script, their "Great Secret." They claimed that their "secret" project was as good as "gold plated securities to put up as collateral":

If it comes off we couldn't begin to overestimate what it might do.... [I]t is not just a Hollywood Dream. The reports upon it so far have been so staggeringly complimentary we could hardly take it....

From [Isherwood's comments] you can see that if there is a slip between cup and lip our ace in the hole is that the thing is eminently publishable, though we would like that naturally to take place in conjunction with the film, not before it....

So—although we are not legally so—we feel as if we were rather in the position of a chap who is holding a thousand dollar bond on Sunday and wants to borrow ten bucks on it. Something final on the subject may in fact come any day. (*Notes*, p. xvi)

About a week later, in thanking Matson for an advance (there was no money forthcoming from Hollywood), Lowry wrote breathlessly: "We still haven't heard from Hollywood but should do so at any moment. In fact there may be a letter at the post office right now waiting for us. Or even a telegram" (*Notes*, p. xvi).

Taylor informed the Lowrys in September that he would be leaving MGM and taking their script with him. A rhythm of diminishing hopefulness continued in Lowry's letters to Matson. In September: "We have not heard yet re the Hollywood venture . . . we still feel very hopeful" (*Notes*, p. xvii). In October: "I hope I was not too optimistic in regard to the Hollywood venture but I feel something must come of it eventually" (*Notes*, p. xvii). In November: "we haven't heard anything from Hollywood" (*Selected Letters*, p. 216).

In response to Lowry's continuing requests for "news," for just "something or other," Taylor wrote in January 1951 that he had begun working for Twentieth Century-Fox and had immediately given the Lowry opus to Mankiewicz who, apparently, showed some interest. Lowry was quick to respond:

I hope and pray Mr. Mankiewicz may go on being aroused.... I pray also he may overlook any possible tangential pretentiousness in the film, and see the real possibilities that are there.... I live in some fear and trembling that he may not like it, praying he make allowance for any peripheral pretentiousness and non professional digressions, and that these may not put him off from what we feel unmistakeably to be *there*. (*Notes*, p. xvii)

But in February to Erskine: "hope for [that . . . long work . . . of which we still can't speak] went up like a rocket the other week, one can't count on more than Bergsonian ashes in one's face this week, though perhaps it'll be different next" (*Selected Letters*, p. 229). And in March to Matson: "We have heard nothing further from Hollywood" (*Notes*, p. xvii).

Taylor's expressions of hope grew dimmer. In April 1951 he wrote to say that Lowry might try his luck again back at MGM, where Fletcher Markle was now a director. In addition to producing, with Gerald Noxon, the radio adaptation of *Under the Volcano*, Markle had also, as Taylor pointed out, done a radio adaptation of some of Fitzgerald's work. But Taylor now stated that Lowry's script, to make it marketable in Hollywood, would have to be revised. (Taylor shuddered a little at how Lowry might react to Markle's likely interest in casting Ray Milland, the star of *The Lost Weekend*, in the Dick Diver role.)

Just after launching *Under the Volcano* with Erskine and Taylor in New York, Lowry had met Markle with Noxon in Toronto in March 1947, and he now agreed immediately with Taylor that Markle should see the script. He responded, too, to Taylor's comments that the script might contain flaws. Anticipating opposition particularly to the script's pronounced deviations from the original and to the extensive additions which give it a tone and structure and rhythm in keeping more with *Under the Volcano* and other of his texts than *Tender Is the Night*, and which are amongst its richest parts, he issued new statements of defence:

I have several times thought we were fooling ourselves a bit in regard to the baby. But I am wrong. It is *there*. It has faults, as you say, of "novelistic" dialogue, Mankiewicz might point out; too much New York, too much ship, an overreaching at the end, though these things had to be written, even if the final intention was for some of them rather to be suggested. But this was in part caused by lack of time, finally, to cut, and it was as if certain metaphors had to be followed through, here and there, to test their validity as suggestions. And unquestionably again it requires further work, for there are no doubt faults of sheer ignorance of the possibilities of the medium. (Though I doubt that they are grave. . . .) But what I felt about it on looking at it severely was that objectively it would be damned hard to find anything better to work on than that script as regards that particular book. In short, whatever anyone may say, I think it's potentially one of the best films I never saw: or rather, for that matter, we *did* see it. (*Notes*, p. xviii)

Markle let Lowry know immediately that he was enormously impressed by the script as it stood, but he made it clear that he would have to proceed very cautiously with it. The upshot of Markle's impossible task is summarized implicitly in Lowry's November

1951 note to Matson: "We have still not heard anything from Hollywood" (*Notes*, p. xviii).

In 1952, feeling beleaguered by publishers as they awaited new work from him, Lowry finally expressed the hope of "paying [his] way" (*Selected Letters*, p. 308) by submitting a movie scenario to them, either of *Tender Is the Night* or of the one other novel he had for a few years wanted to adapt—*Under the Volcano*. In the late 1920s and early 1930s he had observed at close hand, with Noxon at Cambridge, the publication of filmscripts as experimental literature in the "little magazines" that flourished in that period. His interest in writing a filmscript of *Under the Volcano* in 1952 was reinforced by his conviction that his "Tender Is the Night" was, as Isherwood had said, strong as a *literary* text: "Frank has a masterpiece of ours," he wrote to Erskine (then at Random House). "That too is publishable perhaps" (*Selected Letters*, p. 295). In April he contacted Matson about the possibility of his writing a publishable scenario of *Under the Volcano* (*Selected Letters*, p. 311), and he discussed with Erskine, once again, the literary potential of his "Tender Is the Night" script:

Whether or not [the film we did for Frank, which is still supposed to be secret] would be feasible as a quid pro quo for a third completed book within that allotted period—what with the difficulties of copyright and the joint authorship—I don't know, but its existence is at least an earnest of what one can do. We did it in seven months and have not ever accepted or borrowed any cash on it and indeed it, alack, did not do for Frank what we had hoped: but perhaps that wasn't its fault, and it may yet. And certainly it wasn't Frank's fault. Shall I write to Frank to send it to you? I dropped *Dark as the Grave* to write this.... It is by no means an ordinary kind of script. The film of course is "Tender Is the Night" and I know Frank won't mind my mentioning it. In fact by writing it for him we felt we were in some sort "keeping in the family." The result was just the beginning of our three years' heartbreak: but at least we keep a-tryin'. (*Selected Letters*, pp. 308-9)

In the summer of 1954 the Lowrys left their home at Dollarton for the last time. In Sicily in November, in a letter to Matson about the script, Lowry made reference to David Selznick, the producer whose interest in Fitzgerald's novel actually led to the eventual production of a version of *Tender Is the Night* by Twentieth Century-Fox in 1962. (Taylor had sent Lowry's script to Selznick and scriptwriter Ivan Moffat after Selznick, who had earlier sold the screen rights to the novel to MGM, bought them back. However, Selznick and Moffat apparently did not, according to Taylor, read Lowry's script.) Lowry spoke to Matson with philosophic melancholy and resignation now, but he still clung to his unbroken faith in the essential greatness of the work:

> It was too long, and we should like to cut and re-work much of it, if Selznick were interested, but even so, we feel it a bloody fine piece of work. . . . I'd like to make it clear, further, that our script of *Tender* was written in 1949 during a sort of doldrums of the American movie and in that script is a sort of prophesy of its recovery. We missed lots of hurdles in our script, and part of the ending is probably tripe, and as I said, it's far too long. We love the work we did, however, and I feel we might possibly deserve, quite practically—for Selznick's sake too—a crack at the version they propose to make in any event. Despite all our mistakes we solved nearly every difficulty of transposing a long sprawling novel into the different medium of the film, and few people can possibly know so much about that book by now as we do. (*Notes*, p. xix)

Though his "heartbreak" continued to the end, so did his belief in the value, even imminent commercial success, of his script (so, too, his ambition to write a script for *Under the Volcano*). As late as 1956, just months before his own death and with Margerie hospitalized from a nervous collapse, Lowry could write cheerily from his last home, the White Cottage in Ripe, England, to David Markson in New York: "We may be film magnates . . . yet: a producer has just paid me $500 for a 6-months option on the *Volc*. And just as Margie went into hospital there was a note (which Fitzgerald would have appreciated) just arrived re Selznick offering some hope re our M & M version of *Tender Is the Night* for Frank" (*Selected Letters*, p. 390).

It was partly his interest in cinema in general, partly his hope of turning *Under the Volcano* into a film, and partly the opportunity to work with "family" that attracted Lowry to the *Tender Is the Night* project. But the fact that Lowry could work so closely on the project not only with Taylor and with Margerie but also—to speak only partly figuratively—with Fitzgerald must have played a strong part in his obsession with the script, too. As he had with other collaborators, he effectively declared Fitzgerald a "family member," appropriated him as a kind of brother, and got down to work with him, as it were, in writing the *Tender Is the Night* story as Lowry felt it should have been written.

The affinities between the two writers—even their interest in Hollywood—are numerous, and they must have contributed to Lowry's conviction that Fitzgerald, were he still alive, would approve of Lowry's attempts to carry the story to its richest possible form. In the

1920s and early 1930s, as well as from late 1947 to early 1949, Lowry had actually come to know at first hand most of the European locations Fitzgerald used as his settings (though locations of his own, from an expressionistically and surrealistically realized New York—where Lowry lived in grim circumstances from 1934 to 1936—to his several sea voyages, become as dominant in the script as Paris or Antibes). In fact, he had been in Paris in 1926, the very time and place of much of the *Tender Is the Night* narrative.

From Fitzgerald Lowry appropriated material in which he found contours of a vision congruent with his own. Yet for all their affinities, the two writers were dissimilar enough that Lowry felt free to adapt and develop that vision along his own lines. Lowry felt he could dissect Fitzgerald's novel and reconstruct it within the context of his own aesthetic. "[H]e says," wrote Margerie about her husband, with the project well underway, "he is Learning a Lot About the Novel in tearing this one to pieces and recreating it" (*Notes*, p. xiii).

When he compared Lowry's achievement with Fitzgerald's, Taylor suggested that the impact of the script "was much, much greater than that of the novel" (*Selected Letters*, p. 441). Isherwood, who had always liked Fitzgerald's novel, was also overwhelmed by Lowry's rewriting of it:

I'm not trying to flatter you when I say that your version of it was a complete revelation of new meanings and of a greatness which was certainly in the book somewhere, but which you made evident. When I'd read you, I was really haunted for several days by the greatness of the themes. It has every bit as much right as Dreiser's to be called *An American Tragedy*—and all your changes and developments on Fitzgerald fill it out and add significance to it. (*Selected Letters*, p. 443)

Despite Taylor's and Isherwood's support for his realignment of Fitzgerald's novel, Lowry was ever sensitive to possible criticism of his somehow having been "unfair" to Fitzgerald by "depriving" *Tender Is the Night* of some of its material, and he continually sought to justify his approach:

There will doubtless be those who may have good reasons for thinking this was a perfect enough book anyway and that it is mere impertinence to have tampered with it as we have done and with this view we sympathize. However we have tried sincerely to have regard for the great American artist who wrote it and where possible even to imagine what he would have done were he trying to make it into a film: as a novel he would have agreed it would have stood some tampering with: as a film it *has* to be tampered with, certain sacrifices have to be made, for which we . . . try to make due compensation, but in terms of what [one] might call Fitzgerald's own buried intentions, or what we conceive them to have been. ("Preface," p. 13)

Lowry's oft-articulated sense of what he strongly felt was the imperfect and relatively raw state of Fitzgerald's novel reinforced his satisfaction in reworking it. In arguing that his script possessed as much artistic integrity and legitimacy as any other serious work of art and that his de/reconstruction of Fitzgerald's work should be thought of as an act of homage to Fitzgerald, Lowry was reflecting his specific sense that the story would actually work best in film form. "What you will receive will be good and noble," he wrote Taylor when he and Margerie were about to finish their writing, "and I never spoke with such conviction and passion in my life" (*Notes*, p. vii). When it was finished he added: "We put our all, our everything in it" (*Notes*, p. vii). To his literary agent, Harold Matson, he stated: "we have a deep instinct that what we did was too good to be written off, Hollywood or no Hollywood" (*Selected Letters*, p. 216).

The filmscript supports Lowry's claim of having put "all . . . everything" into it, for it is a significant text in its own right. Having used Fitzgerald's novel as his stimulus, Lowry fit his script firmly and convincingly into his own canon as a continuation and extension of his other work, a signal of the direction he wanted his later fiction to take. It was a way of illustrating that film was on a par with literature as a medium through which to move an audience toward a new vision of human existence. "Is there any valid reason," he asked, "for literature and the movies to portray a man as ignoble and mean?" ("Preface," p. 8). He was convinced that in this text he had produced, without being maudlin, what post-war audiences were seeking: "some sort of powerful reflection of the true dignity of man" ("Preface," p. 10).

If Lowry had already used "cinematic" techniques in *Under the Volcano* to provide a narrative that was as direct and palpable as possible, the actual filmscript format now gave him the ideal chance to develop and state and apply a "cinema" aesthetic in a more literal way. By its formal means, his filmscript renders elements of his general aesthetic visible. The reader/viewer, "equipped with his own head-camera and the expertise of Laruelle," who can become "co-director of one of this century's most cinematographic novels" (Kilgallin, p. 131), *Under the Volcano*, can now become co-director of the "cinematographic" filmscript created by its author.

Even Lowry as man/writer becomes surprisingly palpable in the script; he seems to see and feel the film, to enter into a kind of tactile relationship with it, and so give himself a kind of visible form. In 1965, noting the "essentially cinematic" quality of *Under the Volcano*, Stephen Spender observed that "[t]he cinema is kinetic. Lowry . . . borrows from it for his own kinetic writing. He seems to write with every faculty which is active, or observes action: the calf muscles, the throat swallowing, the frank outward-looking eye observing, the memory re-enacting." There is in his prose a "fusion of muscular mental energies of body and intellect" (Spender, p. xv). Spender's words anticipate the Lowry of the filmscript, where Lowry's bodily reactions seem to be writ large as they are written into the text. With Lowry's kinetically and spatially conceived cuts, dissolves, music, and noises erupting savagely here, triumphantly there, with his visual technique persistently determining just how "we feel" (as Lowry says in the script, with reference to not just emotional but also his own and his audience's physical response), Lowry's reader/viewer enters with him into what seems like a physically realized environment. Lowry used the mechanical options and conventions and imperatives of cinema, even the actual inner space of the movie house itself, to give muscular form to his new universe, to give it a sense he had felt in childhood, when movies first engulfed him in their electrifying perils and magical pleasures. He reached for effects that would be "shattering" upon the audience. In his use of *Daddy's Girl*, the film within the film in which a car-ride sequence echoes other such sequences central to the development of the film, for example, he illustrates his method and desire: "We get a tremendous horrendous sensation of increasing speed and the exhilaration of being on the road ourselves, which ever recedes beneath our very chairs. In sequences of this type one often used to wish that such a scene would go on and on beyond the breaking point where the cut is made, and here we get our wish" (see Section 12).

As his filmscript opens, the panoramic camera technique brings to mind the "cinematic" opening of *Under the Volcano*. The camera at the end of the filmscript (carrying through to the final moments of the film Lowry's desire to privilege camera-truth in relation to subjective truths of individuals) brings to mind the explosion of images and movement in the concluding paragraphs of Chapter Eleven, as also of Chapters One and Twelve, of *Under the Volcano*. As we read the filmscript we are struck by innumerable other narrative and formal elements which echo the elements at work—themselves often evoking Eisenstein and his use of montage—in *Under the Volcano*: there is the Mexican doctor, José, echoing Dr. Vigil (based on

Lowry's friend, Juan Cerillo, who had played in Eisenstein's *Que Viva Mexico!*, of which the *Thunder Over Mexico* section was released in 1933) of *Under the Volcano*; there are the words of the chorus performing in *Antigone* in New York, echoing the first epigraph of *Under the Volcano*; there are the Alps echoing the volcanoes, various abysses and cliffs echoing the barranca; there are the Ferris Wheel and, more significantly, the car, echoing the infernal machine.

The car as motif is central. Lowry repeatedly pointed out why he had discarded Fitzgerald's original incest motif and replaced it with the symbol of the car: because of obvious reasons as far as Hollywood censorship was concerned but also because he felt Fitzgerald himself had failed to utilize the car in an organic enough manner in his novel. In Lowry's script, it is the car which represents the source of Nicole's illness and precipitates much of the action; it also lets him explore the possibility of freedom and hope. While the car represents illness, doom, and menace at the beginning of the story, it finally stands as the sign of Nicole's freedom when she drives, alone, from the beach to the Villa Diana near the end. The car becomes that which marks the transformation from damnation to redemption.

The script, replete with cinematically impressive sequences and with discussions on the nature of those sequences and on the nature of film technique more generally, explicitly "quotes" or draws upon the larger world of film as well as the other arts. Through references to many works, Lowry manages—as he also does in *Under the Volcano* and other of his texts—to maintain a running commentary on the characters and on the action. He will place a reference to Murnau's *Sunrise* here, a glimpse of a theatre notice advertising Bernard Shaw's *The Doctor's Dilemma* there. These and many other references and quotations, all enriching the texture of the narrative, add layer after layer of multiple meaning to the text.

Technically and aesthetically, sound—and silence—are exploited by Lowry in his script. Already in *Under the Volcano*, as for that matter in much earlier texts such as *Ultramarine*, there had been a veritable pot-pourri of background noise: people speaking, dogs barking, guitars playing, bells ringing. In the filmscript, music (to select from amongst the many sounds Lowry suggests) drives the pace, pegs characters, suggests moods, introduces and repeats themes. But never does Lowry utilize music as mere background; his soundtrack is woven into the text so that, as with even the apparently most incidental visual images, it becomes an integrated part of the very scene it comments upon. Bix Beiderbecke's haunting piano composition *In a Mist*, for example, not only creates the desired mood whenever it is played by Abe or simply heard in the background; its own bittersweet quality and the tragic history of its alcoholic and (at least during his lifetime) unappreciated composer are comments upon Abe and, by extension, upon Dick as well. Probably the best example of Lowry's multilevelled use of music is the tune *Frère Jacques*, "the result of twenty years' search for an onomatopoeia for a ship's engine" (*Notes*, p. 44). Lowry had conceived of this children's song as an imitation of the sound of a ship's engine when he and Margerie voyaged to Europe in 1947; he employed it in *October Ferry to Gabriola* and in short stories such as "Through the Panama," "Present Estate of Pompeii," and "The Forest Path to the Spring." In the script it is used not only as realistic sound, but also, for example, as a symbol of Dick's nostalgia for his family, and finally it is made to represent "a kind of rhythmic link, or rhythmic base, or strong beat sounding away in the depths of the picture sometimes, neutral only in the sense that one could depart from it musically in any direction one wished" (*Notes*, p. 55).

Of course, a reader/viewer need not pursue all the symbolic connections to enjoy the filmscript on its immediate level. Lowry hoped that his film would be as accessible and appealing to a child as to the most informed critic. Referring to his use of Gluck's *Orféo* in one scene, for instance, he wrote that for some members of the audience knowledge of this opera would add a level of meaning to the narrative; but (as he put it to Taylor) those "who do not get the point at all will have heard some supernaturally good music in exactly the right place by someone they have thought was on your payroll" (*Notes*, p. 24).

Although it was a subtly crafted and vibrating sensorium into which Lowry wanted to immerse his movie audience, it was the directly visual/spatial idiom of film that he explored with most relish. In grappling with the problems of narrative perspective in *Under the Volcano*, Lowry had already demonstrated not only his penchant for the panoramic, but also for incorporating the visually minute and specific alongside the general and abstract. Not hesitating to employ artistic possibilities suggested by film technology (though it was to be a black-and-white film), Lowry seized upon the camera as the very instrument with which to communicate a complex view of reality. He knew he could utilize the camera's ability to provide simultaneous images and effects with an immediacy—and objective spatiality—that the written word could not imitate. Even words should appear for their visual impact as much as for their meaning. The parallels with *Under the Volcano* are obvious. Indeed, as Lowry said to Downie Kirk, who often helped him with the translation of expressions, the French translation for the film, *Daddy's Girl*, "should be ironic, if possible. It appears as an advertisement (much as *Las Manos de Orlac* does in the *Volcano*)" (*Selected Letters*, p. 195).

Lowry liked to exploit what he saw as the camera's dual, paradoxical role as both objective and subjective voice. Given the ambiguity and untameableness of the written word, Lowry had, in his previous work, been faced with the authorial paradox created by his simultaneous desire to control language and to ensure its plenitude. In Lowry's script (as Lowry himself pointed out), the camera possesses the ability to act, on the one hand, as a power dominating reality through the objective image projected on the screen; Sigbjørn Wilderness "tried hard . . . to see the situation as objectively as if he were watching a film," Lowry wrote in *Dark as the Grave* (*Dark*, p. 166), outlining, as it were, his technique in the filmscript. The camera—which Lowry always felt should subvert the efforts of theatre to ruin cinema—operates, as he put it, as "the old Greek chorus" throughout. On the other hand, the camera acts as an agent of plenitude or a multiplier of meanings as it conveys its own subjective viewpoint or that of one or another character. And Lowry's camera creates not only disparate points of view, but also the intervals between them; it invites the reader/viewer to manufacture new perspectives and involves the reader/viewer in co-creating the "reality" begun by the film.

Not surprisingly, amongst films of the period, Lowry was particularly struck by *Rashomon* (1951), with its brilliant examination of opposing perspectives. In one of his many references to *Under the Volcano* as a kind of film, he thought of it as a little like *Rashomon*, that is, as a "five dimensional movie" (*Lowry and Noxon Letters*, p. 40). The last two chapters, occurring simultaneously, reminded him and Erskine of one of the first instances of multidimensional storytelling he had ever seen: *Intolerance* (1916).

It can be argued that at the root of Lowry's fiction—as critics such as David Falk have suggested—is an autobiographical impulse towards self-mastery. Lowry must have felt some ambivalence about using cinema—with the relentless linear continuity it was dangerously capable of imposing on narrative by means of its tyrannically mechanical apparatus—as a vehicle for self-mastery. As he suggested in *October Ferry to Gabriola*, Ethan's life had been "less a life than a sort of movie, or series of movies" (*October Ferry*, p. 42). Ethan's experience in seeing again a half-remembered "lousy movie" (*October Ferry*, p. 132) only galvanized his sense of angst, of the absurd in his own life, as, hounded by his own foreknowledge, he helplessly watched the hero of the movie meeting (as the reel unwound) his disastrous end: "against such a predetermined doom, as against one's fate in a nightmare, finally you rebel! How? when the movie will always end in the same way anyway" (*October Ferry*, pp. 132–33). Yet Lowry could argue also in his fiction that a director can accept cinema technology, though it be a twentieth-century metaphor for the infernal machine, and produce through it work that defies its ominous mechanical logic just as his novel *Dark as the Grave Wherein My Friend Is Laid* and his filmscript could defy his own cyclical story of "predetermined doom," *Under the Volcano*. So Lowry insists, as he does through Sigbjørn's thoughts in *Dark as the Grave*, that the individual may determine the course of his life, may find salvation despite the odds against him: "Were we not empowered as the director [who changes the ending of a film] . . . to turn the apparent disaster of our lives into triumph?" (*Dark*, p. 249)

In *Under the Volcano* Lowry had projected into the Consul all that he felt was destructive and damning within himself, hoping thereby to lay his personal demons to rest. The character, however, at times almost overwhelmed his creator, threatening to join Lowry's destiny with his own. Much of the fiction that followed *Under the Volcano* may be seen as Lowry's attempt to avoid such a fate. What Lowry needed to find was not a way to banish the Consul—creator and created were far too close for that kind of complete denial—but a way to integrate him into a universe that would provide for the upward spiritual movement of man. In adapting and rewriting Fitzgerald's *Tender Is the Night*, Lowry was able to find psychic and mythic resonances to establish such a universe.

Lowry was well aware that Hollywood conventions placed limits on the degree to which darkness and despair might be seriously explored in a film. Yet he argued that greatness in art freed a work from all forms of censorship and other strictures, even those imposed by Hollywood. Just as Lowry found that the "passion and scholarship and artistic devotion" of Joyce's *Ulysses* served as a model of technical brilliance ("Preface," p. 9), so he found a film such as Welles' *Citizen Kane* exemplary. But he saw that it had a parallel in *Timon of Athens* rather than *King Lear*, and he wanted now to insert into film history a work whose intention the public would not mistake:

Citizen Kane you might call a sort of filmic *Timon of Athens*. *Timon* is one of Shakespeare's finest plays, but also his most demeaning and most unpopular: there is room for the demeaning as even perhaps for the depressing, in the movie as in nearly all art, especially when accompanied by genius, which is exhilarating anyway, but isn't that rather putting, in this case, the cart before the horse? That the cart might be filled with sheer filmic gold to a real film lover is quite by the way, save to him and for history; unschooled, the public might mistake its contents. *Timon* was preceded by most of the great plays. ("Preface," p. 10)

Under the Volcano was Lowry's *Timon*. When that novel begins, the Consul is already dead. He is resurrected, so to speak, in Chapter Two—where "M. Laruelle's film" begins—but only with the reader's knowledge that he will be dead at the end of the novel. The Dick Diver who endures the death-in-life existence at the conclusion of Fitzgerald's novel is (in the filmscript) resurrected by Lowry. With Abe North, Dick's alter ego, carelessly murdered in the story (and thereby bearing something of the identity and burden and fate of the Consul in *Under the Volcano*), Lowry develops the structure of Dick's situation in a direction different from that in Fitzgerald or from the Consul's. It is in his treatment of Dick that Lowry marked his most dramatic departure from Fitzgerald and made the most pronounced and significant narrative statement of the script. Fitzgerald, Lowry insisted, had failed in his novel to provide a focus for Dick's conscience ("Preface," p. 8); he had abandoned Dick at the end of the novel, left him to live absurdly an altogether too dingy existence (the kind of existence already demonstrated by Abe North). For the post-*Volcano* Lowry (himself in danger of collapsing personally), Fitzgerald's ending was too preoccupied with absurd forces of a tragedy of disintegration that had governed *Under the Volcano*: "in the subterranean part of the book, Abe—the duel—Peterson—Abe's death—Dick becomes Abe—there is a law of cause and effect going on that works out almost like a collaboration between the Buddha and Sophocles," Lowry said of the resemblance between Dick and Abe in Fitzgerald's novel ("Preface," p. 14). Convinced that Fitzgerald had failed to follow his own best intentions by letting the tale wither into pathos, Lowry established a ground on which Dick (as also Nicole, who stands in contrast to the Consul and Yvonne of *Under the Volcano*) could be reborn. Refusing to release Dick to the bleakness of a death-in-life, Lowry finds for him a means of spiritual realization in the end.

The Consul of *Under the Volcano* retreats into solipsistic despair when faced with the reality of human ambiguity and the vision of his own fate. Dick's vision (in Lowry's script) is obviously redemptive. In making his sacrifice for Nicole, Dick finds a way out of his moral cul-de-sac, out of the claustrophobic impasse which the Consul had been unable to escape and instead felt compelled to validate.

Lowry's Dick Diver finally has an opportunity for heroism different from any available to the Consul or Fitzgerald's Dick Diver. Lowry's March 1951 letter to Clemens ten Holder is revealing: "I had to go apparently *under Under the Volcano* myself in order eventually—as is now my intention—to redeem the Consul. I am now trying to redeem him" (CTH, p. 63). Though Lowry was here referring to his work in progress, to his "The Voyage That Never Ends," his statement brings to mind the filmscript. Lowry's Dick Diver, in the process of turning away from his own woes and insisting—though it will mean his death—on the salvation of his fellow man, achieves (not only for himself but also for Lowry's audience—even for Lowry) the very object Lowry now explicitly sought—the ennoblement of man.

In the sequence of stories that was to comprise his projected "The Voyage That Never Ends," Lowry hoped to affirm "evidence of . . . the survival of the soul" ("Voyage," p. 97). "The Voyage, of course," Lowry wrote in 1951 in a statement that again might as easily have referred to Dick Diver's journey as to the movement of characters within his entire prose corpus, "is life itself, the meaning of which and purpose of man herein this author takes to be primarily (among other more pleasant factors) ordeal, going through the hoop, an initiation, finally perhaps a doing of God's will" ("Voyage," p. 75). Lowry saw "The Voyage" ending on a decidedly happy note, "with the Wildernesses [his protagonists] watching the tide bearing the ships out upon its currents that become remote, and which, like the tide, becoming remote, return" ("Voyage," p. 97). Interestingly enough, Lowry does not allow Dick Diver the comfort of quite such a serenely happy future as he gives the Wildernesses. Perhaps in 1949–50 Lowry was not yet ready to risk a "happy ending" in his story, and Dick's voyage has to end in order that his moment of triumph is not eclipsed by Lowry's temptations to set in motion the mechanics of the absurd.

That the links between Lowry's filmscript and his other work are richer and more numerous than with Fitzgerald's novel invites further notice. Certain images—like the *Frère Jacques* motif—and entire scenes from the script are echoed in Lowry's stories, just as the long New York sequence (the middle one-third of section 29 in our edition) recalls *Lunar Caustic*. Dick's visit to Keats' house in Italy in the filmscript (in section 32 of our edition) is a variation on a similar scene in "Strange Comfort Afforded by the Profession." His chance meeting with Rosemary in Rome finds its counterpart in "Elephant and Colosseum," in which a character wonders whether he will have a romantic encounter in Rome with someone from his past. (He does have an encounter of sorts—although Rosemary turns out to be an elephant!) Lowry's cycling of material from text to text, his including the filmscript in that play among texts, confirms the centrality of the filmscript within his work at a time when he was placing his entire canon within the vast frame of his life project, "The Voyage That Never Ends."

Scholars have called attention to the intertextual character and the metafictional vein which run through Lowry's post-*Volcano* work. Sherrill Grace, pointing out how Lowry's use of marginalia in "Through the Panama" creates a rich and complex intertextuality, has also noted a similar interplay of the components in the script. Identical passages and expressions slip in and out of "Through the Panama" and the filmscript; they even have a double presence or coexistence in preliminary drafts, where pages of "Through the Panama" appear on the verso of pages of the Atlantic-crossing sequence of the filmscript (comprising the last one-third of section 29 in our edition). Certainly the filmscript is rich in inter- and also intratextual play. There is a wealth of provocative material formally placed by Lowry *within* the primary text of the script (and reprinted below): comments on Fitzgerald, on the characters, on matters of technique, discussions of literature and film and drama, all carried on alongside the narrative as part of a running dialogue with the reader. (As discourse, the filmscript is at one level epistolary in form, a long letter to Taylor and others in Hollywood; therefore, it is not surprising that a reader should always be directly implicated in Lowry's comments.) This extranarrative material of the filmscript (bringing to mind the post-modern structure of Lowry's short story, "Ghostkeeper") offers a self-reflexive commentary stimulating and complex enough to establish the script as perhaps the most outstanding demonstration of Lowry's metafiction during the years following *Under the Volcano*. (We must not forget to read it, on another plane, as metacinema too, an essay on film so richly cognizant of film traditions that Taylor's assessment is appropriate: "everything that has been thought, written and recorded on and about film is preparation for and prelude to this creation" (*Selected Letters*, p. 441).)

As metatext, in structure as in theme, Lowry's filmscript may be taken as a partial enactment, if not a formal segment, of his planned epic, "The Voyage That Never Ends"—what Lowry called the history of a human imagination ("Voyage," p. 6). Originally meant to resemble a kind of Dantesque trilogy, Lowry's projection of an interrelated sequence of stories included virtually everything he had ever written and might yet write, or revise. As Ronald Binns and Sherrill Grace have indicated, Lowry hoped that the stories in the proposed "Voyage" would escape stasis as each text rereads those which precede it and is in turn glossed by them, creating in the process an intertextual and metafictional dynamic.

The filmscript can be taken—although its status as part of Lowry's canon has so far been ambiguous—as an echo of this whole. In fact, the script's explorations of post-modern concerns, both within its own textual boundaries and in relation to Lowry's entire corpus, together with its stature as the only major work finished by Lowry after the mid-1940s, mark it as the apotheosis of Lowry's creative life after *Under the Volcano*.

"Here she goes. We don't know how to title it but perhaps that won't matter," Lowry wrote Taylor as he sent it off to him in April 1950. "Step right inside and see! Sex! Drama! Thrills! What should a doctor do? How should a doctor feel—with a human soul at stake! . . . We hope it will fire your imagination. So perhaps we should term it: an adjustable blueprint for an inspiration for a great American film" (*Selected Letters*, pp. 202, 205).

Works Cited in Preface and Introduction

Binns, Ronald. *Malcolm Lowry*. London, New York: Methuen, 1984.
Bradbrook, M. C. *Malcolm Lowry: His Art and Early Life—A Study in Transformation*. London: Cambridge University Press, 1974.
Burra, Edward. *Well, Dearie! The Letters of Edward Burra*, ed. William Chappell. London: Gordon Fraser, 1985.
Costa, Richard Hauer. *Malcolm Lowry*. New York: Twayne, 1972.
Day, Douglas. *Malcolm Lowry: A Biography*. New York: Oxford University Press, 1973.
Dodson, Daniel B. *Malcolm Lowry*. New York and London: Columbia University Press, 1970.
Falk, David. "Beyond the Volcano: The Religious Vision of Malcolm Lowry's Late Fiction," *Religion and Literature* 16 (1984): 25-38.
―――. "Self and Shadow: The Brothers Firmin in *Under the Volcano*." *Texas Studies in Literature and Language* 27 (1985): 209-23.
Fitzgerald, F. Scott. *The Portable F. Scott Fitzgerald*. New York: Viking, 1945 (includes the edition of *Tender Is the Night* used by Lowry).
Grace, Sherrill E. "'An Assembly of Apparently Incongruous Parts': Intertextuality in Lowry's 'Through the Panama.'" *Proceedings of the London Conference on Malcolm Lowry, 1984*, eds. Gordon Bowker and Paul Tiessen. Waterloo and London: Wilfrid Laurier University and University of London, 1985, pp. 135-65.
―――. "Malcolm Lowry and the Expressionist Vision." *The Art of Malcolm Lowry*, ed. Anne Smith. London: Vision Press, 1978, pp. 93-111.
―――. *The Voyage That Never Ends: Malcolm Lowry's Fiction*. Vancouver: University of British Columbia Press, 1982.
Kilgallin, Tony. *Lowry*. Erin, Ontario: Press Porcépic, 1973 (cited as Kilgallin).
Lowry, Malcolm. *Dark as the Grave Wherein My Friend Is Laid*. eds. Douglas Day and Margerie Lowry. Toronto: General Publishing, 1968 (cited as *Dark*).

———. "Elephant and Colosseum." *Hear us O Lord from heaven thy dwelling place*. Philadelphia and New York: J. B. Lippincott, 1961.

———. "Ghostkeeper." *Malcolm Lowry: Psalms and Songs*, ed. Margerie Lowry. New York and Scarborough: New American Library, 1975, pp. 202-27.

———. "Letter to Clemens ten Holder," ed. Terry Hilton, *The Malcolm Lowry Review*, 21-22 (Fall 1987-Spring 1988): 41-47 (cited as CTH).

———. *Lunar Caustic*, eds. Earle Birney and Margerie Lowry. London: Jonathan Cape, 1968 (1963).

———. *October Ferry to Gabriola*, ed. Margerie Lowry. New York and Cleveland: World Publishing, 1970 (cited as *October Ferry*).

———. *Selected Letters of Malcolm Lowry*, eds. Harvey Breit and Margerie Bonner Lowry. Philadelphia and New York: J. B. Lippincott, 1965 (cited as *Selected Letters*).

———. "Strange Comfort Afforded by the Profession." *Hear us O Lord from heaven thy dwelling place*. Philadelphia and New York: J. B. Lippincott, 1961.

———. "Three Letters to John Davenport," ed. Terry Hilton, *The Malcolm Lowry Review*, 21-22 (Fall 1987-Spring 1988): 18-30 (cited as JD).

———. "Through the Panama." *Hear us O Lord from heaven thy dwelling place*. Philadelphia and New York: J. B. Lippincott, 1961.

———. *Ultramarine*. London: Jonathan Cape, 1963 (1933).

———. *Under the Volcano*. Harmondsworth: Penguin Modern Classics, 1963 (Jonathan Cape, 1947) (cited as *UV*).

———. "The Voyage That Never Ends." *The Malcolm Lowry Review* 21-22 (Fall 1987-Spring 1988): 72-99 (cited as "Voyage").

Lowry, Malcolm, and Margerie Lowry. "A few items culled from what started out to be a sort of preface to a film-script," ed. Paul Tiessen. *White Pelican* 4, 2 (Spring 1974): 2-20 (cited as "Preface").

———. *Notes on a Screenplay for F. Scott Fitzgerald's Tender Is the Night*, ed. Matthew J. Bruccoli, introd. Paul Tiessen (pp. v-xix). Bloomfield Hills, MI, Columbia, SC: Bruccoli Clark, 1976 (cited as *Notes*).

Lowry, Malcolm, and Gerald Noxon. *The Letters of Malcolm Lowry and Gerald Noxon, 1940-1952*, ed. Paul Tiessen, with Nancy Strobel. Vancouver: University of British Columbia Press, 1988 (cited as *Lowry and Noxon Letters*).

Noxon, Gerald. "Malcolm Lowry: 1930," *Prairie Schooner*, 37 (1964): 315-20.

Spender, Stephen. "Introduction," to Malcolm Lowry's *Under the Volcano*. Philadelphia and New York: J. B. Lippincott, 1965, pp. vii-xxvi (cited as Spender).

Tiessen, Paul. "Malcolm Lowry and the Cinema," *Malcolm Lowry: The Man and His Work*, ed. George Woodcock. Vancouver: University of British

Columbia Press, 1971, pp. 133-43 (published earlier in *Canadian Literature*, 44 [Spring 1970]: 38-49) (cited as Tiessen).

See also:

Tiessen, Paul. "A Canadian Film Critic in Malcolm Lowry's Cambridge." *Flashback: People and Institutions in Canadian Film History*, ed. Gene Walz. Montreal: Mediatexte Publications, 1986, pp. 65-76.
———. "Something Forgotten, Something Lost: Gerald Noxon and the Creation of *Under the Volcano*." *Autobiographical and Biographical Writing in the Commonwealth*, ed. Doirrean MacDermott. Barcelona: Editorial AUSA, 1984, pp. 229-34.
———. "Here the Camera Must Be Our Shakespeare." *Canadian Drama/L'Art dramatique canadien*, 5, 1 (Spring 1979): 61-64.
———. "The Critic, the Film, and the Astonished Eye." *Figures in a Ground: Canadian Essays on Modern Literature in Honour of Sheila Watson*, eds. Diane Bessai and David Jackel. Saskatoon: Western Producer Prairie Books, 1978, pp. 125-40.
———. "Malcolm Lowry: Statements on Literature and Film." *The Practical Vision: Essays in English Literature in Honour of Flora Roy*, eds. Jane Campbell and James Doyle. Waterloo: Wilfrid Laurier University Press, 1978, pp. 119-32.
———, ed. *Apparently Incongruous Parts: The Worlds of Malcolm Lowry*. Metuchen, NJ: Scarecrow Press, 1990.
Tiessen, Paul, and Miguel Mota. "Introduction," to *"On Malcolm Lowry" and Other Writings by Gerald Noxon*. Waterloo: *Malcolm Lowry Review*, 1987, pp. iii-viii.
———. "Re-writing Fitzgerald: Malcolm Lowry's 'Tender Is the Night,'" *Transformations: From Literature to Film*, ed. Douglas Radcliff-Umstead. Kent, OH: Kent State University International Film Conference Proceedings, 1987, pp. 30-35.

A Note on the Text

Malcolm Lowry's manuscript, "Tender Is the Night," is a 455-page typescript which Lowry wrote in the period from July 1949 to April 1950. A carbon copy is housed in the Special Collections Division at the University of British Columbia Library. We have checked this copy against the original, which is located in the private Margerie Lowry collection in Los Angeles; the two copies are identical.

Parts of the typescript more or less simply follow the texture and text of F. Scott Fitzgerald's 1934 novel *Tender Is the Night*. In other places, thirty-eight in all, the typescript is largely original to Lowry; indeed, it often plays upon passages of his 1947 novel *Under the Volcano* or (as we note above) evokes passages from other of his works, especially *Lunar Caustic*, "Through the Panama," and "Strange Comfort Afforded by the Profession." It is the scenes and the authorial notes which are largely original to Lowry which we have edited for this scholarly edition. It is these sections that contribute to our sense of Lowry's aesthetic, his method of composition, and our reading of the themes of the larger Lowry corpus. We have omitted those scenes which Lowry drew more or less directly from Fitzgerald's novel (scenes which in any case are governed by copyright regulations preventing our using them here) and have summarized them within our brief editorial comments which precede each of the thirty-eight individual passages that comprise the "Lowry-text." These passages of "Lowry-text" vary in length from less than one page to over one hundred pages (in the case of the twenty-ninth passage). Readers will note that within our comments we have included references to the page source in Lowry's filmscript and to the sections in Fitzgerald's novel where corresponding passages can be located. In several cases where Lowry's version of the story deviates notably from Fitzgerald's in the narrative summarized in our comments, we have drawn attention to the variation or quoted directly (with page references to the filmscript) from Lowry.

In our own notes, which follow the filmscript, we have concentrated on people and works in areas to which the filmscript draws attention: especially film, theatre, literature, jazz and other music, and general culture of the 1920s. We have not supplied notes concerning persons readily recognized by the reader nor on the many place-names of the text (for example, streets or clubs in Paris, New York, or Rome) because in most cases they are self-annotating or adequately described by Lowry. For the same reasons, we have avoided commenting upon the expressions in languages other than English.

We have also included in our notes references made elsewhere by Lowry himself, notably in *Notes on a Screenplay for F. Scott Fitzgerald's Tender Is the Night*. Neither *Notes on a Screenplay* nor "A few items culled from what started out to be a sort of preface to a film-script" (a work from which we quote several times in our Introduction above) was incorporated by Lowry into the completed typescript. Rather, they were regarded by Lowry as instructions and observations designed to follow his submission of his 455-page manuscript in 1950.

There are virtually no typing errors or punctuation slips in the original typescript; in those two or three places where a minor slip has occurred, we have emended it silently. At the same time, we have deliberately retained Lowry's sometimes informal style, even a few inconsistencies in format here and there, to convey a sense of the filmscript's epistolary tone.

Finally, we must say that in dealing with the filmscript (as is the case with virtually all of Lowry's work after 1939) it is difficult to separate the writing of Malcolm Lowry from that of Margerie Lowry. The title page of the original manuscript for "Tender Is the Night" states that Margerie Bonner [Lowry] and Malcolm Lowry are the writers. Notations in the manuscripts of Lowry's letters and commentaries about the filmscript show that Lowry's "I" has often been changed to "we," his "me" to "us." In our Introduction, we have referred at times to Lowry alone, at other times to the Lowrys as seemed fitting. It should be remembered, however, that when we speak of Malcolm Lowry, there is always at his side the significant figure of his collaborator, Margerie; at the same time, when we refer to the Lowrys as co-writers, Malcolm Lowry's primary role should be borne in mind.

*A Scholarly Edition of Lowry's
"Tender Is the Night"*

A Scholarly Edition of Lowry's "Tender Is the Night"

1

Lowry's opening scene, technically reminiscent—with its succession of shots from extreme panoramic to medium close—of the opening paragraphs of Under the Volcano, *draws attention to Lowry's literary and cinematic preoccupations in the filmscript: the tactile treatment of sights and sounds as envisioned on an imaginary screen mingles with abstract, metaphysical, at times poetic evocations. His use of the collective "we" here, as many times throughout his text, unites camera, character, writer, and reader. Indeed, Lowry's reference to audience draws our attention to his desire to create through his text a single community comprised of himself, Margerie his collaborator, the readers/viewers of the filmscript, and the imagined viewers of the film he could see and hear and feel. This opening sequence ends with one of Lowry's own "notes" (the first of several which he incorporated into the filmscript, and which we include in this edition), in which Lowry explores some of the complexities in the relationships within the community of artists and audiences which he strove to create.*

The picture opens in dead silence with a tremendous shot of the night sky, the stars blazing.

It is a protracted shot, held long enough for us not only to feel the majesty of the night and the stars, but also how these last are mysteriously connected with man's destiny, with the destiny of earth, of God.

Then we become aware that the silence is not complete, and of a faint yet steady rhythmic throbbing sound as of a ship's engine; perhaps its pulsation is that of a ship's engine, but the sound seems as it were set wordlessly and remotely to the rhythm and even the ghostly melody, in a deep bass sense, of the old canon, *Frère Jacques*: yet at the same time we almost feel this to be more, to be perhaps the faint music of the universe itself, of the spheres, in the imperceptible endless motion of their courses.

A bright sailing moon now appears, is dominant, then disappears behind curdling clouds.

The camera seems to be bearing down upon us, so that the sensation we have is of receding downwards from the sky and the moon, and from this rhythm, to the earth.

The next instant the clouds become smoke coming out of a tunnel from which we see a train emerging into morning sunlight; the next we are in this train, in a first class compartment, with Rosemary Hoyt and her mother, watching the landscape of the French Riviera out of one window. Immediately we draw almost to a stop before a sign standing in a field on which we see in huge Greek capitals:[1]

ΑΝΤΙΠΟΥΙΣ

Meantime, as the camera comes closer, we see as much as is necessary in French and English of the sign itself, which reads in full as follows:

Touriste Américaine! Vous vous approchez maintenant de la ville ancienne d'ANTIBES. Original Greek: ANTIPOLIS

ΑΝΤΙΠΟΥΙΣ

Originally Greek, founded by the Greek Phoenicians, in the 3rd century, its latest walls were built by the great Vauban, and up till 1860 marked the Italo-French border.
HOTEL DES ETRANGERS, ANTIBES, 5 km. Confort Moderne.
Patron: Charles Gausse. (son delicieux couscous)
Beach clots—vins—liqueurs—Bar—
Everything for the American tourist at popular prices![2]

Some sign painter—who catching sight of the Hoyts and perhaps feeling they are Americans, smiles almost beckoningly at them—is just putting the finishing touches to this sign, so that it is apparently new.

Of these two in the compartment, Rosemary Hoyt is 18, and has a beauty of the sort that depends mostly upon her radiant youth, though she is seductive enough. Her mother is pretty too, with an expression both tranquil and aware. On the other hand, as they look out of the window, we feel that if they are not actively bored, they are both rather consciously blasé.

Mrs. Hoyt: (cheerfully) Rosemary, something tells me we're not going to like this place . . . The guide book here says it's scarcely worth the trouble of a visit.

Rosemary: I want to go home, anyway, Mother.

As the train now forges on, the camera goes beyond the sign, and in contrast to the feeling aroused by these remarks, takes in a shattering landscape: the Bay of Angels, at Antibes, and now, beyond it, the Alps themselves, clear and terrible, cutting the suddenly empty sky with lance points and spearheads like uplifted templars' swords.

Cut to the sea, thundering in Homeric majesty against the beach; but in such a way that we feel we are still behind the camera, still entering Antibes. Upon a promontory we see a conspicuous lighthouse, higher up a church: the camera moves along to a beach, takes in a deeply bronzed figure, diving into the surf, returns immediately to the lighthouse, with the church above, which is Notre Dame d'Antibes, and, always with the Alps in view, begins to travel swiftly up the street, marked by chapels, the stations of the cross, that leads to it: we see the name of the street: Via Crucis, the Way of the Cross. Then the camera goes briefly into Antibes itself: narrow and quiet streets, massive doorways with Gothic arches—corbels—and crowning everything, two ancient square towers, one taller than the other, one adorned with curved horns, like a Norseman's helmet; the whole impression is, dramatically, of massiveness, of antiquity, and militance.[3]

But the primary impression is that Antibes is a walled city, a fortress, with the solid towers rising above the walls, and the Alps always in the background: the camera comes to rest at a point by the more lofty tower where a guide is indicating a stone with an inscription upon it, also in ancient Greek, to two American tourists, a shabby-eyed, pretty woman, and a rather scrawny man of about thirty, both wearing espadrilles and in rough dateless indiscriminate holiday clothes, though they are not as yet suntanned. They seem decent kindly people, by themselves, yet there is a hint of motiveless tension between them. From a window in the tower—doubtless still a barracks—we hear a gramophone playing jazz music very faintly: Gershwin's *Somebody Loves Me*.[4]

The Woman: Albert—we're already late for the beach—

The Man: (rather importantly, in a way) I was just going to ask him this, Violet, (to the guide in rather bad, not too bad, French) est-ce-que le romancier français, Guy de Maupassant, a écrit un—

The Guide: Ah oui—de Maupassant—ah, Monsieur, he lived here—and I am going to show you, the house where he lived, and the very room—

The Man: No, no—but didn't he write something about someone who shut a woman up in this tower?

The Guide: Ah that is a true story, Monsieur, of Antibes, well known here. When Antibes was a garrison town, after the war of 1870, (the camera takes in the tower with the horns, the gate, the walls) a girl here is married to a man who kept her shut up here, but the captain of the fortress is her friend-boy, and in order to have one kiss—Madame—while her husband is in Nice one day, the captain orders the gates of the city closed by the army . . . So when the husband returns the soldiers will not let him into the city, and the friend-boy, c'est l'amour, vous savez—but her husband, now, he is locked out, outside the city, at the station—

Cut to the station of Antibes, outside the walls, where the train we have seen before has just drawn in. Rosemary and her mother get out and cross the platform toward the sortie. Meantime a handsome tall American wearing a jockey cap and a fisherman's jersey, dungarees and espadrilles, and an unusually beautiful woman in slacks, accompanied by two children, all of whom are deeply tanned, are observed seeing off an expensively dressed woman leaning out of a Wagon-Lit carriage.

The Woman Who Is Leaving: (to the others) But I do feel you are so dreadfully cooped up here. Nicole, my dear—

The Man: (as the train begins to move) And Baby, if you do run into Gregorovious, by any chance in Zurich, tell him I want that pamphlet back. I wrote him twice . . . Tell him not to get lost in the edelweiss . . .

As the train pulls out we see signs in the Antibes station, in French, Italian and English: Défense de traverser les voies, E proibito traversare i banari, It is forbidden to cross the lines: also some travel advertisements, for Cannes, Nice and Paris, and lastly, Zurich, Suisse, with the Alps as background in the poster.

Cut to Rosemary Hoyt and her mother in a horse cab which is trotting down a steep dusty hill toward the sea. Dusty poplars line the hill, beyond which can be seen a few old villas, and below and beyond, the Mediterranean, with smoke from merchantmen hull-down on the horizon. The walled town of Antibes with its towers is visible through the trees to one side. The Hoyts' victoria is passed at considerable speed by an Isotta-Fraschini, containing the man in the jockey cap, the woman, and the children, and driven by a chauffeur. The Hoyts have to hold their hands over their faces against the dust the Isotta cannot help raising. The dust clears away for us to see before us another sign for the hotel we saw advertised from the train, standing in a garden among trees: Hotel des Etrangers, P. H. Gausse, (son delicieux couscous) etc. The victoria has turned in at the road entrance of the hotel itself. Then the Hoyts, followed by a bus boy, are walking through the hotel lobby to the desk: near the desk we see a calendar: Juin 1926.

Cut to Rosemary, still in her travelling clothes, standing alone on a verandah of the hotel looking down at the crescent of beach and the sea.

The camera regards the beach, from Rosemary's viewpoint. It is almost deserted. In the immediate foreground are three British nannies, knitting and gossipping; about the middle of the crescent are two groups of people under striped umbrellas; at the water's edge some children shouting; a little way out to sea is an empty raft, rocking, with a high diving board.

Rosemary and the camera now become more concerned with the people on the beach; the more interesting group belongs to the umbrellas on the left: three men, a woman, and two beautiful children, all deeply tanned, the latter, and one of the men, being the same people we saw at the station, though we don't know whether Rosemary saw them or not.

(Note: So far as possible in this first section we are within Rosemary's mind and vision, and increasingly it is the intention to share her curiosity and subjective feeling—without the camera and ourselves playing truant to these. Nonetheless, since it has proved detrimental entirely to maintain this, after all, purely literary fiction— even Fitzgerald could not maintain it as that in a book—the consistency has been deliberately and objectively broken at the very outset. There is of course a slight division too between the camera and ourselves: we know slightly more than Rosemary, and less than the camera has suggested. But this establishes from the beginning the right of the camera to see a little more than Rosemary later, when it wants to, and ourselves to see and hear more. But the privilege is not abused: the camera's role is rather that of a sporting clairvoyant who, while knowing the story backwards and forwards, doesn't want to spoil it by letting the cat out of the bag, yet simply can't resist letting the cat just poke a whisker out now and then. In this way we will not question later the precedent the camera has thus subtly established for itself to insinuate meaning.) (Lowry, pp. 1–7)

2

Lowry, now basing his text on Fitzgerald, follows Rosemary as she walks to the beach and lies down between two groups of people. In the one are the American tourists from the tower, Albert and Violet McKisco; with them are an older woman, Mrs. Abrams, and two rather effeminate young men. The other group consists of the young family from the train station (their two children now playing a sand-game that involves trying to sing Frère Jacques*) and two other men, Abe North, a pianist and composer, and Tommy Barban, a soldier. McKisco points out to his wife the walled house where he says the other group is staying, a house which reminds him of the de Maupassant story. (See Lowry, pp. 7-9 and Fitzgerald, 1, i.)*

Lowry's own note follows in the filmscript.

Note: The tempo is important before anything: some of the dialogue is overlapping, some not: it is up to the discretion of the director what parts can be most effectively stressed and how fluid the camera is, but the feeling should be on the one hand of such intensive realism that we feel ourselves actually to be on the beach, in contrast to the greater dramatic selectivity of the opening, and on the other, imperceptibly, of more selectivity still, so that we feel ourselves gradually drawn by a thread into a curiosity about the Divers, and some mystery in their life: actually in this first beach scene we have two such threads beside the camera, there is the quasi-literary ficelle of McKisco, who enjoys a position of near subjectivity at one point, though he is of course subservient to Rosemary, who is the camera dominantly, and the prime "subjectivity:" in the second beach scene we do not need McKisco in this role, for he is in the process of becoming a more objective character, and the observation is all Rosemary's and the camera's; however it is in the second beach scene, where there is deliberately seemingly more irrelevant dialogue, that the question of overlapping is the more important: here the tempo has to be slightly speeded up, but the effect will be lost if every line is a home run. (Lowry, pp. 9-10)

3

From her spot on the beach Rosemary watches the group with the young children, focusing first on the woman, beautiful yet severe at the same time, then on the man, who at once captures Rosemary's interest. Mrs. Abrams approaches Rosemary, whom she has recognized as the actress whose latest film, Daddy's Girl, *is currently popular and also much admired by the McKiscos. Rosemary swims out to a raft, followed by the McKiscos. The beautiful woman in the other group, the McKiscos inform Rosemary, is Mrs. Diver, of the rich Warren family from Chicago, and the man is (much to Rosemary's disappointment) her husband, Dr. Diver, currently a non-practising psychiatrist.*

Rosemary swims back to shore and falls asleep. Cannes hovers in the distance like a mirage, its reflection shimmering in the water, a sailboat and sleeping gulls adding to the feeling of noonday peace. In the distance a school of sharks moves across the sea just beneath the water. Rosemary wakes to see Dr. Diver standing above her; he warns her not to get too much sun on the first day.

Later, Rosemary has lunch with her mother in the hotel. The McKiscos pass by, and it is obvious that Rosemary does not like them very much. She tells her mother that she has fallen in love with Dr. Diver.

On the beach the next day, Rosemary watches excitedly as Dr. Diver performs stunts on an aquaplane. She dozes off and again wakes up to find him standing above her. He invites her to join his group and introduces her to his wife, Nicole, as well as to Tommy Barban and Abe North. (See Lowry, pp. 10–18 and Fitzgerald, 1, i-iv.)

Lowry's note follows.

Note: the dramatic and spiritual choreography of this scene is now as follows: Dick has managed the introduction so that Rosemary's name isn't mentioned, but letting her know that they have recognized her, (presumably from her photographs in magazines, etc.) while respecting the completeness of her private life. Rosemary is enchanted with the Divers, who are in fact enchanting people. If Dick, by reason of his effortless charm and high spirits, is the dominant figure, Nicole is clearly the central and most dramatic figure, and seen at close quarters the qualities we have observed, her beauty, her indrawnness, her distinction, are accentuated. It is apparent, if not immediately obvious, too, that North and Barban are in love with her and she accepts their homage quietly, in a friendly manner, and without the slightest hint of flirtatiousness. Nicole Diver is quiet and self contained, intent this morning upon some sewing, and keeping an eye on the children—who are playing the Frère Jacques game again, in the surf, a half-built castle appearing nearer in the sand—yet the focus of her being, her serious attention, whatever may occupy the surface of her mind, is always directed toward her husband. Barban conveys a kind of disgust and impatience with the general environment yet gives the impression of being the most serious person present. The general tone of the scene is easy, informal and gay. (Lowry, p. 18)

4

Dick, Nicole, Tommy Barban, Abe North, and Rosemary exchange pleasantries and small talk about the other people on the beach, poking fun at the group with the McKiscos. Dick, working with a rake to get pebbles out of the sand, slowly makes his way up the beach in the direction of the McKiscos. The Divers' children, Topsy and Lanier, are building an elaborate sand castle with a large moat. The castle, Lanier points out, is supposed to be Topsy's father's castle, and the big moat is meant to keep people out. He must rescue Topsy, he explains, but the sharks in the moat prevent him from doing so. Listening to all this, Rosemary finds herself gazing at Dick, now working his way back to the group, and she sighs with clear and obvious infatuation, as Nicole notices. Nicole's mood changes at once, although subtly; she seems on the verge of becoming vitriolic, almost dangerous, as she complains that there are far too many people now on this beach, which she claims Dick himself has built out of a pile of pebbles. Lowry emphasizes that Dick's expression here hints that he is uneasy at something in Nicole's mood and wishes to distract her in some way. In fact, Lowry claims, Nicole may have unconsciously given Dick the intimation that she wants him to interfere with her mood and show his authority. Suddenly, Dick decides that he will invite the McKiscos and their friends to dinner, a decision which, for the moment, terrifies Nicole but which at least has the effect of disrupting her previous mood.

Dick and Rosemary go down to the water and meet the McKiscos, whom Dick invites to dinner that evening at the Divers' villa. Dick, Rosemary, and Barban swim out to the raft, where Dick performs some complicated dives in front of Rosemary.

Again, the scene changes to Rosemary having lunch with her mother in the hotel dining room, and she once more tells her mother how much she is in love with Dick. She likes Nicole, too, she says, but adds that Nicole never laughs.

The scene changes to Nicole's unsmiling face at the Villa Diana. She is making her way toward Dick's workhouse at the far end of the garden. Lowry suggests that although, on the one hand, she does not dare disturb him, her look of piteous doubt may be caused by his absence from her—she feels that she must be near him. Nicole walks through the beautiful garden, past the workhouse, and stands at the wall at the back of the garden looking down over the precipice to the Mediterranean below. Dick emerges from his workhouse with a telescope, which he uses to gaze first at the sea and then at Nicole. Picking up a megaphone (though Nicole is easily within hearing distance),

Dick bellows out to a now rather good-humoured Nicole that he has invited Mrs. Abrams to the party as well and that he will invite also the two effeminate young men from the McKiscos' group. (See Lowry, pp. 19–26 and Fitzgerald, 1, iv, vi.)

The camera moves up to Tommy Barban on the terrace where he is smoking a pipe and engaged in cleaning his pistols with oil and wadding and occasionally sighting through them. Behind Barban, through the open French windows, we see into the house where Abe North is sitting at the piano, leafing through some music. He has a drink beside him on the piano and an ashtray crammed with cigarette stubs. Also on the piano, in a folding leather frame, are two photographs: Nicole, as a young girl, and Dick, in the uniform of a captain in the U.S. Army, Medical Corps. The following exchange of dialogue is overlapping.
Barban: (shouting) If you're going to invite the Neverquivers I've got to have Geneveva de Momus. We can phone her long distance to Vevey.
Dick's Voice: (through the megaphone, directed at Nicole) I want to give a really *bad* party. I mean it. I want to give a party where there's a brawl, and women going home with their feelings hurt and people passed out in the bathroom . . .
Barban: (mutters to himself in French, obviously vaguely irritated, then) Do you hear that, Abe?
Abe, looking melancholy, takes a sip from his glass. He has not heard.
Dick: (as the camera comes back to him) . . . You wait and see! (with a final admonitory gesture he puts down the megaphone and returns abruptly into his workhouse. The camera follows him inside.)
We see books everywhere on every kind of nervous disorder, some by himself with highly technical titles, some in German, published in Zurich, then, upon a desk, his work in progress, entitled: Psychiatry for You.
Dick shakes his head, goes to a shelf, takes out a far more complicated and serious-looking work on pre-Krapelin cases, also by himself, also in manuscript, and also unfinished. We see the phrase: "As Dohmler, then as Gregorovious, his pupil, disclosed . . ." He glances at it and puts it back. We form the swift, unsubtle inference, that something has caused him to discard the more serious work for the more popular. In the corner, the camera sees an old fashioned gramophone with a large horn, that does not seem much in use: there is a 12 inch German record upon it, with a highly technical title, that has

to do with the Psychopathology of Verbalistics: lying half hidden under some modern records, Dick's eye falls on an old dusty American jazz record, of the tune *Smiles*.[5] Dick half picks it up, reveals another old record, of the *Japanese Sandman*,[6] replaces it. He frowns cheerfully, it would seem, for an instant at his work, then taking his telescope goes back outside. As Dick raises his telescope we see Barban, in the background on the terrace, perform a similar action with his gun, sighting down the barrel. Then we are looking through Dick's telescope again at the freighter, which is now much nearer. She appears, from the Greek lettering on the hull, a battered old Russian, or Greek, steamer, but Dick's instrument is sufficiently powerful for us to see—or we make it do so—the washing hanging between the derricks and even some of the crew off watch. On the bridge the quartermaster at the wheel is striking five bells: the lookout man on the foc's'le head strikes his bells five times, mutely. A blackened stoker comes on deck from down below and stands, in his shuddering flimsies, taking great breaths of air. Huge clouds of spray break over the ship, from which we now see that an officer scanning the coast is apparently watching Dick through *his* telescope. Dick smiles, for there is even a huge megaphone on the ship's bridge, and we read the vessel's cryptic name: she is unmistakeably Greek. As Dick finally makes it out we see the Greek lettering of its name on the hull: ΟΙΔΙΠΟΥΣ ΤΥΡΑΝΝΟΣ dechristen itself into its English counterparts: *Oedipus Tyrannus . . . Piraeus*.

Dick shifts the telescope before we have "got" all the *Piraeus*, and the deserted beach before Gausse's hotel comes into focus, then the road of the opening shots of the film, leading up through the poplars to Antibes station. Long shadows lie across the road, now seen in the most beautiful light of day, the long, level light of approaching sunset, behind, the towers and walls of the old town, behind that the Alps. We have the feeling, though the time it takes is fractional, that none of these images is quite art for art's sake: perhaps Dick will find himself taking a freighter like that one day; the beach will mean something for him again, and ourselves, and so will the road, leading as yet to abstract departure. Nevertheless all this has created a lyrical mood in ourselves, and apparently a happy one in Dick. Nicole is now seen again through the telescope still leaning over the precipice with her back to the camera and Dick takes the megaphone once more.

Dick: (barely whispering through the megaphone) I love you so much . . . (we cannot gauge the abstractness or concreteness of his expressed feeling, whether it is directed toward life, the home, or Nicole. But for some reason Nicole turns around.)

Nicole: Dick, the gulls!

Dick puts down his megaphone and runs to her. In the garden, a scarcely observed, tiny little snake wriggles away from him into the bushes. The gulls, a straggling undulating marathon of them, are flying home out of the west along the coast and it is evidently a ritual for the Divers to watch them in the evening. They pass with a soft persistent whispering sound. Dick puts his arm around Nicole's shoulder. Somewhere a clock strikes the half hour, thus confirming to the initiate, who knows it must be about half past six, the time mutely struck on the ship. In the house Abe starts to play a strange and melancholy piece on the piano, like the best kind of jazz, a thing of many twelfths in the left hand, but again not precisely jazz per se. He plays it rather slowly and from any point of view expertly, and it is significant that he plays this piece and no other. It is *In a Mist*, by Bix Beiderbecke.[7] Those of us who bother about such things recognize it as by Beiderbecke and that, even more than Gershwin, he perhaps sums up the "jazz age," more, because there was in him, like Abe himself, the tragedy of a wasted life. Moreover this is one of the few wordless jazz pieces in existence which seems to sum up such a life and can reasonably be called tragic. But even those of us who do not know it, recognize its beauty and that it is haunting to the point of mania.

(Note: Since writing this we learn of the coming production of *A Young Man With a Horn*, from Dorothy Baker's book, about Beiderbecke.[8] It would seem that anyone who knew his music must have used this piece, doubtless even as the theme of that film, so that we cannot know whether it will conflict or not. It is just possible however that the makers of *A Young Man With a Horn* have had to concentrate on Beiderbecke entirely as a trumpet player and band leader, and not at all, or little, as a composer, in which case it would be reasonable for them to have left this piece out, which is simply for the piano, and unadaptable to an orchestra in any form. If Beiderbecke will not do, one of the very different compositions of Willard Robison[9] would nearly as well here, but it is to be hoped that this does not invalidate the use of an obscure companion piece of Beiderbecke's later on in the film. It is wrong to imagine "such a thing," as easy to compose, however, even by a genius: its effect is unique and hard to come by, by which is meant also that just any good jazz of the period will not do at all, the idea being here to suggest finally, and establish a haunting and underlying serious quality in, or motif for, the jazz age itself, like desperation, but as different from what usually is meant by desperation in that connection, even the desperation as evinced occasionally in Gershwin being serious—who is used elsewhere, however, from time to time—as chalk from cheese.)

Dick and Nicole stand together, silent for a moment, listening to Abe's music, watching the gulls, and watching too the long, sunlit scroll of wash from the Greek freighter rolling toward them across the bay.

Nicole: What's that Abe's playing? You know I don't like jazz as a rule, but that's good . . . But I don't know why, the music makes me sad tonight.

Dick: Do you remember when you said that to me before?

Nicole murmurs affirmatively and leans against him.

Dick: Poor old Abe. He's feeling pretty gloomy these days.

Nicole: At going away, you mean.

Dick: (seriously) Well . . . and because of his work. He hasn't done at all what he intended to—who has, have they?—do we? It's nearly seven years ago—Lord, Nicole, (the wash from the freighter begins to break against the cliffs) when I first knew him in New York—

Nicole: But you remember years ago, when he was one of our only friends, how gay and assured he could be. (The wash now breaks more thunderously against the rocks below the precipice, sending up its recurring crash and boom through the remainder of the dialogue.)

Dick: (his tone changing, and looking over the precipice) He's sad . . . maybe a bit acrophilic at the thought of all those skyscrapers yawning below him—or above him—after so long . . . Hear the wash . . . It's from that Greek freighter out there, you can scarcely see it now . . . It's got a good name for a ship too, I made it out through the telescope. (chuckles) *Oedipus Tyrannus*—eh? Tyrannus is right.

Nicole: But you're not sad, are you?

Dick shakes his head and kisses her.

Nicole: Dick . . . The Rosemary girl's coming tonight with her mother, isn't she? Will you like that?

Dick: I thought she might cheer poor Abe up a little . . . Don't you like that?

Nicole: I don't like ickle durls. Especially when they're so tweet. (She hides her head in Dick's coat while Abe goes on playing.)

Cut to the lanterns hung in the trees: their lights go on. It is twilight now, just turning to night, the magical hot sweet night of the south. We see firefly sparks riding the air and hear a dog baying far away, probably at the moon, which has risen over the sea and now shines full on the garden. The bell over the door in the garden wall tinkles, and we are outside in the road, on the other side of the door, where Mrs. Hoyt and Rosemary are standing and a victoria is just turning round. So far in this sequence we have been playing truant to Rosemary. (Note—though with rather more philosophic justification, so to speak, than Fitzgerald, especially with the addition of Barban and Abe at least to suggest some slight censorship of the expression, or their expression too loudly, of secret thoughts which so far are unknown to ourselves and to Rosemary.) Now, gradually, we begin to see with her eyes again. We see the wall, thick with roses, the name of the house, Villa Diana, over the door, and the moon rising. (Lowry, pp. 26–33)

5

Dick, his coat over his arm like a bullfighter's cape, with something of the rebel and adventurer about him, greets Mrs. Hoyt and Rosemary at the door of the Villa Diana. Nicole runs out to greet them too, and Mrs. Hoyt makes notice of the beautiful garden, which Dick claims is Nicole's very own. (See Lowry, p. 33 and Fitzgerald, 1, vi.)

Lowry's note follows.

Note: It is important that the following scene should be dominated by the moon and by moonlight. The moon, riding higher and brighter in the sky as the evening goes on, is used as the double symbol of love and madness, and also, occasionally, of remoteness, the ideal, the unattainable. In a psychological sense this last usage of the moon has a profundity of its own: for it is precisely the pretence that this unattainable ideal exists as a tractable reality (the living phantasy of the unconscious) which is held to be one prime cause of neurosis and madness: on these symbolic terms therefore, psychological reality coincides with the ancient belief that the moon itself does cause madness, so that the moon is also cause and effect at once. The moonlight is used predominantly, over the light of candles and lanterns there is moonlight, and the camera should be employed to evoke all the witchery, poetry and magic of a moonlit garden, with the underlying terror implicit there too. Shadows should be used, sometimes circling, sometimes greatly attenuated, sometimes vast and menacing, and when there is a gust of wind in the trees, suddenly they gallop. Yet shadows caused by moonlight are different from other shadows, peopling the night in a way of their own, rendering it a sort of nocturnal day, and should a shadow be menacing, it conveys no ordinary or obvious menace. We should be aware too, if possible, though in no "Little Theatre" sense, of a gnarled fig tree,

and an ancient black cypress, the one is life, the other death, though their reality and beauty as trees is more important. Through the trees, always behind, above, is the militant, prison-like yet dramatic town. There is yet another light, that we have made no very specific directions for, but which—though it should be used sparingly—is almost as important. This is distantly supplied by the lighthouse of Antibes itself, far down below and out on the point that we saw at the beginning of the film—which occasionally is seen flashing a beam across the night. The lighthouse invites the storm, but also lights it—but the idea here is that it is this man-made light, that flashes an occasional ray of sanity across the proceedings, a beam of hope across the moonlight and the sea—the sea during the film is established as a symbol of the unconscious itself. Were this a poetical tragedy such images would be the substance of one's poetry here. They are in fact still, but not in words. Though a little later people discuss the night, and implications are made, we can't afford to say anything as pertinent as we have suggested, besides the dialogue is mostly ironical. The camera's rôle therefore here is of an interpreter whose intensity of awareness is far in excess of anyone's present; however the camera cannot wander far afield on its own and its behaviour is nearly always simultaneous with the action and it does not need to suggest too much—in fact it is absurd to suppose it should *deliberately* suggest as much as this. On the other hand the more purely photographic beauty there is in keeping with what is relevant, the more room our creative imaginations have in which to move: perhaps only a fraction of these things could or should emerge into our full consciousness, all one is saying here is that the camera's evocative power is much greater than that of words, for it can say several things at once, and, though this last is scarcely news, we ventured to think that a citation of some of the possible evocations here might be helpful for the director to work upon. Murnau's intention in *Sunrise*[10] cannot have been as complicated and extreme as this, yet the complexity and intensity of the emotions aroused by one single very short sequence of moonlight at the opening have stayed with us for over twenty years. At the time, however, one was moved simply by its sheer beauty. Perhaps by identifying the truth with the latter Keats meant something like this. Perhaps too when we have said the intention was complicated, all we really meant is that it should seem simple, above all, in execution, be moving.
(Lowry, pp. 33-36)

6

The McKiscos arrive at the Villa Diana to join the others, and McKisco points out to his wife that Diana is the moon goddess, also known as Luna, the symbol of lunacy. Dick, ever the devoted parent in a way that Nicole appears not to be, kisses his children goodnight; but before they can go off to bed, Abe asks them to sing a song and accompanies them on the piano. (See Lowry, pp. 36-37 and Fitzgerald, 1, vi.)

Lanier and Topsy, standing hand in hand, sing:

>Au claire de la lune
>Mon ami Pierrot
>Prête-moi ta plume
>Pour écrire un mot
>Ma chandelle est morte
>Je n'ai plus de feu
>Ouvre-moi ta porte
>Pour l'amour de Dieu.[11]

As the children begin to sing, the camera moves from their faces to the moon, climbing the sky, giving us a sense of purity and simplicity without. Within, however, Abe plays the accompaniment, adding very softly some terrifying harmonies and dissonances of his own, so that the complexity within contrasts with the purity without: indeed the simplicity outside has terror within. On the word "Pierrot" we see, from Rosemary's viewpoint, beyond the children, Abe playing, and as the camera moves swiftly up to him the song seems relevant to Abe himself, who has composed no music for so long; and yet by the time we hear "morte" it might as well apply to Dick, whom we suspect of having abrogated his higher self also, and Abe accentuates the two chords on which "morte" falls. Immediately the camera has come up to Abe we hear him murmuring the words in English to himself. This he does flatly, even sardonically, without self-pity, and as it were against the music: "Lend me your pen, to write a word, my candle is dead, I have no light." On "Je n'ai plus de feu, ouvre-moi ta porte," a tragic plea that everyone can apply to themselves, the camera moves back from Abe, playing and saying: "My candle is dead, I have no light, open thy door, for the love of God," through the literally open door to the children's faces and then, with the supplication of "pour l'amour de Dieu," takes in the sailing moon again to which, with its bilingual significance of love and madness we feel always a certain ambivalence, and finally on the "Dieu" moves back to the whole night sky and the stars, thus holding up the whole little scene against eternity, as though the screen had broadened out, which spiritually and dramatically it has. Thus, in the space of less than half a minute, even those who have not understood French, have experienced the effect of every known form of irony, including the Socratic, and some unknown. The intention however is that it should be a moment at the same time so intensely moving, so exquisite, that all the characters stand motionless, as if in a crystal. Nor should we see—or at least it would be very risky—people's rapt faces, least of all the McKiscos or the "Neverquivers." Immediately the song is over we see the children smiling, and running away to bed, and beyond them, through the window, Abe, who takes a drink from his glass on the piano and, glad to be alone, goes on playing for a while. He plays Bach. Anyway the applause is not for him.

We cut right through scattered clapping, Barban's "Bravissimo," Dick's "Thank you, that was fine, now off to bed," to Rosemary and Barban alone by the table near the precipice. The lighthouse on the point throws a beam against the night. In the background on the terrace and strolling in the garden in groups we see the others. Dick is everywhere tactfully assimilating, separating, rearranging, offering drinks, thinking of his guests' happiness and comfort. (Lowry, pp. 37-39)

7

The party continues, with the guests scattered, mingling throughout the villa. Barban informs Rosemary that he is going off to war the next day. Staying with the Divers, he tells a confused Rosemary, always makes him want to go to war. Later, when she is alone with him, Rosemary tells Dick that she fell in love with him the moment she saw him, a declaration that Dick accepts as a formal compliment. Still later, during dinner, Rosemary notices that for the first time since she has met her, Nicole is suddenly laughing and gay; but when Dick's eyes find Nicole's she becomes calm and withdrawn again. Barban notices the momentary tension and tries to keep the conversation going in order to draw attention away from it. Near the end of dinner, the group talks about Abe's recent attempt to saw a waiter in half with a musical saw. (See Lowry, pp. 39-42 and Fitzgerald, 1, vi-vii.)

McKisco: (to Dick) Now then, Diver, what kind of complex would that give a waiter, do you suppose, to be sawn in two.

Barban: (quickly) He said waiter, not writer.

Rosemary: (for McKisco's sake, to Dumphrey) But no, Mother and I do a lot of walking in Hollywood, don't we, Mother?

Mrs. Hoyt: (to Rosemary) *You* do. (then to Dumphrey) I suppose she must walk five miles a day on the set.

Campion: Did you walk five miles a day on *Daddy's Girl*?

Rosemary, noticing Nicole seems strained, is thinking of something to say when Mrs. Abrams, eyeing the moon sailing above the trees, comes to the rescue in a moment's pause.

Mrs. Abrams: (rapturously) Tender is the night.[12] . . . How does it go on, anybody?

Dick: (as the moon goes beneath a cloud) But here there is no light.

McK: (to Dick) Save what from heaven, no. Keats surely meant moonlight was the only light there was . . . But haply the moon—haply the—Keats seemèd obsessed by the moon—my wife was asking—had you that in mind, these moonlight nights I mean, when you called this the Villa Diana?

Barban: (noticing Nicole's increasing excitement) Didn't Keats write a song about four fairies?

Dumphrey: (looking at Campion) *Four*, my *dear*!

Mrs. Abrams: (brilliantly, being surrounded by two of them herself) And haply the Queen Moon is on her throne, clustered round by all her starry Fays.

There is loud laughter at this, Dumphrey and Campion being especially delighted at so much attention.

Abe: Here where men sit and hear each other groan (taking a drink) Where youth grows pale and spectre thin and dies.

Barban: To thy high requiem become a sod.

McK: (to Dick) Aren't you a friend of Van Duren Biana—I mean Van Buren Denby?

Dick: (shaking his head politely) It seems we all know our Keats, eh, for some reason. (We hear the sea pounding suddenly, but getting rougher) But how about our Homer? We shouldn't forget that it's the Mediterranean, still old Homer's Mediterranean.

Rosemary: That's just what I said to Mr. McKisco—

Abe: You mean it's Gausse's Mediterranean.

Dick: The Mediterranean of the *Odyssey*—or should we? (we hear the surge and thunder of the sea, and see, momentarily, the moonlit Mediterranean)

McK: (while the camera is still on the sea) That's right. Poor old

Oedipus. (the camera comes back to McKisco) That's all he's become now, a complex—

Abe: You're thinking of Stout Cortez, McKisco.

Dick: I'm not sure there isn't wisdom in your words, Mr. McKisco—this town had gotten on very well for fifteen hundred years or whatever without remembering it was Greek—I suggested to Gausse—your patron, Mrs. Hoyt—something might be made of that; next thing we know they're putting up a sign by the railway.

Mrs. Hoyt: Yes, we saw it—

Dick: The next thing is the merchants come—are beginning to come—

Nicole: But Dick, the idea was—

McK: (to the table in general) Say, did you ever read that story about Antibes by de Maupassant, guide we had the other day said it was based on a true story in 1870—about a man who shut up some woman in this town here, in Antibes—that is, de Maupassant doesn't say it quite like that—he just has the husband shut up, I mean shut out, but in true story, when Antibes was a garrison town, some man has a woman shut up here—

Barban: (helpfully) Just shut up.

Abe: Stout Cortez, McKisco. Oedipus wasn't mentioned in the *Odyssey*.

Barban: No, he is thinking of Ulysses.

McK: Eh? I never said that Eulipus was in the Odysses. (to Dick) But can't there be a Ulysses complex too?

Barban: Yes, but confined to writers, isn't that it?

Mrs. McK: (who has been getting quietly tight) That's very rude. My husband wrote the first—

Barban: (right across the table) Dick, who was the Greek that smelled?

Dick: (smiling) Philoctetes . . . He was a good shot.

Cut to the table and the precipice with the sea below and the lanterns alight among the trees. Two picturesque oil lamps are alight on the table. Barban and Dick are together by the wall, drinking brandy and smoking cigars. Abe and McKisco are a little apart from them but McKisco seems on the point of breaking into their conversation while Abe is staring gloomily out to sea. Next to them Nicole is talking to Mrs. Hoyt: then Rosemary and Mrs. McKisco. Mrs. Abrams and the young men are on the terrace, laughing, with their drinks. Down below the Mediterranean is growing rougher and surges and booms against the cliff. There is troubled moonlight on the sea, and the stars above. The lighthouse sends out, intermittently, its remote beam. We see the moving lights of a ship, as of the obscure lights of the human soul itself out there in the darkness.

Barban: Why shouldn't I bring in God? Is the thought disgusting?

Dick: I merely said that Freud had said he never felt that oceanic feeling himself.

McK: (tightly) Das grosse Machiniste—I don't follow either of you. What the heck, the Mediterranean isn't even an ocean.

Dick glances at Nicole, who is pressing on Mrs. Hoyt a beautiful evening bag she has admired. In the moonlight we notice again a remote, staring quality in Nicole's beauty. It is as if the obscure but multiple emotional associations of which she is in some way, we feel, the victim, are becoming too much for her. Yet in the excited manner in which she overwhelms Mrs. Hoyt with attention, while disturbed by Rosemary's presence, we seem to see an almost frantic generosity of nature rather than a neurotic one. Moreover by doing this she seems also, perhaps, trying to conquer her necessity (anti-social in this case) always to be near Dick. Another cloud comes over the moon. (Lowry, pp. 42–46)

8

Nicole sweeps into Mrs. Hoyt's evening bag all the little articles to go with it that she can find. Amid the first rumblings of a summer storm, Dick's eyes meet Rosemary's and, suddenly, Nicole excuses herself and goes abruptly up to the house, Dick watching her with concern as she leaves.

A very tipsy Mrs. McKisco also goes to the house to powder her nose. While Barban and McKisco argue over politics, Dick tells Rosemary that the fun is over in Antibes now that Barban and Abe North are leaving, and he asks Rosemary to accompany him and Nicole to Paris to see Abe off to America. Back in the house, the guests are suddenly confronted with an excited Violet McKisco, returning from upstairs, who says she has stumbled upon an extraordinary scene. Before she can say any more, Barban sharply rebukes her, and there is heard a piercing scream from upstairs, which is suddenly muffled. Abe North plays In a Mist *furiously on the piano. As the weather worsens, the music, says Lowry, merges from* In a Mist *"into a cross between something like Prokofiev's music before battle, or a gathering storm in* Peter Grimes.*"*[13] (Lowry, p. 51)

Later, as the guests are leaving, Dick assures a concerned Rosemary that Nicole will be all right. Mrs. Hoyt and Rosemary leave in the hotel car, and everyone else, including Barban and Abe, piles into the Divers' Isotta-Fraschini. Along the way, the Isotta pulls over to the side of the road; as the hotel car passes it, Mrs. Hoyt and Rosemary overhear Barban and McKisco arguing violently.

Back in the Hoyts' hotel room, just before dawn, Rosemary is looking out of her open window when she overhears Abe and Barban on the terrace below. She gathers that there is going to be a duel, and Mrs. Hoyt encourages her to go and see what is going to happen. When Rosemary arrives on the hotel terrace, Barban excuses himself and it is left to Abe to explain to her the strange turn of events. A flashback shows the Divers' car once again on the road back to the hotel and Mrs. McKisco bringing up the subject of what she saw back in the Divers' home. Barban once again sharply tells her to be quiet, and in the argument that follows, McKisco says that there still ought to exist the code duello, whereupon Barban promptly slaps McKisco, challenging him to a duel. (See Lowry, pp. 46-55 and Fitzgerald, 1, vii-x.)

Cut to the verandah of the Hotel des Etrangers. The stars have gone, the moon is setting, the sea is calm and still as a white mirror beneath the white sky, white mists hang motionless among the trees; the hushed, yet expectant sense of early dawn. This is a scene of exquisite eerie loveliness, and contrasts with the desperate fatigue of those still hag-ridden by the night behind them. A taxi stands in the driveway, the chauffeur yawning at the wheel as Rosemary, Abe, and McKisco come out of the door and down the steps. Only Rosemary, by reason of her youth, is still fresh and pretty. The two men's faces are lined and shadowed by exhaustion and dissipation. The attitude of the three is as follows: Rosemary, excited by the romantic idea of a duel, doesn't really want to stop it, (though of course she isn't consciously aware of this) she goes on making conventional protestations to which the men pay little attention. Abe, though quite drunk, is still the only practical one of the three. Nonetheless we feel he could have—should have—stopped the duel, should be trying to stop it now. Abe's "practical" behavior is really self-destructiveness in a vicarious form, something that manifests itself more objectively, clearly and dangerously later. McKisco is terrified and bewildered, yet somehow, finally rather admirable. This whole sequence is, in essence, fantastic, and is played like a fantastic nightmarish farce which neither the characters involved nor ourselves can quite believe—albeit it is very important we do believe—is happening, yet which at any moment may topple over into tragedy; the sort of experience which is at the time exciting and horrible and later becomes material for an irresistibly comic story. The characters are all figures in a farce, yet serious: and symbols too of an idiotic destructiveness. And the tension is nearly unbearable, exactly as if we ourselves had been called upon, tight, to fight a duel. The seriousness is accentuated by the conformity to strict realism throughout, and by the beauty of the scene itself. The moonlight in the previous scene on the terrace lent its note of insanity to the insane proceedings, and that mood must be carried over and sustained. As this scene on the verandah opens we hear, so faintly at first we are no more conscious of it than the beating of our hearts, (it is similar in its primary appeal, though in one way worlds apart from, the sound we heard at the very beginning of the film, for it is the motif, or one motif, of the unconscious) the sound of far-off, muffled drums, and this sound grows slowly but steadily louder. (Lowry, pp. 55-56)

9

On the way to the scene of the duel, a quite frightened and very drunk McKisco wonders how he became entangled in this mess. But, he says, his wife has already called him a coward, and he cannot back out now.

At the golf course where the duel is to take place, McKisco and Barban stand at some distance from each other with pistols; when Abe drops the handkerchief, they fire, both shots missing their target. "Though we see this scene in the main as through Rosemary's eyes," Lowry writes, "we do not see Rosemary herself again, save very fractionally perhaps, until the end, her dominant recurring presence anyhow would seem an artistic intrusion and a mistake" (Lowry, p. 60). Barban complains that he is not satisfied, though Abe suspects that he has missed purposely. Lowry suggests that there is something in Barban's voice that hints that he is not entirely serious as he speaks. McKisco, however, seems proud of himself for having gone through the ordeal and tries to play down Abe's suggestion that a great deal of his bravery was the result of the fact that he was extremely drunk. Abe, now alone with Barban at the edge of the fairway, asks him whether he missed McKisco deliberately. (See Lowry, pp. 56-62 and Fitzgerald, 1, xi.)

Barban: It must have been that literary conversation we had last night. (As he speaks, we follow the amused eyes, first of Barban, then of Barban and Abe, to where McKisco has abruptly broken away from Rosemary and, with a handkerchief pressed to his mouth, is running into the bushes.) I suddenly remembered I'd played Othello at school in England. (Barban is both serious and laconic here, yet as if half absent-minded, making his quotation, he is not ridiculous, nor above all striking a pose.)

> Though in the trade of war I have slain men
> Yet do I hold it very stuff o' the conscience
> To do no contrived murder: I lack iniquity—[14]

Abe: (the two men do not take their eyes off each other) Yeah. It must have been a very enlightened school. Are you sure you don't mean Iago?

Barban: Anyhow, it wouldn't have done Nicole any good.

Abe: No. You're right there.

The drums have never ceased and now, as they grow louder, we cut from someone playing a full brassy shot from the exact spot where Barban and Abe were standing on the golf course: the flag on the green becomes a flag on a Moroccan fort: the drums become real drums played by black troops: a soldier on a parapet blows a bugle: Barban in uniform beckons: there is a crush of rifles: the camera takes in the desert with a group of soldiers, lost, there is a mighty burst of music as the soldiers rush toward a mirage of water, with palms, a vision of the sea with waves crashing: the mirage turns into the skyline of Paris as it appears to Rosemary, Abe, Nicole, and Dick through the windscreen of the Divers' speeding Isotta-Fraschini: the Eiffel tower grows nearer and we see the Paris streets with people: the drums become the drums of the negro orchestra at the Café Chagrin where Rosemary, Abe, Nicole and Dick are having lunch to the violently hot and stentorian accompaniment of a tune whose name we see on the scattered band parts in the orchestra, to which the musicians however are paying little attention: *Whispering*.[15]

Outside the restaurant the metro sign Sèvres-Babylon is placed in such a way that the word Babylon, seen through the window, possesses a certain emotive force. Though we are being treated to a form of excellent jam session, and Abe seems mainly interested in the orchestra, the latter outfit now recedes to a point in the background where we can reasonably hear what the protagonists are saying, and also see the people in, and coming into, the Café Chagrin. There is a sudden burst of laughter between Dick and Rosemary. The waiter is taking their luncheon and bottles of Beaujolais away and they are drinking coffee and liqueurs. It is a dark restaurant with isobars of smoke rising to the ceiling. (Lowry, pp. 62–64)

10

Dick amusingly points out what he calls the lack of repose in all the men who enter the restaurant, who never fail to make some kind of nervous gesture when they suspect they are being watched. Rosemary and Abe join in Dick's jesting, but Nicole refrains from giving in to their merriment. Meanwhile: 'The band has stopped playing **Whispering** but has immediately started *again to play, more quietly, Joe Venuti's* Going Places,[16] *perhaps, we feel, since some of its members look hopefully in his direction for Abe's benefit, for it is a breakdown of a melody by Debussy"*[17] (Lowry, p. 64). *Rosemary, eager to find a print of* Daddy's Girl, *leaves the group to make a phone call.* (See Lowry, pp. 64-65 and Fitzgerald, 1, xii.)

Meanwhile the orchestra has stopped playing without having even given *Going Places* its routine length. There is a moment of sheer exhausted dissonance, the pianist playing a run against the saxophonist playing a break. Although the drummer keeps up the momentum of the scene by practising away to himself, it is a jangle that seems to match what, by now, we feel is the jangle of our protagonists' lives. Abe gets up and leaving a cigarette burning in one of his monumentally overflowing ashtrays, goes over to the negro orchestra and is seen a moment later shaking hands with some of its members and talking to the pianist who, evidently on Abe's suggestion—for Abe is striking a chord or two himself—plays *In a Mist* while speaking to him. This is not an orchestra piece so the others do not join in, though the guitarist and violinist are interested and come over to the piano. All this goes on in the background while Nicole and Dick are left alone at the table. Dick takes her hand across it; Nicole looks lovely, but still bears traces of strain.

Dick: Rosemary's seeing if she can get them to run off a print of her film for us ... Are you interested?

Nicole: (nobly but doubtfully) If you are. (Nicole suddenly sniffs Abe's ashtray, extinguishes Abe's cigarette in it, and fails to catch a waiter's eye in order that the ashtray shall be removed.)

Dick: (while Nicole is doing this) I've no idea what it's all about. (looking round momentarily for a waiter himself) The title sounds pretty forbidding, I admit. (directly to Nicole again) It's probably terrible ... But it might do her good.

Nicole: Dick ... How many have there been?

Dick: How many what?

Nicole: People you've "worked over" in the past year? How about the French circus clown? And then that actress from the Grand Guignol, those dancers, that crazy fellow from the Russian ballet, the tenor we staked to a year in Milan—

Dick: *We* staked. We shot a bear.

Nicole: And then Abe himself ... (the camera falls on Abe's ashtray, by now almost a synecdoche of Abe himself, Dick sees a waiter out of the corner of his eye, and passes him the ashtray over his shoulder) ... and now Rosemary?

Dick: Well, although I'm not practising I guess my dominant principle goes on displacing energy as if I thought I once had. Or should I say generating? In fact I have all that extra energy, professional energy, and somehow or other one has to use it. (Somehow this strikes us as being almost exactly what he has told Rosemary about herself, moreover that it was what Nicole and Dick had decided about her.)

Nicole: Dick . . . But how much good has it done them? You know, you speak about your repose . . . But there's one thing you can't resist.

Dick: What's that?

Nicole: (but she says this as lovingly as she does sardonically) Your charm . . . Your wonderful, wonderful charm . . . Nor can I.

The waiter's hand is seen returning a clean ashtray to the table, Dick and Nicole are standing up, Dick is smiling, they are going out: Abe is seen still with the negro musicians, where fleetingly and ironically among the scattered and pencilled band parts on the piano can be seen now the title of yet another piece, in fact the alternative title of Beiderbecke's *In a Mist*: *Bixology*. Cut to the hinterland of the café and Rosemary phoning in a semi-booth. (Lowry, pp. 65-67)

11

After finishing her telephone arrangements for the following afternoon's screening of **Daddy's Girl**, *Rosemary steps into the vestiary, where she is taken aback at overhearing Dick and Nicole passionately expressing their love for each other. Dick wants Nicole to go back to the hotel with him, but Nicole says that she has promised to go shopping with Rosemary, and they decide to meet at the hotel that afternoon at four.* (See Lowry, pp. 67-68 and Fitzgerald, 1, xii.)

The voices move away along the corridor. Rosemary follows them and meets Nicole and Dick at the restaurant door, through which we see the Isotta waiting outside with the chauffeur. Abe is still with the orchestra, gesturing to and absorbed with the musicians, who are playing, with the violinist playing like Venuti himself, Joe Venuti's *Going Places*.

Cut through and into a suggestion of this nostalgic violin music, Venuti-cum-Debussy, following them, to Rosemary and Nicole driving along in the Isotta. We are in the car with the girls as they pass Les Deux Magots, the spire of St. Germain des Prés, the statue of Diderot, then they are going along the Quai Malaquais and we see the Louvre across the river, dappled light beneath the plane trees, a barge going downstream. What we want to feel here, for a moment, is a sense of their purely youthful relation to the flowing world, the superb and indestructible vitality of Paris, to life itself.

(Nicole's true feelings about Rosemary are complicated: she is jealous, but that jealousy has a deeper source than Dick's interest: she sees herself in Rosemary as she was—or could have been. Also she does not like Rosemary as a person, though Rosemary is not aware of this. Nicole is pleasant and polite but never intimate, keeping them on a formal footing.)

Nicole: Dick tells me we're going to get an opportunity to see your picture.

Rosemary: Tomorrow afternoon. If that's all right with you?

Nicole: (rattling on) Fine—that'll be interesting—Dick and I must be the only people we know who haven't seen it, except Abe, of course—I never heard of him having seen a movie at all—of course we have to go all the way to Cannes when we want to see a flicker—

Rosemary: I noticed your movie house was only open twice a week—professional interest, I guess.

Nicole: Do you know, I went through a period of wanting to be an actress, though it seems a very long time ago—

Rosemary: (generously) You'd make a wonderful actress, you're such a dramatic person. (Lowry, pp. 68-69)

12

During the shopping trip, Rosemary buys carefully and deliberately, very aware of what she can and cannot afford. Nicole, on the other hand, buys extravagantly and carelessly from a list two pages long, adding to it anything that she sees and likes. Nicole is truly part of the rich upper class, around and for whom industry and commerce revolve. In a quick succession of images, Lowry shows the crew of a half-foundering steamer trying in vain to secure the shifting cargo, a ship being loaded, men and women working in factories. The main emphasis—along with trying to "relate the film to some economic factor" (Lowry, pp. 70-71)—is on Nicole's extravagance, not of the general kind opposed in some way to honest toil, but of a more personal nature, representing perhaps some sort of revenge that Nicole is taking to compensate for something she has either lost or never had. As four o'clock approaches, Rosemary, remembering the appointment that Nicole is to keep with Dick, grows rather tense, and Nicole finally leaves for the hotel.

The next afternoon, Dick, Nicole, Rosemary, Abe, and Collis Clay, a friend of Rosemary, are watching a screening of Daddy's Girl. *"[W]e hear the flickering noise of the projector. [. . .] [W]e have become aware that the silence—the sudden total absence of music, with nothing to be heard save the whining projector—constitutes a dramatic element in itself"* (Lowry, pp. 71-72). *Rosemary is playing a schoolgirl who adores her father; father and daughter seem to do everything together.* (See Lowry, pp. 69-72 and Fitzgerald, 1, xii, xvi.)

A subtitle: That night. (though on the screen it seems to be broad daylight.)

Abe snores. Dick nudges him. Rosemary anyway is so narcissistically delighted by her own face she does not notice these reactions.

On the screen, a dance, with people jerkily doing the Charleston. (This however is the only place—and it is doubtful even here—where the Charleston should be "guyed") Rosemary is doing the Charleston with a callow looking youth in a dinner jacket: with Rosemary on the scene the dance appears, as it sometimes was—and is—not ungraceful.

A subtitle: Faster.

Rosemary and the youth do the Charleston faster. Daddy and Rosemary appear on a verandah; Daddy looks a little hipped about something, perhaps the youth.

A subtitle: I love you best of all, Daddy, unless it's . . .

The alternative seems to be a shiny new roadster in the street below. Daddy and Rosemary are in the roadster, Daddy is driving and now it really is night. A road in bright moonlight stretches before us with telegraph poles flashing by. In the audience, Dick half looks at Nicole and strikes another match for his cigarette, which has gone out.

A subtitle: (as from Rosemary) Faster.

We see the car driving faster.

A subtitle: We do everything together, don't we, Daddy?

But now in the car Rosemary has her hand on the wheel too, with her father's, and we begin to feel that this part of *Daddy's Girl* is rather good. Rosemary's hair ripples out behind her like the solid hair of a tanagra figure. Now we can see only the road ahead of us and the hood and the two hands on the wheel, then only the road and part of the hood, but particularly the road. We get a tremendous horrendous sensation of increasing speed and the exhilaration of being on the road ourselves, which ever recedes beneath our very chairs. In sequences of this type one often used to wish that such a scene would go on and on beyond the breaking point where the cut is made, and here we get our wish: we are carried down that rushing road until beyond the breaking point of exhilaration and excitement we are interrupted by a burst of not quite hysterical laughter from Nicole, a murmur from Dick, another sobbing laugh and stern admonitions from Dick, as they leave hurriedly, Dick swiftly apologising to Rosemary on the way out; as Abe wakes up and lights a cigarette and leans over to say something to Rosemary, cut to the inside of a taxi, indeed the speed on the screen merely telescopes us into the speed of the taxi. (Lowry, pp. 73-74)

13

Dick, Rosemary, Abe, and Collis Clay drive around Paris in the taxi; Nicole is noticeably absent. Dick apologizes to Rosemary for Nicole's behaviour, explaining that she had once been in a car accident herself: "It was just one of those diabolical coincidences you can't explain" (Lowry, p. 74). Abe gives his own background in movies: "I saw Buster Keaton in Seven Chances—*I saw* Intolerance.[18] *But I never slept right through one before. I mean I never saw right through one before . . . What I mean is, I once played a piano in a movie house to annoy my father" (Lowry, p. 75). Rosemary tells Dick, much to both his and Abe's concealed amusement, that she is sorry only that there has been no time for Dick's screen test, which she had arranged in the hopes of some day having Dick join her in Hollywood to play her leading man in a picture. Dick and Rosemary drop off Abe and Collis Clay, who go their separate ways. A final glimpse of Abe here dissolves into a shot of a park guardian signalling the park's closing by ringing his bell: "since Abe has not quite faded from the picture the feeling is that it is ringing Abe's doom" (Lowry, p. 76).*

Dick and Rosemary go on to an art exhibit where Dick is to purchase a few pictures from a friend in need of money. While there, Rosemary overhears three women speak of the Divers in uncomplimentary terms, and she grows tense with indignation. Lowry has the gossips actually turn into cobras hissing and ready to strike: "This age old device, usually employed to make us laugh, should produce here an objective moment of terror and evil" (Lowry, p. 77). Once again in a taxi with Dick, Rosemary, her loyalty to and passion for Dick aroused as a result of the malicious gossip she has just overheard, confesses to Dick that she loves him.[19] (See Lowry, pp. 74-78 and Fitzgerald, 1, xvi-xvii.)

Dick, who has been flirting lightly with Rosemary, is flattered, also slightly taken aback. He has not meant to elicit anything serious—or so at least he persuades himself—and he is disturbed by a threatening "situation." At the same time he is kind, he is decent. But he appears in an unflattering light, one dislikes Dick a bit here, as one dislikes anybody visually employing their charm—employing that charm which "he can't resist." The scene should be done subtly, even, finally, sternly: Dick and Rosemary have not been lovers, nor is there a hint that they have; on the other hand Dick is scarcely innocent of having invited Rosemary's emotion. Rosemary for her part should not be too serious or pathetic, but pathetic too, just the same, at one point even ridiculous. She is ambitious and hard for all her youth, adult in some ways beyond her years. If we feel though that all this simply represents la condition humaine, one might well suspect something wrong with that condition itself in its contemporary phase of the nineteen-twenties at least, if Dick represents it at its best, with all his integrity, and despite his undoubted decency at the end of the scene. What is wrong is not his behavior, but that he should be in this position at all, the essential ugliness of which is disclosed in the scene which balances this one, much later on in the film, in Rome. (Lowry, pp. 78-79)

14

Dick kisses a sobbing Rosemary lightly and comforts her. He tells her that he is very much in love with his wife and that she mustn't be hurt. He adds that his love for Nicole was responsible, in a way, for the duel between Barban and McKisco. Rosemary, surprised at Dick's knowledge of the incident, asks how he found out, and Dick replies that one should never confide a secret to a man who drinks. The most important thing, Dick repeats, is that Nicole mustn't suffer. Swept away momentarily by his own rising passion, he kisses her once more, but he quickly draws away again, begging her to understand that his relationship with Nicole is a complicated one, that she is not as strong as she seems. Dick and Rosemary, on foot now, enter Notre-Dame Cathedral and stand watching the lighted candles and the people at prayer. Outside, they gaze at the façade of the cathedral: "we see a close up of one of its most hideous gargoyles which seems as though it is about to fall down upon us: this image, against the stormy sunset, dissolves in turn through the sombre tolling of bells, and now the louder beat of drums again and a terrific burst of jazz music, into a bar later that evening" (Lowry, p. 81).

Dick, Nicole, Rosemary, Collis Clay, and Abe are in the bar, as is a Miss Smythe, a girl Abe has picked up. Abe is rather drunk, and all seem to be enjoying themselves. (See Lowry, pp. 79-82 and Fitzgerald, 1, xiv, xvii-xviii.)

At this moment it is as if a cymbal or gong, which fills the whole screen, is struck a tremendous splintering crash. The gong becomes a kind of cornucopia-shaped vortex into which, as if into the screen, or as though it were the centre of a musical tornado that extends into the screen, all the characters and ourselves are sucked. The momentum of the picture violently increases, (though not too much, for it has to increase still further at the end of the sequence) accompanied by unending and relentlessly good hot jazz, largely dominant over more indigenous French music—this is the jazz age, in Europe too: scenes, sometimes linked by hot breaks, are punctuated by shots of the intersecting planes made by lobby lights, of glass doors, of glass doors revolving, buses and taxis rushing by—this last gives a partly false impression, so we supply a note here, meantime asking you to imagine we are already beyond it, in the scenes in question.

(Note: In so far as there is an element of phantasmagoria about this party, it differs from other such movie phantasmagoria in that its form is thematic, and, paradoxically, it is clear: that is, some characters may get tight as guinea fowl but the camera, if none too sober, is nonetheless intent upon writing a sinister and beautiful little poem full of meaning: the party not only can be seen, in little, as the form of Abe's life, but also, subtly, of Dick's. It illustrates symbolically, through the principle of cause and effect that runs right through the picture, some of the major mistakes they have made, or are to make, in their lives. Another manner in which it differs is in the use of signs, words, advertisements, seen as we rush across Paris. Cinematically speaking we might indeed here be right back in the phantasmagoric world of Murnau, or Murnau's imitators—though this is indeed the world of that period—but for one important development, as a consequence of which we are only there in part technically. That is we can use his genius here as a touchstone, if we like, but only as a touchstone of genius, for our intentions are quite other. In the description of the aforementioned signs, we might well have said, we see the signs Moulin Rouge, Grand Guignol, et cetera. We wish to emphasize, minimal though its importance and the time it takes may seem to be, that we are not saying et cetera. We suggest a development from this: here the signs are not only historically accurate—your research department being at the moment the memory of one of your writers—*Ça Qua Ça Gaze*, for instance, *was* the French name given to Reginald Denny's *California Straight Ahead*,[20] which *was* playing in Paris in 1926, and so was Kuprin's *Pit* (*La Fosse aux Filles*)[21] at the Grand Guignol, and *Paris en Fleures* at the Casino de Paris, but these have a fleeting psychological significance and irony, and even interplay of irony of their own (like the windmill and Don Quixote) and to push the matter further we can even half remember that Dick (les 10 Fratellinis, Grock[22]) had "helped" a circus clown: similarly with Grand Guignol, which word however contains also a foreshadowing implication of our drama. While all this is passing at such great speed it does not have time to sink into our minds, in fact some of these things may be only half seen, nonetheless it all contributes to what one might call the subconscious life of the movie itself, thereby rendering it the more organic. More than that, such attention to detail, philosophically speaking, gives the film a sort of solipsistic world of its own which, if expressed in accordance with strict realism that in turn is in accordance with the actual historical facts, will inevitably increase our response to it by appealing to facets of the consciousness not usually called into play. This appeal is by no means directed to the most intelligent or to the aficionado amongst us. On the contrary it is, especially with the nature of the accompanying music, largely primitive. Thus the argument that "not 2 people in the audience are going to get this," falls down. Many emotions may be evoked in the spectator without their being aware of how, or without, even, being consciously aware that they are being so evoked, which all add up to the impact and final impression. And since, finally, there have to be some signs, etc., why not, without overdoing it, some (as there are in life) significant ones? With this in mind, this technique is used elsewhere too where most effective, to heighten the drama, though in a more routine manner. As the evening progresses each character reacts to this party in his or her different way. Nicole for once is glad to be gay, yet we see also that, hating certain aspects of this kind of party, she is forcing herself to be sporting on Abe's account and also in a more complex manner, upon Rosemary's. Moreover we see her, as it is important we do see her, behaving with fortitude and wisdom in the face of a situation that might become dangerous, and might be frightening to any woman, (as it is to Rosemary) in contrast to how Nicole has behaved, and will behave, on the face of a direct psychological precipitate, or an accumulation of precipitates, of which the incident in question can finally be seen as one. Rosemary, happy to be with Dick, almost forgets her heart is broken over him, and sees this night mostly as "life," as really "seeing Paris," for the first time. Dick himself is giving the party for Abe, he is always the organiser, mainly conscious and considerate of the other's pleasure and the point of balance. Abe's actions are in a direct line: psychologically motivated away from life and towards death he has become almost a living symbol of destructive force. Clay is the conventional American in Paris making inoffensive whoopee. Abe's evanescent sidekick, Miss Smythe, is, in the book, his wife—whom we have cut out altogether—in another form, and does as well, since for him emotional life has become impossible. In the book the party is not confined to the people we have mentioned; at the speed of a slapstick comedy it moves through the night: they are six, they are twelve, they are sixteen, they are quartets in separate motors, and so forth; and here, especially so far as concerns the speed, this too is the general effect it sometimes has. Nonetheless it should be emphasized, this is only a general effect, for if the kaleidoscope is merely a rhythmical and emotive background against which is dramatised the specified and typical, hence particular behaviour of the main characters, it is also controlled in itself, and interwoven with that behaviour. Very little, in short, is here that has no bearing on the story either immediately or as a foreshadowing: chords struck here are resolved later, and the arbitrary is at a minimum—though it is understood that if here as elsewhere we have occasionally written beyond a point where a more effective condensation or cut could be made by the director, we have assumed it would benefit the cut itself if he knew what was in our minds.) (Lowry, pp. 83–87)

15

The party moves to a houseboat restaurant, then out to the street past a cinema with electric bells ringing to signal standing room still available inside. The advertisements outside the cinema, the Eden, show that the movie playing inside involves a speeding car. The party moves down to a basement bar—also called the Eden—next door to the cinema. In the bar Dick humourously explains to a slightly tipsy Rosemary that it is not because of any professional disgrace that he is currently a non-practising doctor of medicine, and Rosemary tells him again that she loves him—and Nicole. (See Lowry, pp. 87–89 and Fitzgerald, 1, xv.)

Cut to the bar of the café; Nicole and Dick alone drinking, Rosemary dancing with Clay, Abe with Miss Smythe. The band, very hot, mixed white and negro, is playing *Sweet Georgia Brown*, with a guitar worthy of Eddie Lang or Django Reinhardt.[23] Abe, while dancing, is smiling and nodding with some of the band members familiarly.

Dick: I don't want you to tire yourself out, darling. Don't you think the Casino de Paris and Montmartre will be a bit much for you?

Nicole: No. No. Absolument non. I'm having a really good time. It's

Abe's last night, it's Rosemary's birthday, and I'm tired of being a wet blanket . . . Oh, listen! (the band has started to play *The Japanese Sandman*, the verse, though without singing, and Nicole and Dick exchange a long look of love and recognition. She takes Dick's hand and after a moment continues, speaking quietly and listening to the band) When I'm tired I'll let you know. (she kisses him) Cher Capitaine. (the band has now reached a place between the verse and chorus, though played very hot, that is marked by oriental sounding bells) Ah! That's the bit I like.

They smile at each other with some intimate remembrance of this, and then dance.

Cut into the Isotta circling out of the screen, with the sound of the electric bell again.

Abe: It's a device the French have so the Americans won't look at their change.

Electric signs circle or whizz by, advertisements, or upon the theatres themselves: Folies Bergère, the word Trinité, nearby on the Metro is held a moment: Maurice Chevalier's[24] grin: Les 10 Fratellinis: Grock: a café sign: La Vie en Rose.

Cut to our party getting out of the taxi in front of the Casino de Paris. We see the billboards with posters of Chevalier—the show is *Paris en Fleures*.

Cut to the inside: there is no dialogue among our party for the show is going on: a glimpse of sumptuousness and an ocean of applause. Abe is seen briefly in the wings shaking hands with and saying goodbye to the orchestra as they come off stage, and we recognize some of them from the Café Chagrin.

Immediately we cut back into the Isotta again, already on its way: lights pick out the words: Grand Guignol, then on a darker sign swept by the headlights, the name of the main piece playing there, *La Fosse aux Filles*, (*The Pit*) de Alexandre Kuprin. Then more signs: Kub and Dubonnet: and always at intervals, the vertical sign which marks the seemingly ubiquitous Eiffel Tower: Citröen. Now we are in the Rue Blanche and we pass Zelli's and the Poet's Cave and stop where the two great mouths of the Café of Heaven and the Café of Hell yawn across the street at each other. (see notes)[25] As we stop the last contents of a tourist bus is disappearing into the Café of Heaven: three Germans, a Japanese, and an American couple looking rather frightened. Our party turn away. Cut to the threshold of the Café of Hell. Abe and Nicole incautiously put their heads inside and quickly withdraw from the blare of noise and light, but the Maître d'Hôtel swoops at them.

The Maître: Crowd just arriving, sir?

Dick: (turning away) You have to be darn drunk.
Abe: That's just what I said. That's just where you're making a mistake.
Rosemary: Oh let's be happy!
Clay: That's what he meant.

Cut through this to the Place Pigalle, with its merry-go-rounds and steam music: the red meccano windmill of the Moulin Rouge revolves, the word Don Quixote is seen on kiosks. It has been raining and the streets are glistening.

The whole party, something like the principals of a revue before a first act curtain, is seen dancing down the street arm-in-arm, then, in the next flash, dancing back again in the other direction, during which we have a sense of real gaiety.

We are in Montmartre, hearing the sound of *Valentine*[26] coming out of a basement, played on a concertina. Then the stamping music of a bal musette. Another party in evening dress gets out of a taxi before the brilliant sign of the Bal Taborin. Cut to one of the merry-go-rounds in the Place Pigalle circling, oddly, above an aerial view of the Seine at night, thus contrasting momentarily two kinds of freedom, true and false, that of the flowing river, and a false, mechanical round, but again, in the latter symbol, fractionally linking us to eternity: this, almost before it is seen, is dissolving through the one word "Babylon," of the geographically dislocated Sèvres-Babylon metro, into a shot of sinister bleak hotels and narrow dark medieval streets and alleys, with cocottes prowling singly or in pairs, and we see that our party have left the Boulevard and struck off into the section behind it, heading for some place like Le Lapin Agile. The white dome of Sacré-Coeur looms nearby. A long shot of our group going down the street, disposed thus: Rosemary and Nicole are walking together behind, Abe we now see, as would happen with Abe, has lost, or ditched, his girl and walks with Dick, Clay is alone, ahead. Occasionally from a cabaret we hear a single, tremendous hot break, mingling into a muted dissonance of various caught musics, and the environment renders the scene, shortly to become humourous and after that dangerous, slightly sinister.

The camera comes up to Abe and Dick. Walking swiftly beside them now on the inside of the pavement, is an American bum, trying to pick them up. (Lowry, pp. 89–92)

16

The bum tries unsuccessfully to sell Abe and Dick some pornographic

postcards. The whole party moves into another basement cabaret, this one called La Nocturne, for which they are clearly overdressed, a fact which draws looks of jealousy from some of the patrons and of indifference or contempt from others. When the bum reappears and once again accosts Dick and Abe, Dick gives him a wad of francs. (See Lowry, pp. 93-95 and Fitzgerald, 1, xxi.)
Lowry's brief note follows.

Note: it should be clear that no slight is intended to the French. It is the universal attitude anywhere one goes slumming. Any misconception of an apparently unfair attitude toward the French is more than compensated for elsewhere. (Lowry, p. 95)

17

Abe grows progressively more bitter as he grows drunker, and after a dance with Nicole, he suddenly grabs the bum, whom he has noticed at the bar, and shoves him against a couple standing next to them. (See Lowry, pp. 95-96 and Fitzgerald, 1, xix.)

Instantly there is confusion, and a fight starts in which Collis Clay can be seen vainly trying to restrain Abe, while the barman comes appeasingly from behind the bar. On the other hand there is something tentative about this fight to begin with, the band has started to play again, perhaps an encore to *I'll See You in My Dreams*,[27] some people are dancing, while others merely calmly take their drinks out of harm's way. This renders the subsequent reaction on Nicole's part both plausible and natural. As for Rosemary, frightened though she is, you feel that had it seemed worse, with Dick actively threatened, she probably would have stayed anyhow, while the same is true, though for a different reason, of Nicole.

Dick, Nicole, and Rosemary are now seen approaching the door, through which we can see the Divers' Isotta standing outside; the chauffeur, who has been half asleep jumps out and opens the door. We see that Rosemary is scared stiff but Nicole seems harshly amused and is even trying to calm Rosemary when they go out.

Dick: (to Nicole, almost pushing them through the door as he speaks) I'll handle Abe. You and Rosemary take the car and go to the Ritz. Wait for us there.

We see the girls begin to get into the Isotta, then Dick plunges in to get Abe out of the fight. It is not so much that Abe is yet fully involved in the fight, but as nearly always happens with the instigator of such things, is still trying to get into it after it has started. However the point now is made that the commotion which Abe has precipitated is nothing to the chain of reactions that goes into motion now Dick interferes and tries to drag Abe from the brawl and put a stop to it. Now the whole business does become dangerous and ugly. In the ensuing push and press and tug one glass knocks down another the length of the bar, one fight begets another, someone brings out a knife, and the fight spreads to the orchestra where a concertina dropped to the floor giving a detumescent growl, frightens a dog that has strayed in and who now dashes out of the back entrance where a taxi, in trying to avoid it, piles, as police whistles blow, into a wall. On the other hand, just before this, matters have become ironically hilarious—or have at least to ourselves watching them—at closer quarters among our protagonists. Abe has half taken off his coat and at one point in the scuffle his wallet falls out of his inside pocket to the floor. The bum, seeing this, reaches his hand down furtively to pick it up. Dick observing this motion on the part of the bum, forestalls him and rescues Abe's wallet from him. Abe, seeing this and catching the bum off balance, with infuriated dexterity relieves the bum of his own rusty wallet containing the cartoon and Dick's pourboire. Dick in turn snatches the wallet from Abe and with consummate justice throws it back, not before, however, having taken back some of his own pourboire himself, to the bum who—for this is the moment that the gendarme's whistles start blowing—is making good his escape but still manages neatly to catch it. Collis Clay meanwhile has got a taxi and while trying to hang on to its reluctant driver can be seen beckoning from the door.

Cut from this to Nicole and Rosemary in the Isotta circling down from Butte Montmartre.

Nicole: Don't be nervous, Rosemary. I have the utmost confidence in Dick.

Rosemary: (who is still frightened) I feel like a coward.

Nicole: Nonsense. Pull yourself together.

The Isotta has reached Place St. Pierre and through the window Nicole sees the funicular that comes down from Sacré-Coeur to Place St. Pierre. There is one car descending just as they pass by.

Nicole: (in a strange voice) The funicular . . . I'd like to have come down on the funicular . . .

Cut to Abe, not too dishevelled, Dick and Clay in their taxi. They are passing the Grand Guignol, and now we see the words, Grand Guignol, even more macabre with the lights out.

Abe: No, no. I don't feel like the Ritz. I'm going to get out here.

Clay: (smiling and indicating the Grand Guignol) I don't think you'd have much fun in there.

As the taxi slows a little going through a by-street we see another quite dimly lighted bar whose interior we can't see but from which is floating cheerfully if monotonously the strains of the *Bolero*.[28] In the shop windows the taxi headlights pick out such phrases as Solde, Réclamé, and then nearer the bistro, more sombre announcements: Vêtements Ecclésiastiques, Déclaration de Décès, and Pompes Funèbres. This but testifies, however, to the universal law of supply and demand, for without knowing it we are near a cemetery also.

Abe: Going to get out here. Friends of mine . . . (he gets out while the taxi is still going and makes for the bistro)

Dick: All right, but then stay there. (he stops the taxi and calls from it) Do you hear that? I've got to get Nicole home, she can't put up with this sort of thing. I suppose you realise it's your last night and you may not see her for a long time. (as the taxi moves off again) And remember *I've* got your wallet. (as the taxi stops of its own accord, before moving off again) Do you hear that? You've got exactly eight hundred francs—(pleasantly) just what I gave that bum—minus four hundred.

Abe: (by the door of the bistro, as the *Bolero* grows louder) Tell Nicole sorry and I'll shee her at the shashun tomorrow. (as the taxi drives away) And go to—!

Lap dissolve into the interior of the bistro. It is a hideous little place with a savage-faced frightening-looking old harridan half asleep behind the bar while the source of the *Bolero* is discovered to be its sole other occupant, a hunchback in black clothes, playing very well on a mouth organ and looking mournfully over the lace curtains that veil the lower half of the window. We now see that behind the bar are also numerous stopped clocks and two jam-pots in which tiny carp are swimming. In one corner of the room is an old black-fanged piano and between the curtains which divide it from a back room we see with Abe a hideously life-like wax figure with one arm missing. The woman who (we observe) has been playing some kind of card game on the counter, seems too drowsy to take immediate notice of him and the hunchback takes absolutely no notice and goes right on playing. Abe sits down quietly at the piano and plays a strange accompaniment for the *Bolero*. This tiny scene is not comic, but somehow mournful and tragic and at the same time frightening: we feel that this is the ultimate bar and Abe's ultimate audience and that the hunchback may be death.

Cut through a shot of the stopped clocks and the carp to Collis Clay and Rosemary entering the bistro where Abe is still playing and the only difference is that he has a drink beside him on the piano, one of his ashtrays beginning, he is playing and singing *The Kerry Dancers*,[29] and the hunchback has gone.

Clay: (looking round) Ugh! (then catching sight of the wax figure through the curtains) My gosh! is that her husband?

Rosemary: (to Abe) Oh, I'm so glad you're alive.

Abe: (still playing) Who told you I was alive?

Rosemary: Dick's seeing Nicole home and is going to meet us at Les Halles. He said you'd insist on going to Les Halles anyway.

Cut to Abe standing up and looking at the carp.

Abe: Come and see the royal carp. They live a hundred years in a bottle.

Dissolve through the sluggish but swimming carp to a shot of the card game on the counter, with the cards arranged in five columns; the camera picks out in the third column the ace of spades upside down half overlapped by the ten of clubs; perhaps the woman was telling fortunes, in fact it is the gypsy combination for death, but we feel its ominousness: cut swiftly from the ace of spades into a speeding taxi again, with yet more jazz music coming out of passing cabarets in spasmodic bursts and the drums sounding at a more urgent speed: slowing once, the headlights fall on a tombstone in the passing cemetery: fade in to Les Halles, the market, with its loaded stalls of fruit and flowers, in the early dawn, Rosemary, Clay and Abe eating onion soup and drinking coffee in one of the fruit merchants' bars. There is the thunder of hooves on the cobbles outside. Almost immediately Dick comes in. The dialogue is swift, overlapping, half thrown away.

Abe: (sheepishly) Hullo.

Dick: (to Rosemary) Nicole was worried about you. We feel responsible to your mother. (when the others are not looking he kisses the inside of her elbow quickly, then, to Abe) Here, you may need that. (gives him another two hundred francs.)

Abe: (taking the money) What's that for? (to Clay) Still, that gives me an idea, what you said about making use of hangovers . . . I'm going to invent a machine.

Dick: (in Abe's direction) A reward for staying where you were told to.

Clay: I didn't say anything about hangovers. But I know one thing, I'm going to have a beaut.

Rosemary: (laughing) What kind of machine, Abe?

Abe: A machine for keeping your hand still, so that composers like me can write music. (Lowry, pp. 96–102)

18

Rosemary, Collis Clay, Dick, and Abe ride down the street in a vegetable cart full of carrots. The cart is being drawn by a splendidly dressed horse and driven by an equally splendidly dressed Indian named George T. Horseprotection. Rosemary tells Dick she is happy to finally have been part of a wild party but adds that it's no fun when he's not with her. (See Lowry, p. 102 and Fitzgerald, 1, xviii.)

Cut into the party approaching Notre-Dame through the dawn, though Abe is straggling behind.

Dick: Everything wears out.

Rosemary: Only love does not wear out. Tell me love doesn't wear out!

Dick: Love is not the garment. It's love itself that grows out of its clothes . . . Was that profound?

Abe: (from behind) Everything is profound when you're tight.

Cut to the sound of bells ringing for matins and a shot right through the open door of Notre-Dame into a soft blast of candles burning before the altar and figures standing and kneeling. The camera comes back out of the cathedral and we see its mysterious, wonderful, begargoyled and be-angeled façade in the half light: in the dawn the gargoyles seem actually alive.

Dick: (suddenly) Where's Abe?

We see Abe is no longer there, see the gargoyle for a moment that earlier had seemed to be falling down on us, then the camera goes briefly in search of Abe, who is found some distance away, still on the right bank, in a doorway around a corner, in a small square, apparently hiding. Again we hear the sound of drums and see a negro, whom we recognize as one of the players at the Café Chagrin, approaching, carrying an instrument in its case under his arm and singing softly to himself: (if this is not an obvious anachronism)

> And I saw my father the other day
> And I gave him my right hand
> But before ever ma back was turned—

The Negro: (catching sight of Abe) Hello . . . Abe! Mistah North. (shaking him) You sick, boy?

Abe: Hullo, Satisfied. No, I'm not sick. I guess I just want a drink, that's all.

Satisfied: Excuse me, I thought it was the other way round . . . Can I help you? That's right, boy, take my arm. Mistah North, you sure is becoming an integral part of the night we inhabit. (The negro has generously piloted Abe to a café bar chiefly for negroes we now see into, from which hot jazz now bursts again and the pounding of drums rises at us with an almost voodoo intensity)

Satisfied: (now introducing Abe at the bar) Let me introduce you to a fellow who goes to really great lengths to tell you how far it is from down to down. (remote names in the background; Mr. Crawshaw, Mr. Peterson, etc.)

Cut back to Dick, Rosemary and Clay crossing the Pont au Double over the Seine which appears mournful and beautiful in the early dawn, Notre-Dame in the background.

Dick: Well, it's no use looking for him. He'll just drink himself tired and then show up in time to get to the station. I know Abe. Besides he'll have to—anyhow, he's over twenty-one. Or is he?

Rosemary: And I'm over eighteen.

Clay: Abe's twenty-first birthday must have been something.

Cut to a shot of old newspapers blowing down the street and then, in the first rays of sunlight striking up behind the towers, the pigeons breaking over Saint-Sulpice, as the party walk by, their footsteps echoing loud on the pavement.

Cut to Abe just finishing playing the piano in another bistro or café frequented by negroes in the early morning. He is in shirt sleeves, his coat over the back of his chair; he feels the inside pocket of his coat and imagines he has lost his wallet.

Lap dissolve to a shot of the park gate opening, the attendant, the first children coming for the swings, the attendant swinging them; the good morning, the day has begun; the children swinging fades into the Divers' suite at the Hôtel Roi George, and Nicole being awakened by a knock at the salon door. On a table we see the photograph of Dick and Nicole that we saw on the piano at the Villa Diana. (Lowry, pp. 103-5)

19

A policeman arrives at the Divers' suite and enquires about Abe. He tells Nicole that a gentleman by the name of Abe North has claimed that he had been robbed the night before and that a negro has been arrested in connection with the alleged robbery. The police now need Abe to identify the man and make the proper charges. Dick, emerging from the bathroom, speaks to the policeman before he leaves while Nicole answers the phone; it is Abe himself, and Nicole promptly hands the telephone to Dick. Abe is in a crowded bistro where he is crammed into a small booth with a number of negroes, some of whom also get on the phone to speak to Dick. They are all obviously quite drunk, and the conversation quickly becomes a confusing babble out of which Dick can make little sense until finally a respectable, sober black gentleman grabs the phone at Abe's end and tells Dick that if he is Abe's friend, he will come down to the Café Mephisto and take Abe away at once. An exasperated and angry Dick gets dressed, tells Nicole to bring Rosemary and meet him at the train station, and takes a taxi to the Café Mephisto. The moment Dick leaves, the phone rings again. It is someone from the front desk, informing Nicole that another black gentleman, a Mr. Crawshaw, is there to see them about some injustice that has been done to his friend, Mr. Freeman. Nicole, beginning to panic, says she knows nothing about the matter, hangs up, and leaves for the train station with Rosemary: "In the travel agency's window a little advertisement in a sort of box, even in daytime, flickers on and off, saying: Passez vos vacances au mer. *Near them also, and at one moment right above Nicole, is a huge holiday advertisement for Switzerland: Zurich, Suisse, with the Alps, a lake, an individual with a feather in his hat picking edelweiss, etc."* (Lowry, p. 111).

With the help of a flask of liquor, Dick manages to direct Abe to the train station: "In a flash we see the words Rue des Frères *on the street wall, simultaneously hear a wordless snatch of* Frère Jacques *on the sound track in bass jazz rhythm. Although Abe is tight he speaks quickly, if not so quickly as Dick, and also in some respects reasonably. (This also has been true during most of the previous night and his slowness has only been apparent during some of the phone conversation. This seems all-important for the tempo, as true to life, and applies to the acting too. Nevertheless gradations of the sacred state must be observed, and here Abe is, while tight, in one of those unholy intermediate stages of tightness, in which he has horrifying glimpses of his own possible sobriety; these glimpses, which spasmodically reestablish his sense of decency, succeed in practically giving him a form of parenthetical hangover, a condition considerably aggravated by Dick, who, as shall be shortly seen, takes his flask away from him)"* (Lowry, pp. 111–12). *There had been no robbery. It was Dick, of course, who had taken Abe's wallet from him the night before for his own protection, and what little money had been taken from Abe at the bar had been taken in order to cover the cost of his own drinks. The problem now, as Abe sees it, is what the other negroes will do to a certain Mr. Peterson who had helped Abe in wrongly identifying the culprit. At the station, while Dick and Rosemary are gone to get Abe's tickets, Abe says* to Nicole that he is tired of them and they are tired of him. Dick comes back and, handing the flask to Abe, is finally able to get him on the train. As the train pulls out of the station, with the goodbyes still ringing in his ear, Abe tries to jerk open a window in the corridor, but the window, falling and breaking, cuts Abe's hands. "The train gathers momentum," Lowry writes, "then almost immediately is going at a tremendous speed which we glimpse from the receding rails and converging gantlets outside, the receding slums of Paris, a local train which keeps pace a moment, then has dropped behind" (Lowry, pp. 116–17). As the train pulls out of Paris, Abe is left standing by the window, staring at his hands full of blood: "From Abe's bloody hands the camera travels obliquely over the flying rails, over the embankment and signal boxes, and diagonally back over the fields and vacant lots and appalling suburbs of Paris, back towards Paris itself again, as if we were abroad a too low flying plane, into and through, suddenly, the wash of the Oedipus Tyrannus beating on the precipice below the Divers' house in Antibes once more (the latter of which might be in Abe's mind, for we hear In a Mist again briefly) but the sea coils its fading waves in an alley where a negro is half-running, half-walking, and glancing furtively over his shoulder" (Lowry, p. 117).

Rosemary, Dick, and Nicole have returned to their hotel, only to have Peterson himself, looking rather timid and carrying a box of materials under his arm, arrive at their suite asking for Abe. Peterson is being persecuted now by those he accused while trying to help Abe, and he tells Dick that Abe had promised to set him up in business with the shoe polish formula that he is carrying in the tin box. "The quality of the direction at this point till the end of the sequence," Lowry explains, "should be that of a hyperactive Fritz Lang.[30] The film goes now at tremendous speed, with dialogue spoken quickly and overlapping, and as it gathers momentum, cuts should seem to tear the screen apart, music is dynamically but sparingly used, noises accentuated, etc., all this not merely being for effect, but because it is the dynamic of the unconscious itself which is coming to the fore again to win its irrational (and paradoxical) triumph" (Lowry, p. 120). In the general scene of confusion that follows, Nicole grows more and more hysterical, and Peterson feels more and more neglected, until, thinking that they have forgotten him and will do nothing to help him, he quietly leaves the room. "The negro Peterson must not be overdone," Lowry instructs, "must never be merely pathetic and we must feel too that Rosemary's presence is contributing to Nicole's tension, while Nicole herself, not moved to compassion by Peterson's situation, though this may touch her ethically and hence reach her conscience, is touched less on this score than by the fact that in Abe's defection she now finds a weapon for her unconscious rebellion against Dick—when we know more we can see something like the nobility of a great decision in this—meantime she should not lose more than a little of our sympathy" (Lowry, pp. 120–21). As Peterson

88   "Tender Is the Night"

leaves the Divers' suite, "Abe's train, with Abe drinking wildly, plunges across the screen at us" (Lowry, p. 122). *When the absence of Peterson is finally noticed and before Dick can follow him out the door, a sharp but muffled sound is heard outside the door of the suite. Dick follows the sound into Rosemary's rooms across the corridor, and there, on her bed, he finds Peterson, who has just committed suicide. "It is raining quietly now, there is no sound but the rain: drip, drip, drip, at the window [. . . but] the drops we heard were drops of blood falling on [Peterson's] metal box of materials standing on the floor beside the bed"* (Lowry, p. 123). *Rosemary, rushing in to see what has happened, lets out a scream when she sees the body, and Nicole, following her, sees a part of the scene before Dick can move to block her view. He escorts the badly shocked Nicole back to their room and then, wrapping the dead body of Peterson in a blanket, takes the bloody sheets from Rosemary's bed and exchanges them for the clean ones that he has instructed Nicole (who, Lowry says, is now behaving "almost somnambulistically"* (Lowry, p. 124)) *to get from their own room: "we have a momentary close up of Dick in which we see his real feeling of guilt, remorse and horror"* (Lowry, p. 124). *His hands now stained with blood, Dick pulls Peterson's body out into the corridor and calls Macbeth, the manager of the hotel, to tell him that he has found a dead negro in the hall. When Macbeth arrives with a gendarme, he discreetly assures Dick that the names of his guests will be protected.*

Rosemary and Dick enter the Divers' suite in time to hear terrible screams from the bathroom. Dick, followed by Rosemary, rushes in, only to find Nicole, on her knees by the bathtub, swaying from side to side over the bloody sheets in which she has partly wrapped herself. Nicole, hysterical, hurls nonsensical accusations at Dick; before Dick can push Rosemary out of the bathroom she has caught sight of the scene and runs, horrified, to her own suite.

Later that night, in bed, Dick holds and comforts a subdued but still restless Nicole. Dick's face is at once stern and sad, bitter and tender: "The camera comes up to Dick's face, holding it a moment, then passes him and, as it were, goes out of the window, holding the moon and the night sky" (Lowry, p. 128). (See Lowry, pp. 105-28 and Fitzgerald, 1, xxii-xxv.)

Lowry's note follows.

Note: In the following section there is a subtle change of technique, as of viewpoint. Up till now we have seen the Divers largely from outside, from the viewpoint of another person or persons, chiefly Rosemary. Now we shall see them from inside: we know their thoughts. It should not be forgotten also, that however immediate this may all begin to seem shortly, that this whole section is one long flashback per se, a stylization, on the part of Dick's memory. From Dick's point of view this in part corresponds to the Aristotelian taking stock after a reversal of fortune, but what we have to express here essentially is the tenderness and passion and conflict of a tragic love story.

Lap dissolve from the night sky into the advertisement (we recognize it from the station) Zurich—Suisse. This becomes the one word Zurich, which extends itself to Zurichsee, to which in turn is prefixed Sanatorium; Sanatorium Zurichsee is now the name over a door of a sanatorium; we go beyond this door, preceded by an objective small 1919, down a corridor and through another door with the name Dr. Frederich Dohmler upon it, where the 1919 miraculously refrains from taking up its proper abode in a calendar on the desk, though there is one there all right, from which, as the scene proceeds, we can discover that it is not only 1919, but late March, 1919. This office has large windows, from which can be seen the Alps, and in the immediate foreground the walled garden of the sanatorium. The trees are bare except for one or two flowering ones, just budding into bloom. Against the wall are still patches of snowdrifts; a few crocus and snowdrops blooming in the thin spring sunlight. (Lowry, pp. 128-29)

20

In the office of the sanatorium are the head of the clinic, Dr. Frederich Dohmler, his assistant, Dr. Franz Gregorovious, both Swiss Germans, and a young Dr. Dick Diver in the uniform of a captain in the U.S. Army medical corps. Dick is on his way home to see his father before returning to Switzerland to work. Dohmler tells him that they are awaiting the arrival of a sixteen-year-old American girl of the rich and distinguished Warren family of Chicago whose father has recently been killed in an automobile accident. A car pulls up to the clinic and a small, child-like girl, the young Nicole, is at once escorted to the door by two nurses. With the girl is an older woman, about twenty-six, who is Nicole's older sister, Baby. From inside the window Dick watches as Nicole is led off through the garden by the nurses. "All this is seen through the window in swift dumbshow," Lowry observes, "but this is the first time in his life that Dick Diver sees Nicole, so that it is a 'moment' " (Lowry, p. 132). Baby Warren enters the office and, as a fellow American, Dick is urged to stay during the interview with her.

Baby tells the doctors that there has never been any insanity in her family and provides them with a few biographical facts about Nicole: their mother died when Nicole was twelve; she had few friends; she had been very close to their father. While listening, Dick again looks through the window as Nicole, still escorted by a nurse, comes out of the garden directly toward him. Her movements are slow, as they were, Lowry explains, when she was exchanging sheets with Dick at the scene of Peterson's suicide. She comes face to face with Dick through the closed window, and a strange expression appears on her face—some prescience, perhaps, of the future, Lowry suggests, or a ghost of a tragic prerecognition. Baby tells the doctors that after their mother had died Nicole had wanted to go away to school but their father—wanting to keep her at home with him (like a princess in a tower, Nicole had protested)—had forbidden it. As a way to appease his young daughter, Devereux Warren had given her a new car. (See Lowry, pp. 129-37 and Fitzgerald, 2, i-iv.)

As Baby Warren begins to talk we cut into Nicole and her father, Devereux Warren, looking down at this car from a balcony, and have at the same time a sensation of revelation, not dissimilar to the feeling some of us obtain from reading those sections of Proust which deal with those material occasions when essences recur, yet at once far cruder and more starkly dramatic, as if indeed, almost, this were a species of ghost story. The scene we now see is not dissimilar to and instantly reminds us, in a frightening fashion, of the scene in the private showing of *Daddy's Girl* when Rosemary and Daddy looked down upon Rosemary's new roadster. On the other hand it is completely different as if that scene were merely a parody of the present one, or as if, had time proceeded along an unbroken plane from that moment to this (which is the sensation we have) another spiral had wound its way upward—although this is a point that would be grasped readily even by a child without realizing it, yet it resembles one of those fundamental recurrences common at all periods of life: it is different, for the mise-en-scène—in so far as we see it—is more expensive, dignified, and thoroughly believable, and Devereux Warren, far from a figure possible to ridicule, a figure of tragedy. It is, however, day and not night—a crisp brilliant autumn morning that we can almost feel ourselves. We dissolve into the car, and Nicole and her father go for a ride, Nicole driving, her long hair blowing out behind her. In her youth and enthusiasm, it would appear, Nicole drives faster and faster down the country highway. So far we have the impression that this is simply an objective dramatization of what has actually happened, as Baby at least, is dramatizing it, either from Nicole's history, or what has been reported at the possible inquest, or as it seems to those present now and listening to it: we hear no dialogue at all so far, and never Baby's voice as "narrator," or otherwise until we are through; we see everything as from a silent distance; though the technique is not of course silent as in *Daddy's Girl*: we are near enough to hear sounds, but not to distinguish what they say, which is doubtless an adequate quid pro quo for Baby's presentation: to stylize it further, there is music: on the other hand, not only do the people who are listening each have their different unknown version of it in their minds as the story is in progress, they already know, as do Baby and ourselves, that there *will* be an accident. With this contradiction in mind, as we see the corn shocks and patches of woodland fly by faster and faster, the camera comes back into the office momentarily where without our seeing Baby talking or the others we follow Dick's gaze out of the window to the point at which, though at a greater distance than before, Nicole is still standing, being familiarized with the grounds by a nurse: in a split second we see the nurse pointing out a flower that has bloomed, Nicole turning away disinterested, or crying, and shattered, and we are in Nicole's own mind, for perhaps she too is thinking of the accident: but before we have time to grasp either this possibility or that Dick is imagining that she is so thinking, we are with Nicole herself and her father anyway, experiencing that same sense of almost unbearable exhilaration of speed that we had experienced in *Daddy's Girl*: and at this juncture we hear their voices.

Nicole:—of course I love the car, Dad, but it doesn't change anything. Oh, can't you see! The only thing I asked you was to let me go away to school. (angrily) You're cheating me, that's what you're—you let Baby go.

Warren: (angry himself, hurt, and also righteous) The situation was very different.

Nicole: I don't see how. Just because—

Warren: Nicole!

Nicole: All right, all right, I know, you've given me everything I wanted—except the one thing I really wanted. Someday you'll be sorry—I'll—I'll—

Warren: (still angry, but quietly, sensing danger) Better slow up a bit, Nicole, old girl—

Nicole: (flings him a defiant look) Oh *you*! There's never anybody on this old road.

At this point we shift in a flash to a sort of God's eye view that sees the future, since, as has been said, we know what the fated people in the car do not. We now see the road from the air, looking down, where we are able to observe not only Nicole's roadster but that in the distance, around a corner and also at a great rate of speed, a huge truck is approaching. These two visions of the accident, the one from Nicole's point of view, the other from the air which includes the truck, now begin to alternate: they alternate more and more rapidly, till each lasts only a fraction of a second, until just before the moment when the truck comes into Nicole's field of vision, then we stay with her at the crash.

Warren: Slow up, Nicole, you idiot. Nicole! Do as I tell you—slow up!

Nicole turns a laughing defiant face to her father.

Warren: (yelling) *Look out!* (he seizes the wheel)

Nicole screams.

It is too late. The roadster flies headlong into the huge truck coming round the curve. The impact, while scarcely unexpected, is so sudden and frightful that the spectator feels the shock. The first shock is succeeded by a succession of later shocks, expressed by a series of static, or almost static, instantaneous shots like newspaper pictures, taken from different angles, following in flashes as swiftly as the previous flashes: shots of the whole scene at a distance, from under the cars with spinning wheels above our heads, of objects catapulting through the air, of two people running across a field: we hear a noise like the Blitzkrieg, during these shots, and finally, as we begin to regain consciousness, as it were, with Nicole, lying in the road, badly but not seriously injured, we hear first a dripping of blood such as we had heard on the tin box after Peterson shot himself; then Nicole opens her eyes to see her father being wrapped in blankets (presumably by the people we saw running across the field) the blankets are stained with blood. Broken bottles cover the road for two hundred yards from the truck, on the back of which we read, ironically, Enjoy Columbia Dry at Work. The beautiful joyous autumn day (still there in the background of peaceful sunlit fields and trees) has, in the twinkling of an eye, been turned into a nightmare of horror. As we hear Nicole scream, and scream again, the screen darkens swiftly around us. (see notes)[31] (Lowry, pp. 137-41)

21

Baby concludes her story by saying that Nicole, whom everyone had assumed was suffering only from shock, had become wilder and wilder in her behaviour and had begun to insist that she had murdered her father. As Baby is escorted back to her car, Dick again gazes through the window at the garden where Nicole had been a few minutes before. His face this time, Lowry suggests, shows another kind of prerecognition—a foretaste of future anguish. As Dick prepares to go outside—where a storm is now gathering—Dohmler tells him that he has learned much from Dick's book (as from the work of other Americans, such as William James) and offers him a position at the clinic when he returns from America, a proposition that leaves Dick surprised and delighted. (See Lowry, pp. 141-43 and Fitzgerald, 2, i-iii.)

Dick walks off down the driveway into the storm, fairly swinging along in his joy. At the gate in the wall he stops and looks back at the sanatorium, which now means to him his opportunity and his future, and we have a shot of the sanatorium with its lighted windows against the dark. Suddenly there is a terrific flash of lightning and a roaring of wind and thunder. In this instant of weird and vivid light we see the building, the trees writhing and tossing in the garden, and behind it and beyond, the lashed and jagged peaks of the Alps. Then darkness again and the lighted windows. The camera comes up to focus on one window and we cut to Nicole lying in bed, tortured and terrified by the storm. A pair of hands comes into the screen, holds her arm: she is given an injection as we fade out.

Fade in on a shot of two pairs of hands resting on a desk, the camera comes back and we see Dohmler sitting at his desk with Franz leaning over his shoulder. We see that they are intent upon Nicole's case history. Through the window we can see the garden with the trees in full leaf, showing a lapse of time. It is now full summer, but a cloudy, rather dark, day.

The camera starts forward to focus on the report, and we see what is written, small, but coming closer and larger as we move in. First we see it as over Dohmler's shoulder, written in Gothic German handwriting. Before we have grasped this it has turned to French as we move up towards it:

Diagnostic: Schizophrénie. Phase aiguë en décroissance.

Before we have read even this much it has changed into English so that by the time we have come up to it we can read it clearly:

Diagnosis: Divided Personality. Acute and downhill phase of the illness. The fear . . .

The other words are blurred and while we are reading, the words Divided Personality have changed into the one word Schizophrenia, their anglo-Greek and more terrifying counterpart. The other words all drop away, and on the screen, surcharged with horror and menace, accentuated by music, and coming straight out of the screen at us, the one word:

SCHIZOPHRENIA

At this moment, as if it had been struck by lightning, the screen splits apart, there is a ghastly confused noise, and we enter the terrifying world of schizophrenia itself, or one of those phases of it which symbolizes the states of absence, confusion, and delirium: at the left and right side of the screen appear two white figures small as puppets seen against the darkness, the noises cease and there is dead silence: these figures, both of whom are Nicole, seem far away, yet are standing from our point of view in about the centre of a dark landscape, prodigious in depth, totally barren, and in fact wholly abstract, save for a faint suggestion of whiteness in the sky over the horizon to which it stretches away: the figure on the left is standing, bowed head buried in its hands, giving the impression of the most complete hopelessness, despair and immobility: the figure on the right, on the other hand, seems frantically trying to escape from something, and gestures with hopeless movements of supplication, yet seems unable to move in anything but a circle.

Suddenly and dramatically there is sound again, as from the centre of the screen in the distance—as from over the horizon—a stream starts to come toward us, while it advances making a mechanically harsh chuckling sound, which becomes more dreadful the nearer it approaches, as if it were charged with the emotive character of an imaginary stream of blood rather than of water; this stream which, qua stream opposed to its noise, may be regarded as representing the normal emotions flowing through Nicole's hypothetically integrated and normal personality (which is not imaged) now, and at a point a little way behind the two figures, divides, and begins to run in two channels, the one to our left passing the figure who does not move, the one to our right past the animated figure trying to escape. So far these currents, although some force has divided them, will still find a normal outlet, but at about the moment the channel to the left has nearly passed the bowed figure, a gallows with a rope suspended from it suddenly builds itself directly in its path: as a consequence of this the right hand channel starts to overflow. (This is in part actually a visualization of a Freudian simile for the process of hysterical conversion yet seems to give a dramatic picture of what actually can happen under the general heading of schizophrenia, if not specifically in Nicole's mind: nonetheless it does for that too, for Nicole is at this time often literally "out of her mind," and what she actually suffers is a kind of greatly distorted reflection of this sort of process upon that part of her psyche still capable of conscious suffering; or she is "absent," feels little or nothing, but the process goes on: one ultimate of this, as in dementia praecox, so far as our knowledge goes, is, as it were, a state of simultaneous suffering and dissociation, of suffering and knowing that one is suffering, but at the same time believing one is "absent," though this is perhaps beside the point.) The left channel now represents the point where the emotions became eingeklemmt, or imprisoned, that is to say, where the gallows confronts the helpless figure, but it is the right hand channel, as has been said, which starts to overflow, and, as it is now seen overflowing, rises to engulf the animated figure still frantically trying to escape, and then, seeming to be drowning.

"Tender Is the Night"

At this moment we cut to Nicole herself lying in bed and struggling, it may be the next day, a week, or some months later: we see the barred windows, and that Franz is standing over her—she is obviously heavily sedated, and we have not seen her otherwise, even, perhaps especially, in the garden. (Odd though it may seem, there is nothing contradictory in having put her in the garden, for madness, like mankind, is often not merely content with having its source in bed, it has to be at its most triumphant there too.) Franz merges into a blur, as through Nicole's mind, through which we now see the sanatorium corridors and even the world outside—any world—with people moving down the streets, and in which everything seems a ghostly blur, and only stationary objects stand out plainly, though even they seem unreal. (Note: a similar technique has of course been used in hundreds of movies, with varying degrees of effectiveness, usually to express drunkenness: what suggested its use here—though this suggestion is tentative—were some photographs in an issue of *Life* in which a photographer employed time exposures, of half a second and one second, "catching the blurs with her camera and," to quote the subscription, "transforming the rushing masses into ethereal streams that wave through the city," (New York) something like this would not be mere trick photography here—though we thoroughly dislike that phrase, is not art itself an enlightened trick?—but would actually catch, far better, say, than auditory hallucinations here, the actual quality and meaning of Nicole's illness) All this, which is accompanied by a sort of suitable ectoplasmic half-din or half-music, echoing, merges into perhaps a deserted station platform, or rather—since there happens to be a platform in the pictures mentioned in the note—a deserted wharf with just these words visible: Enjoy Columbia Dry at Work, some symbol of departure or leave-taking and sadness, which changes abruptly into the same abstract landscape as before, with the same two figures, in precisely the same relation as they were at the beginning of the former bit, without the gallows or the stream, but with the same eerie silence: the only difference, as precisely the same drama of contrasted immobility and futile escape begins to repeat itself, is that the landscape is now lit by a maniacal full moon hanging over the horizon in whose light the landscape itself appears awful beyond description and something perhaps like a desert on the moon itself, although it should somehow be anything but a so-called Dali-like landscape. Once more abruptly there is noise, and a gigantic shadowy figure begins to rise over the horizon, blotting out the moon and filling the whole screen: suddenly we see Devereux Warren's face, anguished, frightening, vengeful and bloodstained. On the screen at the bottom to the left, and as the face fades, and in small letters coming towards us, first in German, changing into French, coming towards us the words: Le pronostic doit rester réservé, changing into English as the face fades into darkness, and remains held: on the screen (at the bottom to the left) the words:

The prognosis must be reserved.

Immediately the rest of the screen brightens and we are in Dohmler's office. Dohmler is looking out of the window as the words fade from the screen. Through the window we see the garden: now and then a leaf falls gently, a gardener outside is raking leaves and burning them. It is now autumn. The door opens, we hear a few clanging words in German from outside, and Dick enters. He is now out of uniform and wearing his white doctor's gown.

Dohmler: Ah ha. Well. So you have what one might call, the healing hand, eh? Allow me to congratulate you.

Dick: Don't please—I don't trust hypnosis as a rule.

Dohmler: Still, Doctor Lladislau tells me that there are whole areas cleared up, and that the gnädige Frau Walter will be on her way into the world again.

Dick: I'm proud of myself, I admit—frankly I thought there was nothing much to be done—a family history of neurosis, and nothing stable in her past to build on—how is our Miss Warren?

Dohmler: Ya—well, it was on account of your little compatriot I— Now our friend Gregorovious says—

Cut to a point later on in the conversation, evidently toward the end, for Dick and Dohmler have just risen from bending over some other papers on the desk, on which we see the name Nicole Warren, and are strolling over towards the door. Autumn leaves falling can be seen outside.

Dick: I thought it looked bad.

Dohmler: Very bad. Very typical . . . The prognosis—as you know, the percentage of cures, even so-called social cures, is very low at this age—but unser Gregorovious had the idea, and I agree, that if you, being . . .

Dick bows in gratitude at the trust reposed in him: fade out and fade in on Dick seated by Nicole's bedside in a severer room, with severer barred windows. Without rising, but tilting back his chair, Dick has been saying something to Franz, standing behind him and half in the door, who gently withdraws, this withdrawal being symbolic of the latter's turning over of the case to Dick, but not total relinquishment of it. (In fact Nicole must have passed through the hands of several other doctors too—though we don't see them—if not specifically for the same reason as that for which Dick is present, including at least one French-speaking Swiss, hence the implication

"Tender Is the Night"   97

of the diagnosis in French also, an apparently unimportant point, which, however, subtly increases our belief in the whole thing.)

Outside, through the barred windows, there is a sense of a lowering autumn day. It is rather late in the afternoon and very still. Dick is wearing a white robe.

Dick: (readjusting his chair but leaning back in it in an attitude and a voice calculated to produce the utmost of ease and confidence, even while what he says is half-humourously self deprecating) Well, as I was saying, Herr Dohmler to the contrary, about the only thing I seem to know about Chicago is that it was the home of the Ferris Wheel. And, of course, the World's Fair . . . And ah yes, they edit a poetry magazine, and last but not least, they have produced many excellent psychologists—

As Dick has reached the words Ferris Wheel, the camera reverts to Nicole and we simply hear the soothing sound of Dick's voice. Nicole lies on the bed, still as a corpse, her face turned to the wall. We would think that she does not hear what Dick is saying or indeed hear anything at all. But now we see that if she does not precisely hear or even perhaps at this juncture think, or at least hear or think as we would, the psychological process, nonetheless, is going on, in addition to a collateral, sad, sub-relative of the normal process of visualization. The latter is now figured as follows. We see a static photograph of a Ferris Wheel standing absolutely empty and still in a completely deserted fairground. (Note: no music, save at the very opening, at the moment of the revelation of Dick's presence in Nicole's room, accompanies this sequence.)

Dick's Voice: On the other hand, my home is in Virginia, a little place by the sea . . . In winter the long waves would come thundering up almost into the church where my father used to preach.

Simultaneously, through Nicole's mind, we see a static wintry photograph of long rollers breaking for miles on a deserted beach with the spray held poised.

But at the repetition of the word "home," which has succeeded "psychologists" and is to be succeeded by the word "father," we begin to illustrate the psychological process. We see, through the disappearing static waves, one of those little rooms, square-shaped but built in such a way that it involves distorting planes, used in visual psychological experiments, and which are in some psychological laboratories. (One—and perhaps it is the only one of this particular type, but no matter, was shown in *Time* in the medical section September or early October 1949) In the front, foreground, on the right, we see the figure of Devereux Warren, not covered with blood, but as he would appear at his best, well-dressed, handsome, and smiling, and only slightly blurred. He is dominating the picture to the extent that his head seems pushed right against the ceiling. This room does not take up the whole screen, however, but appears at a distance within it, as if the floor of the room were a stage, though we do not see Nicole. In the left hand, far corner of the room, cater-corner from the other figure, is a tiny figure so blurred that we cannot make it out at all but which seems to be of a man half Devereux Warren's height (which is the psychological point of a room so built, for in fact the impression will be the same if both men are the same height, or about the same height, as they are here). All this too is simply a static photograph with the figures unmoving and unchanging as to expression. This latter and more remote figure, whom we now see in better focus, is Gregorovious, and he is standing with his head as far from the ceiling as would seem to befit his only ostensibly smaller stature.

Dick's Voice: Still does—a trait that I have inherited. Say, you should be doing the talking.

While Dick is saying this the camera comes briefly back to Nicole's face again which likewise has not changed. But now we see the distorted room again. Gregorovious has come into better focus in order to turn into Dick, and now the figure in the far left corner turns into Dick standing in his white robes, an only slightly larger figure than that of Gregorovious, while on the right Devereux Warren still remains unchanged and with a fixed smile dominating the illusion. This all takes place in the moment or so while Dick's voice is heard speaking.

Lap dissolve from Nicole lying on the bed to Dick seated beside her bed; the face on the pillow turned toward him now, watchful yet curiously blank. However this very watchfulness is a species of advance, and implies a role of rebellion again, this time in a more therapeutic form. (We say again in case the half-rebellion at the door of the hospital be thought to amount to one: actually this had bearing only on Nicole's "outside" personal character, for Nicole was then still in the world, where the juxtaposition is subtly different and such a conflict can bring about what amounts to a lucid interval, just as a man with some fatal but obscure injury about to enter a hospital that afternoon, and even perhaps die, can still protest at a bar that he is being served the wrong kind of Scotch) It is still autumn outside, though later, the trees are now bare. Dick says nothing at first, but through Nicole's mind, in a second, we see the same distorted room as before, only this time Gregorovious is not present at all. Dick in his white robes and Devereux Warren are in the same places, but scarcely blurred. Suddenly, in a flash, Dick and

Warren change places with each other. As Warren becomes the dwarfish figure in the further left hand corner his face also changes, however, into a symbol of guilt again: his face is agonized, and covered with blood: the face blurs slightly: meanwhile, on the right, it is Dick's head that seems pressing against the ceiling and it is Dick who dominates the picture. At this moment all this disappears altogether and the camera goes outside the window of Nicole's room where a wild wind rushes through the garden, whirls and spins the dead leaves, and suddenly Nicole breaks into hideous disjointed speech.

Nicole: If you come here again with that attitude base and criminal and not even faintly what I had been taught to associate with the role of gentleman then heaven help you. I've thought a lot about moonlight too, and there are many witnesses I could find if I could only be out of here.

Dick: (quietly, softly, in his long white robes—which accounts for the white cat in the next paragraph) You will be.

Nicole: They said you were a doctor, but so long as you are a cat it is different. My head aches so, so excuse this walking there like an ordinary with a white cat will explain, I think. (Dick places his hand on her head) It was the duty of someone who understood. The blind must be led—

Lap dissolve: Dick seated by Nicole's bed: the room is different, there are no bars on the window. Outside the snow is falling. The face on the pillow shows awakening consciousness.

Lap dissolve from Nicole's face to Nicole, frightened and alone, in another dark, strange, but much less abstract, nearly realistic landscape. She shuts a gate behind her and suddenly realises she is in a graveyard. The graveyard is full of tossing trees, and there is faint moonlight. On one side there is a narrow alley bounded by high walls and turnstiles. There is a shadowy solemn church in the middle of the graveyard but the door is shut. Along the alley comes a dark sinister shadow that gradually extends itself. Frightened, Nicole tries to find her way out of the graveyard, in which there are many tombstones, on one of which seems to be the name Warren, though all she can make out is the word thus: War. There is the muffled sound of guns which cease now that Nicole, still frantic with fright, has escaped from the graveyard. At first she is walking between what seem to be almshouses or low, poverty-stricken houses huddled together—but definitely not tilted or otherwise *Caligari*-like[32] houses, though they could be ruined, as if bombed. Then an enormously long straight road appears ahead of her leading uphill into the distance, and between what might be wild moorland. On either side of this road appear unlit old fashioned street lamps.

Occasionally a light appears ahead over the horizon, suffusing the sky for a moment, and we feel it might be that of a car, but no car appears. On the other hand behind her the sourceless shadow has left the alley and stealthily follows her. Meantime we have seen the name of the road: Warren Drive. Nicole becomes increasingly frightened and we wish that some friendly human being would appear to light these street lamps. Now she is filled with joy as we see, infinitely distant as yet, a small figure come over the horizon. It is the lamplighter, and with his old fashioned lamplighting stick he approaches Nicole who is coming up the hill; as he does so he is going downhill from one side of the road to the other, reaching up with his long torch to set the lamps alight. The figure grows closer and larger and now we see that it is Dick, an expression of great gentleness and wisdom on his face. Only the face is much older than Dick as we know him and he is wearing a uniform that might be identified as military, and hence vaguely with what we have seen Dick wearing at the beginning of the sequence. Having lit the lamp near to Nicole he smiles reassuringly at her and places one hand on her head then goes on downhill lighting his lamps. Nicole watches him and once the lamplighter looks back, waving his hand. Nicole also waves, and we see that the shadow that had been approaching Nicole from behind now merges into the shadow cast by the lamplighter and that it recedes with him as he does from Nicole. But now he is almost gone Nicole is frightened again and though the lamps are now alight ahead of her, she rushes up the rest of the hill. Nonetheless there is a sort of exultance this time combined with her fright. Yet now she has reached the top of the hill we see there are no lights beyond on the other side, only a kind of abyss. As she rushes on now we see that there is something there, like a stone wayside cross placed in her path. The cross is on fire and comes up out of the screen at us. Lap dissolve from the cross of fire to Nicole's face on the pillow.

Nicole: . . . So you see how I stand. And what good can it be for me to stay here with the doctors harping constantly in the things I was here to get over. One doctor in Chicago said I was bluffing, but what he really meant was that I was a twin six and he had never seen one before. But I was very busy being mad then so I didn't care what he said, when I am very busy being mad I don't usually care what they say, not if I were a million girls. The mental trouble is over and besides that I am completely broken and humiliated, if that was what they wanted. My sister has shamefully neglected me, there's no use asking her for help or pity. Well, I think love is all there is or should be.

Dick: (we see that his eyes are holding her, at once supporting and dominating: the beginning of the same look we are familiar with from the first sequence) If so you might begin by trying to understand your sister . . . We must all try to be good. (laughs) You're doing so well before you know it you'll be clearing up her compulsive acts too.

Nicole: If I had only known what was going on like I know now I could have stood it I guess for I am pretty strong, and now when I know and have paid such a price for knowing they sit there with their dog's lives and say I should believe what I did believe. Since you will not accept my explanation you could at least explain to me what you think, because you have a kind cat's face, and not that funny look that seems so fashionable here. . .

Lap dissolve: Dick seated beside Nicole, who is now dressed and lying on a couch in a comfortable, even luxurious and luminous room. Outside it is a calm, bright winter day, with snow everywhere. Through the window we can see people skating in beautiful circles on the lake, vivifying, if we like, even the conception of "circle," vicious in its psychopathological image, and beyond, the Alps. Nicole's expression is still remote, strained, but something in her eyes is alive, and she keeps her eyes on Dick's face with the look of one in desperate prayer toward the altar.

Nicole: I think one thing today and another tomorrow . . . That is really all that's the matter with me, except a crazy defiance and a lack of proportion . . . Here they lie in their bathtubs and sing, *Play in Your Own Backyard*—as if I had my backyard to play in or any hope which I can find by looking either backward or forward.

Dick: Right now it's only by meeting the problems of every day, no matter how trifling or boring they seem, that you can make things drop into place again. How do you like that for one of my father's sermons? Fact of the matter is—

Nicole: They tried it again today and I almost hit the nurse with the weight. I am too unstable.

Lap dissolve: Nicole standing alone by the window looking out. We see that it is early spring in the garden, the trees are still bare, except one which is flowering. There is a knock at the door.

Nicole: Entrez.

Dick comes in. Because of the knock we know she must be much better, but we are scarcely prepared for the change we see in Nicole's face as she turns from the window. Her eyes are clear and candid, there is only a shadow of the strain, and she looks at Dick trustingly as a child.

Nicole: Good morning, Doctor.

Dick: Good morning. Wie gehts es mit Ihnen, heute, gnädiges Fräulein?

Nicole: Bien. Wunderbar . . . I'm coming back to life. (she turns to the window, then back, infinitely touching as she speaks hesitatingly, shyly) . . . Today the flowers, and the clouds . . . I have been watching the tree.

Meantime we have seen the clouds: and again also the snow-drops and crocus, the flowering tree, the other still bare ones.

Dick: Don't watch it too long. It might get frightened and drop an apple on some genius' head, and then we'd all have another Theory to cope with.

Nicole: (laughing) It isn't an apple tree, silly . . . And it couldn't have apples on at this time of year, stupid . . . Oh, I *know* I'm coming back to life . . . And the war has been over a year and a half and I hardly knew there was a war. Dr. Gregory gave me a picture of you in uniform when you went away for a vacation—don't look—(Nicole goes to a small table by the couch, where she finds the photograph in a place where she has obviously kept it so that it won't be apparent to Dick should he come in—it is a picture in a leather folding frame, accommodated for two photographs, and we have seen it before on the piano in the Villa Diana and in Paris, when the vacant space now apparent was occupied by a photograph of Nicole) was it at—Christmas?—I still get a little mixed up . . . There you are. (She hands Dick the photograph, Dick takes it and we see the picture of Dick in uniform.)

Dick: I didn't see any of the war, only its results, so I ain't no hero, I'm afraid. (he hands the picture back to Nicole) Which reminds me we had some shell-shock cases who merely heard an air-raid from a distance. (Dick walks over to the window and stands, looking out) We have a few who merely read the newspapers . . . You know, this time I'm going to say something really intelligent about a tree, Miss Warren. Had you and I been rash enough to have carved our names upon that tree down there at about the same time you arrived among us here in Zurich, the names, by now, like the tree, would have grown larger. (see notes)[33] It's a scientific fact. (Dick begins immediately to go, rustling in his white robes.)

Nicole: (gazing after him with an expression almost of rapture) How kind you have been! You must be very wise behind your face like a white cat. A bientôt . . . (Immediately Dick has gone Nicole rearranges the photograph of Dick in uniform) Mon Capitaine . . .

As Nicole looks at Dick's photograph, on the right in the double frame, we see the empty place beside it filled by Nicole's own photograph, much as we have seen it in fact: this at present expresses a purely romantic, girlish, even "movie" whimsy, as immature an infatuation as Rosemary's love for Dick, and in many respects, considering the obstacles in the path in both cases, analogous to it: Nicole's photograph fades, and almost at once the frame with Dick's photograph is becoming the distorted room again, with Dick on the left in his white robes as he was before when Devereux Warren, now completely out of the picture, occupied the dominant place: but this smaller figure is now by no means dwarfed by the other—he does not have to be, for the other figure is Dick too, in uniform, precisely as he appears in the photograph—he simply smiles, and this is the first time anyone in this configuration has physically moved his features—and fades out, much as the real Dick has just done in leaving Nicole's room, leaving the other Dick in uniform, smiling too, but unmoving as in the photograph, (indeed the other Dick *is* the photograph—a representation of something that does not exist) alone in the distorted room, and in command, and alone on the screen, as the rest of it darkens and we lap dissolve into Dohmler's office.

(This was of course an intended illustration of how an actual transference should presumably be, how it is in fact taking place then or at an intermediate unspecified time, and how it could have been completely effected, but for Dick's tragic flaw, or his moment of weakness, etc. For the point is that the image of Dick in uniform is not essentially Dick, only a mythical Dick, a warrior-captain Dick, in which is subsumed the real Dick, much as the father-image concept was subsumed in the surrogate image of "Capitaine," in the first place, at present only the person Nicole will fall in love with some day, simply an imaginary, but dominant, romanticised teleological objective somewhere in the great world at large, to which she is becoming adjusted, just as she should be, on this plane of reasoning at least.)[34] (Lowry, pp. 143-61)

22

It is May 1920. Dick confers with Franz and Dohmler at the clinic. The two men congratulate Dick on his work with Nicole, and through the open window of the office, they can hear Nicole playing tennis outside. Chasing a ball, she once again comes face to face with Dick at the window; her expression shows not only the love she feels for Dick but also the happiness of one who has been reborn, who has finally come to life. Dohmler notices the look that passes between Dick and Nicole, and he seems concerned although he says nothing. After sunset, in the garden, Dick tells Nicole that she will be leaving soon; she replies that she hopes she will be going somewhere exciting with her sister. Nicole tells Dick that she has some records she would like him to hear and offers to take him to the secret place where she keeps her phonograph. (See Lowry, pp. 161–63 and Fitzgerald, 2, v.)

Cut into a little summer house, open at the front, at the end of the garden, surrounded by flowering trees which glimmer whitely in the soft, exquisite light of the early twilight. The phonograph on the table is playing *The Japanese Sandman*. The summer house we have a mysterious sense of having seen before, vaguely it reminds us of Dick's workhouse at the Villa Diana. Perhaps this is partly because of the old fashioned phonograph, which is the same one we saw there. The singing of crickets threads the intervals between the music. Dick smokes his pipe. (perhaps this reminds us vaguely of Barban)
From the gramophone, a voice, with orchestra:

> Won't you stretch imagination for a moment
> And come with me,
> Let us hasten to a nation lying far
> Across the western sea—

Nicole shifts the needle of the gramophone ahead and roughly to the point where the verse is linked to the chorus by the nostalgic chiming of oriental-sounding bells. And perhaps this reminds us of the scene in the Café Eden, in Paris.
Nicole: (childishly) That's the bit I like.
From the gramophone: (beautifully but with diabolical meaning)

> Here's the Japanese Sandman, stealing on with the dew,
> Just an old second hand man, he'll buy your old days from you.
> He will take every sorrow of the day that is through,
> And he'll give you tomorrow just to start life anew.
> Then you'll be a bit older in the dawn when you wake,
> And you'll be a bit bolder with the new day you take,
> Here's the Japanese Sandman, trade him silver for gold,
> Just an old second hand man, trading new days for old.

Listening to this, Dick and Nicole are not for the moment doctor and patient, but simply seem two young Americans enjoying the music, whatever Dick may read into the words of the song.[35]
(We were able to hear the *Japanese Sandman* six years later because

it is a song that has never dated, and is still popular today among jazz addicts—this is true of many songs that involve destiny. The Sandman's psychological significance is likewise appalling. On the other hand we are able to hear the next piece, *Smiles*, in the Ferris wheel sequence later on largely because fair music is always about six years behind the times.)

Dick: (as the record ends and Nicole takes it off) That's good. Let's play it again. (something about the tune has moved him so he becomes the doctor again) Not enough has been written about the therapeutic value of jazz—

Nicole: (interrupting) Wait, I have another. (she puts on a new record and sings with it, looking at Dick, smiling)

> There are smiles that make us happy
> There are smiles that make us blue—

(she stops singing and dances a bit by herself, then both sings and dances)

> There are smiles that ... something ... something ...
> That the eyes of love alone can see,
> But the smiles that fill my heart with sunshine
> Are the smiles that you give to me.

Nicole stops dancing in front of Dick abruptly, and stands looking at him, suddenly serious.

Cut to a golf ball being savagely driven off a golf tee. The camera, from a position in the rear of the golf tee, now follows the trajectory of the ball, played by Dick, who is playing a round with Franz. Ideally this course should be situated between a single-line electric railway embankment on the left, and the lake to the right, with the Alps in the distance all around. The embankment is divided by a fence from the fairway they are playing down, to the right of which are bunkers that separate it from another fairway going in the reverse direction, which borders the lake; and as Dick plays, a train passes. But it can be any course, so long as it has snow-covered mountains in the background. It is practically deserted and the doctors have no caddies. They are playing with wooden clubs, that is, not steel-shafted ones, and very few of these. It is one of those spring days of sudden light and shadow with a big wind blowing. Both are good players. Dick's ball has travelled a great distance, hanging high in the wind, but, slightly hooked, it seems to be going or have gone over the left hand fence.

Franz: (watching the ball) You-are-out-of-bounds!
Dick: I don't think so. We'll see.

Cut to the two men carrying their clubs, strolling down the fairway but bearing to the left in the direction of Dick's ball. Franz' ball is well placed in the centre of the fairway. Dick's mien is gloomy and preoccupied. The beautiful windy spring day and the accompanying music accentuate the conflict of what we know is haunting Dick. (Lowry, pp. 163–66)

23

During their golf game, Dick tells Franz that he will try to discourage Nicole from developing too close a relationship with him. He says that his plans are to be the greatest psychiatrist who ever lived and that he has great faith in the book that he is currently trying to publish, though Franz questions the wisdom of writing only popular books on psychiatry. Later, in Dohmler's office, both Franz and Dohmler warn Dick of the danger of letting Nicole fall in love with him. Dick admits that he is half in love with her himself and that the thought of marrying her has crossed his mind, but Dohmler insists that if Nicole is to experience a full recovery, the relationship must be terminated, and he suggests that Dick take a vacation, during which time Nicole will be discharged. That afternoon, while discussing with Nicole her plans for her departure,[36] *Dick tells her that he will be leaving on a vacation the next day; though Nicole is visibly upset at the news, she holds up rather well.*

Lowry comments at length on the use of his soundtrack in this scene: "The music begins to play faintly a wordless arrangement—or a suggestion—of the beginning of the fourth act of Gluck's Orféo. *Music lovers will recognize that poignant music toward the end where Orpheus, who has charmed the Kingdom of Darkness and Hell with his music, is now leading his beloved Eurydice out of those regions again, an intention only to be consummated if he does not look back. On his way out though, sadly his resolve can't stand the test, for when Eurydice in turn tells him that she can't bear his apparent indifference, he tragically does turn back to embrace her, and instantly Eurydice assumes once more the pallor of the damned. Unlike most such apposite use of music this recognition of it has to pass through a poetic perception of its application to the story before it is understood: this having been accomplished, another dimension is added to the meaning of the film. While those who do not get the point at all will have heard some supernaturally good music in exactly the right place by someone they have thought was on your payroll but who died in 1787"* (Lowry, pp. 171–72).[37] *The next morning Dick leaves the clinic.*

The scene changes to Dick bicycling on an Alpine road when, suddenly, a tiny bird crashes into him, though it is not seriously hurt. When Dick picks it up, it swiftly flies into the distance. Arriving at the funicular at Glion, Dick checks his bicycle, drinks a beer, and observes the funicular. Water is gushing from the car waiting at the bottom while at the top of the mountain another car, very small in the distance, waits as it takes on water. As the brakes are released, this latter car begins to descend, pulling the car at the bottom upwards. (See Lowry, pp. 166–77 and Fitzgerald, 2, iv, vi-viii.)
Lowry's own note follows in the filmscript.

Note: This funicular process, without seeming precisely symbolic, seems to mean something else. There is more than a hint that one is catching a glimpse or image of a psychological process in it, the one perhaps which one hopes will work with Nicole. Like the funicular, the patient ascends to the higher air of normal consciousness and common sense by virtue of the gradual displacement, but also the weight of the receding father surrogate. Or is it simply our old friend tragic irony? As Nicole goes up, so Dick will go down? Then again, it is merely a funicular working. (Lowry, p. 177)

24

Dick boards one of the cars and, along with another man, a young Tommy Barban, goes to the rear compartment of the funicular. From Barban "we get a much greater sense of youth than from Dick, at the same time of naiveté, power, and experience" (Lowry, p. 178). Just before the door of the car closes, a crowd of passengers hurriedly arrives and settles mainly in the first class car at the front. Barban, whose head is bandaged and who is walking with a slight but noticeable limp, exchanges words with a priest and then strikes up a conversation with Dick; when Dick asks about the bandage, Barban replies that he is a soldier whose business is killing people. Slightly amused at Barban's bravado, Dick retorts that his business is saving them. At that moment two young people scramble from the first class compartment into the rear. One of them is Nicole, and Dick is thunderstruck. Nicole introduces her companion as the Count of Marmora, and Dick introduces Barban, who is fascinated and enchanted by Nicole. When the car stops halfway up the mountain directly opposite the descending car, Dick looks out the window and sees the conductor of his car, whose face so resembles Dohmler's that he actually turns into that man in Dick's eyes. The conductor is smiling, but as the cars once again begin to move, he raises his hand, palm outwards, bidding farewell to his fellow conductor—a gesture which, in Dick's eyes, becomes a clear warning to stop. Nicole has been trying unsuccessfully, to pluck a rose from one of the bushes at the side of the mountain, and as the funicular begins to ascend, Barban reaches out and steals one for her. "Now the two funiculars pass and our car proceeds toward the summit again," Lowry notes. "We pass a forest path, a gorge, and we see the bottom of this gorge. Dick is silent and thoughtful, the others laughing and looking out of the window at the scenery" (Lowry, p. 182). *Nicole and Marmora disappear in the shuffle of the passengers transferring to a mountain train, and Dick is left alone once again with Barban.* (See Lowry, pp. 178–83 and Fitzgerald, 2, viii.)

Barban: (offering a cigarette) You said your business is saving people?

Dick: (indicates he has a pipe, offers Barban a light for his cigarette, lights his pipe) I'm a doctor.

Barban: (laughs his great, good-natured yet scornful laugh we already know) I thought for a moment you must be a clergyman . . . You in the war . . . ?

Dick: (embarrassed by the question, begins to nod, then slowly shakes his head, meantime using the lead to get on to another subject) My father is a clergyman . . . You're Catholic, aren't you? I saw you talking to the priest.

Barban: (smiles) As a matter of fact my family was descended from Knight's Templars[38] . . . (seriously) I try to be a Catholic—a man can have a tough time with his conscience in my profession.

Cut to a shot of the train going round a spiral in the mist and clouds. Cut back to the men at a point later on in the conversation. The following exchange is almost as rapid as if they were discussing football, so inevitably have they fallen into this fundamental subject that concerns them both.

Dick: No, with me conscience has to stand merely as the inner perception of the rejection of certain wishes existing within us, that's all.

Barban: Inner—but why ten more words when you've got one already?

Dick: In my profession—

Barban: (smiling with unerring intuition) Don't tell me you're one of these mental doctors?

Dick: (chuckling, but wryly) Perhaps not exactly mental—yet . . . But you can call me that if you like.

Barban: (after a pause, laughing, the next thought seeming to him too outlandish to be true) If that's one of your patients you just introduced me to I'm tempted to drop the army and join forces with you.

Dick: (smiles, but seriously, returning the conversation to its former strain) It often makes me feel like a priest, nevertheless.

Barban: (the train begins to come alongside the platform) I thought you people left God out altogether.

Dick: (getting up) It often seems to me it's God who's left us out— (throws away over his shoulder, getting out of the train) which would be another problem in psychology, if I knew what that word means. (Lowry, pp. 183–84)

25

Dick and Barban shake hands and go off in separate directions as they leave the funicular. Nicole and Baby—for she is here as well—approach Dick, and Baby asks him to join them in the hotel salon later that evening. As Nicole watches Dick pedal away, the look on her face shows that she is still very much in love with him.

Dick arrives at the salon that night. While Nicole dances with Marmora, Baby, burdened by her worries about Nicole, takes the opportunity to confide in Dick. She does not know, she admits, what she should do or how she should behave; she cannot determine when Nicole might be acting like any normal young girl or when she might be acting strangely. Dick assures Baby that Nicole is completely well and happy and that Baby shouldn't be concerned. As Dick watches Nicole dance with Barban, Baby tells him that she would like to send Nicole back to Chicago where she could make the right friends and perhaps fall in love with a good young doctor. Suddenly, Nicole is nowhere to be seen in the salon, and to pacify Baby, Dick goes to look for her. He finds Nicole outside in the moonlit night with the white crests of the Alps in the background; they both feel electricity between them. Nicole asks Dick to give her a chance to fall in love with him, and flinging her arms around his neck, she kisses him. With the abyss below, a roar of thunder in the distance, and the Alps now blotted out by clouds, Dick and Nicole stand a few steps apart from each other in the gathering storm. He walks up to her, turns her toward him, embraces her, and kisses her as the rain starts to fall. They run back to the hotel hand in hand to meet Baby and Barban; after having a drink with Barban, Dick walks through the rain back to his own hotel. (See Lowry, pp. 184–94 and Fitzgerald, 2, viii–ix.)

Cut to Dick asleep in his hotel room, turning restlessly and muttering. The storm has ceased and a shaft of moonlight coming through the window falls across his face.

Dick: (muttering in his sleep) Nicole . . .

Nicole's Voice: Dick . . .

He is dreaming: Nicole is here, she materializes, as it were, out of the moonlight, kneeling beside his bed, we see her face, half real, imploring, wet with tears, lit by moonlight. Dick takes her in his arms and kisses her. Tormented and tempted by his desire for Nicole, his mind now tricks and tempts him again by making her appeal to him as her saviour.

Nicole: (very softly) I stood waiting for you in the garden holding all myself in my arms like a basket of flowers.

Dick: Nicole . . . my darling . . .

Nicole: Help me . . . Save me . . .

Dick sits up in bed, wide awake: the vision of Nicole has gone. With a groan he gets up and goes to the window. The street below is lit by maniacal moonlight. Nicole seems to be standing in the street, her face turned up to him with a look of supplication. The vision fades. Dick is sleeping restlessly in bed again.

Lap dissolve to Dick and Barban climbing a black, steep cliff in the Alps, below the snow line, that seems difficult, almost impossible to climb, though there is a path. This also is a dream, but a very realistic one. The cliff is the visual image of the difficult decision postulated by Dick's conscience at this moment, and there is a suggestion of slightly closer identity between the two men, for Barban here represents Dick's conscience itself. (For a psycho-analyst in a situation such as Dick's this business of the conscience must be thought of as exacerbated and appalling indeed: not merely is he a trader in such commodities as guilt and the conscience, he has a responsibility analogous to that of a captain of a regiment, or a ship—always he has a whole situation to think of, involving other lives. The son of a clergyman, who has that very afternoon been discussing concepts of the conscience with the Catholic Barban, it is natural that Dick in his dream should revert to the values of his childhood and see his decision in one sense as a matter of religious right and wrong. Nonetheless if his conscious mind has not rejected such principles, his very vocation indeed involves a rejection of them as anything so simple, so that what in fact, in his case, is a clear-cut decision—if a hard one—appears to him in his dream as a complex one too, that requires advice and disguise. What is happening, however, seems perfectly clear to ourselves watching it. If—and here we don't speak in psychological terms—this cliff seems often difficult and steep to ascend (integrity) it looks a whole lot easier to slide down it, even if there is an abyss below (the desires, etc.) This leads Dick to his commonsense though sacrificial decision the next morning that seems final. But as will be seen it is only a half decision or half intention and when fate intervenes—as it so often does at such moments—to make it more difficult of accomplishment in fact, he weakens and allows himself to be pushed once more in the direction of his desires. Much later, with a similar push by fate, he is strong enough to resist, but here he fails.)[39]

Barban throughout this brief scene appears grave and stern.

Barban: How could I advise this man? I'm not the Sacred Penitentiary.

Dick: And if you were?

Barban: I wouldn't be. That's an authority extending to thoughts and deeds unknown to any, save the person concerned and his conscience.

Now we see another climber ahead, who turns and looks at them.

Dick: Hullo, look at that, won't you? (the climber is recognized as the bearded conductor of the funicular) Talk about a busman's holiday.

Dick seems to tire, stops, looks down the other way, where we see the abyss, as Barban goes on climbing. When Dick looks round we see that the conductor's face has become once more that of Dohmler. He waves, but turns the wave into precisely the same gesture of interdiction Dick imagined before, implacable and stern: we have no hint that he is blocking the path ahead and above too; however, the interdiction, if it has more significance than before, seems against Dick's looking down, or turning back.

Lap dissolve to Dick and Barban seated on a rock, with a magnificent angled and sinister panorama of the Alps around them and a shattering drop into the abyss below. Barban is lighting a cigarette, Dick his pipe. We are here more strongly reminded that it is a dream, but its unreality, accentuated by mist, seems also of reality itself.

Dick: . . . but a pipe smoker who takes to cigarettes, I always think, must have left some corresponding quantity of his patience behind him. (He pauses. Barban is regarding him steadily, gravely, as though forcing him to return to the main problem from which he is trying to escape, he does not speak but merely waits. After an instant, almost against his will, Dick returns to the point.) . . . Well, you can see that my problem is interesting, at least from the point of view of the secular conscience.

Barban: Secular conscience! How can there be any such thing as a secular conscience? You can't deprive conscience of its religious character. Any betrayal of your higher self is a betrayal of God, even if you don't believe in God . . . And upon what possible basis of thought has individual sacrifice, or the principle of sacrifice, even been considered a misdemeanor?

Dick: Sacrifice? . . . (Dick looks down into the abyss.)

Cut to Dick restlessly turning in bed, muttering to himself. He gets up with a groan and goes to the window again and stands there, looking out at the high, white, moonlit Alps. (Lowry, pp. 194-98)

26

The next morning Dick receives a note from Nicole saying that she is not ashamed of what happened the night before. Even if she were never to see him again, she writes, she would be happy that it had happened at least that one time: "The camera narrows down to hold the words: even if I never saw you again. Dick has taken the letter to the window, where outside we see the Alps" (Lowry, p. 198). (See Lowry, pp. 198-99 and Fitzgerald, 2, ix.)

Cut to Barban in the bar, otherwise deserted, as Dick enters. Barban is drinking beer and turning over the pages of a copy of the *English Sporting and Dramatic News*. (An illustrated weekly common in Europe at that time.)

Cut to Dick and Barban drinking beer; Dick with one hand, idly, turns the pages of the *Sporting and Dramatic*. He hesitates and we see what his eye has fallen on: a full page advertisement—in every illustrated English weekly at roughly this period—with the caption DAIMLER HIRE. Underneath is a large picture of a Daimler, the make of kingly vehicle in which Baby Warren has turned up at the sanatorium. As we watch the word HIRE seems to come toward us and take on an ironic significance.

Barban: By the way, I want to thank you again for introducing me to little Miss Warren, Doctor. She certainly is a charmer.

Dick: (still gazing at the advertisement) Yeah, she's a nice person.

Barban: I don't want to cut in on you, you know, it's not my habit—but you didn't give me much indication—

Dick does not answer for a moment, still gazing at the advertisement. Suddenly the pictured Daimler changes to the real Daimler standing outside the sanatorium in the rain on Nicole's first night there. We hear the thunder of that time which merges into the thunder of the storm of the previous night here and we see Dick and Nicole running for shelter again. Cut to Dick, still looking at the magazine: the word "hire" disappears and DAIMLER turns into its more immediate assonance of conscience: DOHMLER, coming closer.

Dick: (casually but firmly, as he smilingly finishes his beer and rises) Not at all. You'd be the real right thing for her. You have my blessing. Well . . .

Cut to the two men at the bar shaking hands. Dick has shouldered his knapsack and is obviously leaving. The *Sporting and Dramatic* lying on the counter now has a sort of wry Fitzgeraldian significance.

Dick: (looking round the empty place) It's not the worst kind of place to say goodbye in.

Barban: So long.

Dick: I'll be seeing you. (goes, then turns) Say, remind me one day to tell you about the darndest dream I had.

Barban watches him go out, then turns to the bar.

Barban: Bring me a double war, please.

Cut to Dick, standing beside the bicycle, at the lampstand where they had embraced last night. He puts out his hand and touches it sadly, almost ritualistically.

Dick: Forgive me, Nicole. (Lowry, pp. 199–200)

27

Just as he is ready to leave the hotel, Dick receives another note, this one from Baby Warren. She asks Dick to take Nicole back to Zurich since unforeseen circumstances have called her to Paris. (See Lowry, pp. 200–201 and Fitzgerald, 2, ix.)

Cut to Dick, with a stony, despairing face, looking up from the letter; he leans on the railing, looking down into the abyss.

Lap dissolve to Dick, in the same pose, with an expression almost equally stony, if not so despairing, gazing out of the open window of the train for Zurich. The camera comes back and we see the first-class compartment, which is empty save for Nicole sitting opposite him.

Outside the railway lines are racing back and we see the merging gantlets, as we have from Abe's train. But this time it is an electric train. There are signs in four languages in the compartment and the corridor. On the heat regulator: Froid: Kalt: Freddo: Cold, etc.

Dick is struggling to maintain a formality that is all the more difficult to maintain (even forgetting the previous night) because of the actual friendship, apart from love, that exists between them both and that quasi-friendship just less than formal that has existed for purely therapeutic reasons, or even because they are both Americans in a foreign land. Nicole, on the other hand, is using every feminine wile at her disposal to break down the barrier Dick has imposed. She too is desperately serious beneath the chatter, being deeply, passionately in love with Dick, and seeing this perhaps as her last chance. At the same time she really *is* enjoying the train ride with Dick, and everything *is* new and fresh to her. More tragically, she will have preserved a certain meagre joy in simply going "home," even though home is the sanatorium, less because she can show them there that she has triumphed over her sickness and is shortly to leave, or because it is the only home she knows, but because—more tragically still, since it shows she is really healthy and could do *without* Dick, a matter on which Dick's mind probably becomes increasingly divided—because first she unconsciously *calculates* that the sanatorium will somehow remind her of Dick for a while should she have to lose him, and second because she needs the feeling in advance to put the sorrow in check.[40]

Nicole: (looking out of the window) I never saw such a beautiful spring. I never saw such wild flowers. Look, flowers on the embankment.

Dick: (taking deep breaths) There's nothing like the air of Switzerland. Electric air, electric train—

Nicole: (like a child, almost chanting) Fields of emerald, fields of jade . . .

We see the signs above the window: *Ne Pas Se Pencher en Dehors. Nicht Hinauslehnen. E Pericoloso Sporgesi. Danger to lean outside.* The camera dwells an instant on the word DANGER.

Nicole: Oh look, look at the exquisite lilac-coloured fleur-de-lis. Like bright enamelled jewelry . . . (almost chanting again) Marigolds and morning brides, star-flowers and wild bleeding hearts . . .

Dick: How do you know so much about wild flowers?

Nicole: Oh, I've always known about flowers!

Through the windows we can see the flowers, the tilted fields, an occasional foaming brook, a waterfall, and the white Alps. We pass a sign outside: Attention! *Ne jetez rien par les fenêtres. Vous risquez de blesser les ouvriers travaillant le long des voies.* We see the workmen, and some of them raise their picks in salute. Nicole waves back delightedly. Now there are pine woods beyond the embankment.

Nicole: See the pines. So neat, they seem to be drilling.

(They do, it is a phenomenon of train scenery: the pines circle, seem to stand at attention, then appear to wheel and march off swiftly, the tree at the end of the line waiting for the others.)

Dick: How did you like our friend, Lieutenant Barban?

Nicole: (considering doubtfully) Oooh . . . He's too sure of himself. I think . . . You're the only one I like.

Dick: (as his eye and ours catch a sign flying by, replying mutely for Dick, and in gratitude for our not having thrown objects at the workmen: MERCI) I like him. He's half American, half French, educated in England, a good combination.

Nicole: (looking out of the window) Oh, there's so much in life!

Dick: (grimly) There is.

Nicole: It's all so wonderful . . . Millions of gold poppies and white marguerites . . . Look! A bird.

Dick: (leaning out of the window too, as the camera follows the bird hovering over the pines) It's a hawk, a kestrel . . . I can't make it out, we're going too fast, no, we've gone too far—

As he still leans out of the window trying to catch sight of the hawk again, Nicole sits beside him, watching, so that their heads are close together in the same window. Dick turns away from the window and her face is turned up to his, her look imploring, and full of love. She kisses him, without putting her arms around him, then draws back. She speaks with passionate seriousness, half shyly, but as if she cannot help but speak.

Nicole: I love you. I'll never love anyone else as long as I live . . . Oh, I know you think it's just that—well, lots of women, girls, fall in love with their doctors, but it's not like that, it's not. *They* think, at the sanatorium, that I shouldn't. I know. Oh, they can take my mind to pieces, but what do they know of my heart!

Dick: (he can hardly bear this, but still he controls himself) Nicole . . . listen—

Nicole: Don't say it. I know, I'm only a kid to you—someone who's fun to kiss. Oh . . . (she begins to cry, but with dignity) But it's not like that with me. It's forever.

Dick: (almost sharply) Don't! Nicole—

The train suddenly begins to rush through a station with an awful tumult, while the camera picks out briefly further signs: Sortie. *Change.* Quai 4 Neuchatel. Vallorbe. Sortie. *Change.* Birra. Wührer Qualita. etc. Then, Das *Ueberschreiten* der Geleise ist *Verboten*. *Défense* de traverser les voies. E *Proibito* traversare i banari. It is *Forbidden* to cross the lines. Then: AUSGANG. SORTIE. USCITA. EXIT.

Abfahrt nach
Départ pour   Lausanne Quai 1
Partenza per   Leotschberg Quai 3

Geldschwechsel am Fahrkartenschalter
Change au guichet des billets
Cambio Valute alla Biglietterria
Money *Exchange* at the booking office

We see this, or part of this, all more or less at once. But it is the words CHANGE and EXCHANGE and EXIT and FORBIDDEN that the camera lingers on and emphasizes. But at this point, it is as if we're not quite sure whether we're going through the station or standing stationary while another express train smashes through past us: the impact of the various obviously symbolised aspects of escape and conscience become tremendous. SORTIE EXIT CHANGE coming up toward us again and again; not merely this but as the camera momentarily picks upon the quadralingual sign beneath the communication cord, ALARME NOTBREMSE ALLARME ALARM they begin to make a kind of aural incantation, not exactly in time with the noise of the train, and certainly not in the form of the usual hallucinatory movie whispers: these words, and others we have seen before, while we remain as if still flashing through this eternal station, are pronounced with a certain flatness. (In the film *Paisan*,[41] a dying soldier in a doorway pronounces the words Madre, Padre, in a similar fashion) so that here it is A*lar*me. Not*brem*se. Perico*lo*so. *Dan*ger. E Pro*i*bito. Ver*bo*ten. It is For*bid*den. Att*en*tion. *Aus*gang. *Sor*tie. (and again) Ueber*tra*gung.

Cut from the climax of this to Dick and Nicole finishing dinner in the dining car.

Dick: (almost as if to a child) How do you like the feel of riding on a train again?

Nicole: (all bright again) Oh, so much. I love every minute of it.

Dick: (taking a sip of claret) It's a bit like a life. Hurry and hunger in the morning. Then the afternoon with the journey fading and dying, but quickening again at the end.

The train is going very fast. It whistles prolongedly. The day is darkening outside, the sun is low. There are pine trees silhouetted against the sunset, the Alps again, beyond.

A signal box flashes by: Zurich 7.

Nicole: (almost casually) Oh—we're nearly home! (But her expression changes as her heart sinks at the thought of parting from Dick)

Dick: (realizing what she means by "home") Home—!

Dick bows his head in anguish and love, cut—the camera, like a landing plane, with tragic music, declines on the building of the Sanatorium Zurichsee and pauses before the door. It is now dark.

Dick and Nicole stand at the door, Dick with Nicole's suitcase. A taxi is driving away down the drive.

Dick: It's a sad door . . . And there was I thinking you were through with Dohmler and me for good and all.

Nicole: It's only for a few days, just to see how I took to the outside world, I guess, and then—but Oh, I hate to go in! (now she is desperate, she may never see him again) Could we walk in the garden like we used to, just for a minute? (these words go past us rather than at us)

They walk a little way from the door, pausing in the garden where they are hidden from sight. Further away, are lights in the windows, where people are shut in eternal darkness. But above, we see the trees tossing their dark plumes against the night sky.

Dick: (looking down: Nicole is wearing a pair of light, heelless summer shoes) You'll get your feet wet.

Nicole: (she puts her arms round Dick's neck and stands on his feet, nestling close to him and lifting her face.) I love you.

Dick: (almost as though it were wrenched out of him) I love you, Nicole.

They embrace. The camera goes up to the dark swaying tree tops, returns.

Nicole: (softly, seriously) You love me!— I don't ask you to love me always like this, but I ask you to remember. Somewhere inside me there'll always be the person I am tonight.

Cut to the door again, Nicole and Dick standing before it. Dick is deadly serious. Nicole is serious, but triumphant.

Nicole: . . . then I'll see you tomorrow? You'll come tomorrow?
Dick: Yes.
Nicole: Promise?
Dick: I promise.

The camera goes up again to the trees, tossing against the night sky.

Cut to Dick immediately afterwards, that night, walking the streets of Zurich. In order to identify ourselves with him, we are walking with him, so he is not seen coming towards us. His expression is desperately serious and thoughtful but it is not that he is struggling against his conscience any longer, for with the words "I promise," he has capitulated. That was the brief moment when he transgressed against them both and this long walk is like the foreshadowing of his atonement. Nor is it that he could not break that promise. Something in himself has given way. He walks, past a theatre showing Georg Kaiser's *Von Morgen till Mitternacht*,[42] towards the lake, beyond which the moon rises over the Alps. (Lowry, pp. 201–8)

28

Dick has tea at a place near Zurich with Baby, who has come to pick up Nicole from the sanatorium. He tells her that he and Nicole wish to be married.⁴³ *Baby has some reservations: she knows nothing about Dick's past; Nicole is very rich and could be taken advantage of. Although Baby had hoped Nicole would marry a doctor, she had also hoped to hand-pick him herself. Dick grows slightly angry and frustrated with Baby, but both his anger and frustration magically disappear when Nicole, happy and fresh, approaches their table with a look of adoring love for Dick.*

The scene changes to a lawyer's office where Dick, Nicole and Baby are arranging Nicole's financial matters. Lowry outlines his camera technique and shot composition: "The lawyer and Baby in the background, not sharply focussed, Dick close to the camera in the foreground, that is, the back and side of his head, so that we see he is watching Nicole, who is in the centre and sharply in focus. She is the only one who speaks, for this is completely stylized, as through Dick's memory; her voice is for the most part rather remote" (Lowry, p. 210). *Nicole tells Baby that she is giving her more money than she'll ever need; she claims Dick has enough money for both of them.*

A quick succession of images—"like a procession passing across the screen," says Lowry, "one scene is beginning while another is ending" (Lowry, p. 210) —*shows Dick and Nicole during the first years of their marriage: Dick and Nicole honeymooning on a boat on Como; Dick and a pregnant Nicole celebrating the successful publishing of Dick's book; a 1921 Christmas card with a photograph of Dick, Nicole and the baby; Dick and Nicole buying larger apartments with Warren money; Nicole in a hospital bed holding her second baby; Nicole in the same bed, tossing wildly about, nonsensical and hysterical, with Dick gravely by her side; a quiet but strained Nicole and a watchful Dick vacationing on a boat; Nicole, trying hard to smile, refusing to drive the Divers' car; another Christmas card, this one from 1923, with the children now a little older; Nicole urging Dick to buy a home with her money; Nicole standing sadly at the edge of the garden at the Villa Diana; Dick and Nicole embracing warmly by the workhouse.*⁴⁴

The sequence ends with the beach scene as Rosemary saw it when she first arrived at Antibes, but now it is not Rosemary but Nicole, sitting with Dick, Tommy Barban, and Abe North, who watches the beach and the people on it. She sees Rosemary but doesn't recognize her face or her name. Rosemary is certainly lovely, she says, but there can be too many people on the beach. Lowry again orients the reader: "The scene is changing to the beach of the first beach sequence of the picture, though no one's voice is heard save Nicole's and this time it is seen from Nicole's standpoint: Dick raking, Barban and Abe seated nearby, the children playing or seeming to sing, and Rosemary, who has just seated herself between the Divers and the McKiscos' group—before having been accosted by Mrs. Abrams—in the near background. We observe that while Dick has noticed Rosemary he is also actually watching Nicole, while raking, in a manner that had not been apparent when the scene was through Rosemary's eyes" (Lowry, p. 214).

The scene begins to darken and there is a moon in the sky. Nicole's voice, full of terror and dread, calls out for Dick. (See Lowry, pp. 208-16 and Fitzgerald, 2, x.)

The camera begins to move, as the sky begins to pale, lightening faintly for dawn, then moves back through the window of the Hôtel Roi George.

It is dawn in the hotel room and Dick is still holding Nicole in his arms; daylight grows, she awakens, smiles, has forgotten what has happened temporarily, Dick has placed her under sedatives. He lifts her tenderly in his arms and puts her to bed. We see the double photograph of them in the familiar folder with Dick in uniform, and *La Vie Parisienne*[45] lying idly by reminds us it is 1926.

Cut to the same scene a little later, Nicole sitting up in bed drinking coffee, Dick sitting on the bed, breakfast dishes are on a table nearby. Nicole puts aside her coffee.

Nicole: Dick—what are we going to do? Dick, I'm frightened.

Dick: Hush, darling, there's nothing to be frightened about.

Nicole: (looking at him fearfully, strangely) Oh yes there is. For *me*. You—you're—Dick! *What are you going to do?*

Suddenly, as if in answer to this, there is a sinister, discreet, regular knocking at the door which, although not loud, makes some of us think, perhaps, or think later, of the knocking at the gate in *Macbeth* (quite apart from the fact that a useful Macbeth himself is the patron of the Roi George) for the intention of recall is not dissimilar, though in one way opposite, to that in Shakespeare's play: here we are recalled gradually into the continuity of the picture in *time* and in line with the former Paris sequence, but the night, i.e. the flashback, instead of being insulated, merely falls slowly into step behind it, and becomes a sort of moving arrière-plan that is part of the continuity and inexorably on the heels of every action the protagonists take from here to the end of the film. The section itself however goes very quickly, it being understood that the action is simultaneous with much it is necessary to present in a detail out of all proportion to the time it takes to play.

Dick: (going through the bedroom door into the salon) Don't worry, darling.

Cut to Dick at the door of the salon taking a telegram: we see his astonishment on opening it, then he gives a harsh laugh, tells the boy no answer, then changes his mind and says "Attendez." The boy waits.

Cut to the telegram: on the screen at first just the words in dramatic focus:

ZURICH SUISSE

Then the rest of the words coming into focus:

WOULD YOU CONSIDER MY BUYING CLINIC FOR YOU AND GREGOROVIOUS STOP HAVE BOUGHT FORTY EIGHT HOUR OPTION ON BRAUN CLINIC AT ZUGERZEE STOP PLEASE REPLY IMMEDIATELY REASON RAILROADS HAVE BOUGHT REST OF CHICAGO PROPERTY STOP NOW ACCRUES NICOLE AND SELF WITH SELF TRUSTEE BUT REQUIRES PROMPT INVESTMENT STOP SAW GREGOROVIOUS IN GSTAAD HE BELIEVES SUCH INVESTMENT CANNOT FAIL BE IMMENSELY LUCRATIVE ALL CONCERNED AND BANKER HERE AGREES STOP BELIEVE THIS MAY BE CHANCE YOU HAVE AWAITED ALL YOUR LIFE AND GREGOROVIOUS AGREES STRONGLY ADVISE YOU CONSIDER FOR NICOLE'S POSSIBLE BENEFIT LETTER FOLLOWS
    BABY WARREN

 This shattering opus is held on the screen for a period long enough for us to grasp its salient points but not long enough for us to be more than convinced by the details in the middle. When we have had time to see whom it was from, with which we take in the bit at the end about Nicole, and have read about half of it starting from the beginning, we see Dick's hands more clearly holding the telegram and hear him beginning to laugh again.
 Nicole's Voice: (from the bedroom, hearing him laugh as he, and we, go on reading the telegram) What's the matter?
 Dick's Voice: (from behind his hands) Nothing, darling. (he goes on laughing)
 Cut to Nicole in the other room.
 Nicole: (frightened) Yes there is, there's always something the matter when you laugh like that. What is it?
 Cut back again, this time to Dick reading the telegram and laughing, the boy still standing at the door.
 Nicole's Voice: (continuing) Is it the police again? Is it Macbeth?
 As Nicole's voice proceeds the telegram comes on the screen again, with Dick's hands holding it: this time, though we have probably read it, we don't know where to begin again to grasp it all, as we want to do, so the telegram itself begins to narrow down from top to bottom bringing its two main points at the beginning and the end into juxtaposition, the two points also which are responsible for his laughter on the one hand, and his hesitation on the other, while it

does this, however, changing out of its character as a telegram altogether to a sort of longish subtitle similar to those necessary in translations at the bottom of the screen, which will change as indicated below, and above and through which the room itself with Dick in it reading the telegram and the boy waiting, come into focus again. Thus the words on the screen will not be merely a précis of the telegram—and it is quintessentially important that the words be of precisely the same appearance and type as upon the telegram so that we do not lose the feeling thereof—but in fact an expression of what Dick is thinking too as if thrown on the screen of his brain so that, since we shall see Dick's actions also in so far as they relate to Nicole in action when she appears once more, we shall be a witness, without taxing our brains, to two kinds of thought process at once in the same person, with the resultant saving of time and heightening of the drama. By the time Nicole has reached the word "Macbeth" the scene in the room is clear, (the room is fairly tidy, but with a slight sense of aftermath, Dick must have tidied it himself, since he will have allowed no one in, and there is a bottle of cognac on the table, etc.) with the subtitle appearing below as Dick speaks.

Dick: No, Macbeth's going to be the three obscene little monkeys (Dick throws away in pantomime that the creatures see no evil, etc. then, to the boy, in French) No answer. (the boy goes)

On the screen simultaneously below, the words: WOULD YOU CONSIDER MY BUYING CLINIC FOR YOU STOP. (the subtitle adds) AND GREGOROVIOUS. (these words take their place last between the YOU and the STOP)

Nicole comes running in, in her nightgown, like a frightened child and Dick puts the telegram in his pocket.

Nicole: What are you doing, looking like that and laughing?

Dick: (taking her hands) Calm yourself, darling. It's nothing—just a telegram.

On the screen, simultaneously, below, the words: THIS MAY BE CHANCE YOU HAVE AWAITED ALL YOUR LIFE

Nicole: Telegram? Who from? Where is it?

On the screen, simultaneously, below: HAVE BOUGHT FORTY EIGHT HOUR OPTION PLEASE REPLY IMMEDIATELY

Nicole: Dick! What are you going to do? I know you're—you look so—so—(she begins to cry softly but as if her heart would break.)

Dick puts his arms around her, murmuring tender words of comfort, quieting her, guiding her gently back towards the bedroom. As they reach the bedroom door, there is another knocking on the salon door.

During the above action, on the screen, simultaneously, below, the words of the telegram (but in one place an omission changes the sense to produce a quadruple ambiguity, which may appear also to us, quite directly and correctly, as the simplified expression of the essential antithesis—indeed of the essential conflict of the film): BRAUN CLINIC AT ZUGERZEE . . . IMMENSELY LUCRATIVE ALL CONCERNED . . . THIS MAY BE CHANCE YOU HAVE AWAITED ALL YOUR LIFE BUT STRONGLY ADVISE YOU CONSIDER FOR NICOLE'S POSSIBLE BENEFIT . . . BABY WARREN

Nicole can be heard crying like a child in the bedroom but stifling her sobs. The commotion of the knocking goes on but this time Dick hesitates even to answer the door.

On the screen, simultaneously, below: STOP

The subtitle adds the words before it: WOULD YOU CONSIDER MY BUYING CLINIC FOR YOU AND GREGOROVIOUS (and after—the STOP this second time having coincided with Dick pouring himself a drink and about the climax of his and our exacerbation about the knocking) LETTER FOLLOWS BABY WARREN

Dick having poured himself and drunk part of the drink we have mentioned, goes to the door and takes yet another telegram from a boy whom he immediately dismisses. He rips it open and instantly the second telegram appears on the screen.

On the screen, the second telegram, appearing as did the first, but with even more dramatic impact, save that the words Zurich Suisse are not this time a dramatic value in themselves, but simply appear in their right place, at the end:

RICHARD DIVER HOTEL ROI GEORGE PARIS FRANCE CONSIDER YOUR SISTER IN LAWS PLAN SO MARVELLOUS AND IT WILL BE THE MAKING OF US TWO STOP IF YOU ARE FREE SERIOUSLY ADVISE YOU DECIDE WE UNDERTAKE IT TOGETHER DOHMLER IS RETIRING NEXT YEAR STOP IT WOULD NOT BIND YOU TOO TIGHT STOP YOU COULD STAY IN RESIDENCE HALF THE YEAR AND WRITE YOUR TEXTS DIRECT FROM CLINICAL EXPERIENCE AND FOR THE CONVALESCENCE IN YOUR FAMILY THERE IS THE ATMOSPHERE AND REGULARITY OF THE CLINIC AT HAND STOP INNOVATIONARY STEPS WILL TAKE ONLY FRACTION OF PROPOSED INVESTED SUM WHICH YOUR SISTER WILL HAVE TOLD YOU IS THREE HUNDRED THOUSAND DOLLARS STOP WHILE THE CLINIC IS A GOLD MINE GESUNDHEIT
FRANZ GREGOROVIOUS ZURICH SUISSE

This telegram is held on the screen per se as a telegram for slightly longer than the first one had been held on its first appearance, during which and the following scene from the bedroom we can hear Nicole's stifled yet heartbroken and terrified sobs: but we canalize from the shot differently: the shot of the telegram itself merges into one of Dick reading the telegram but reflected in a mirror: Dick raises his face from the telegram, as does the image of Dick in the mirror, which now becomes a close up on the screen, the expression of which Dick seems, we feel, to be searching, like ourselves are searching in another way in Dick, for some sign of equivocation: the telegram has of course disappeared but, though we are not inclined to take our eyes wholly from Dick's mirrored face, the subtitles reappear below: these subtitles, at first wholly from this second telegram, change with a rapidity that bears little relation to Dick's change of expression—indeed it would be a great mistake if they bore too much—the converse of this being even more true though an exception is made at one point and perhaps another; nonetheless this scene is better expressed visually as if there were such a continuous and direct relation; and in fact there is, to the words. When we say "first close up" it is understood that there are, strictly speaking, only two close ups, with very minor variations, and each is held on the screen while the silent changing words go on bombarding us like hailstones.

Close up on the screen of Dick first raising his face to the mirror.

On the screen simultaneously the words, below: CONSIDER YOUR SISTER IN LAWS PLAN SO MARVELLOUS AND IT WILL BE THE MAKING OF US

The subtitle adds to this the word: TWO

Close up of Dick still in the mirror.

On the screen, simultaneously the words, below: DOHMLER IS RETIRING NEXT YEAR STOP

Close up of Dick's face still in the mirror: on it we see sadness and deep worry, but no equivocation.

On the screen, simultaneously the words, below: FOR THE CONVALESCENCE IN YOUR FAMILY THERE IS THE ATMOSPHERE AND REGULARITY OF THE CLINIC AT HAND STOP

Cut from the close up of Dick's face in the mirror to a close up of Dick's face over by the window; as he lights a cigarette the close up shows a face as honest and good as the one we saw in the mirror, but less full of conflict, and with even a hint of sardonic amusement in it again.

On the screen, simultaneously the words, below: PROPOSED INVESTED SUM WHICH YOUR SISTER WILL HAVE TOLD YOU IS THREE HUNDRED THOUSAND DOLLARS The subtitle adds the word: STOP

Same close up of Dick still smoking his cigarette.

On the screen, simultaneously the words, below: YOU COULD STAY IN RESIDENCE HALF THE YEAR AND WRITE YOUR TEXTS DIRECT FROM CLINICAL EXPERIENCE . . . STOP IF YOU ARE FREE

Cut to Dick's hand swiftly pouring himself a drink: then immediately a close up of his face again, he is about to take the drink, but hesitates at the last moment.

On the screen, simultaneously the words, below: IT WOULD NOT BIND YOU TOO TIGHT

The first five words vanish, leaving sardonically just: TOO TIGHT

The subtitle adds to this the word: STOP

Close up of Dick still held but taking his drink after all.

On the screen, simultaneously the words, below: GESUNDHEIT FRANZ GREGOROVIOUS

Close up of Dick smoking again by the window.

On the screen, simultaneously the words, below: FOR THE CONVALESCENCE IN YOUR FAMILY THERE IS THE ATMOSPHERE AND REGULARITY OF THE CLINIC AT HAND

The first three and last two words vanish leaving the words: IN YOUR FAMILY IS THE ATMOSPHERE AND REGULARITY OF THE CLINIC

Close up of Dick—he savagely stubs out his half smoked cigarette in an ashtray.

On the screen, simultaneously the words, below: WOULD YOU CONSIDER MY BUYING CLINIC FOR YOU STOP

Then: HAVE BOUGHT FORTY EIGHT HOUR OPTION . . . PLEASE REPLY IMMEDIATELY

The words are replaced by: IF YOU ARE FREE

Cut with the abruptness of a sudden decision to Dick going into the bedroom: we feel that Dick has probably made up his mind (see notes).[46] He looks very tenderly at Nicole, who, though still crying, immediately and gallantly gets up on her knees on the bed.

Nicole: (as Dick takes her hands) Oh Dick, do say we can be happy and good again—

Dick: (tenderly) What would you say if we were to—(the phone rings) Half a minute—

On the screen, simultaneously the words, below: DOHMLER IS RETIRING. The words fade as Dick goes into the salon, closing the door behind him. Cut to Dick at the phone in the salon.

(Note: this scene should be played absolutely as fast as possible for it to be still believable and lucid, the object at this point being to whip a sort of tourniquet round the film itself, with the further

"Tender Is the Night"

object of stopping the flow of emotions from the lesser conflicts for the time being, so that we can concentrate on the most vital one.)

Dick: (on the phone) Hullo . . . Oh, hullo Baby (Dick lowers his voice and looks round to make sure he's shut the door) Yes I did. I'd rather . . . You can't wait . . . Sorry . . .

As Dick speaks he takes the telegrams out of his pocket, sees apparently he has got Baby's, and the whole of the first telegram is thrown on the screen again, but already in process of condensation once more from top to bottom, so that it appears—the words preserving as before the character of a telegram—while Dick is seen phoning, as a subtitle again at the bottom of the screen, as follows:

WOULD YOU CONSIDER MY BUYING CLINIC FOR YOU AND GREGOROVIOUS HAVE BOUGHT FORTY EIGHT HOUR OPTION PLEASE REPLY IMMEDIATELY SUCH INVESTMENT CANNOT FAIL BE IMMENSELY LUCRATIVE ALL CONCERNED CHANCE YOU HAVE AWAITED ALL YOUR LIFE STRONGLY ADVISE YOU CONSIDER FOR NICOLE'S POSSIBLE BENEFIT BABY WARREN

Dick: Yes, I did . . . No—I gave orders last night we weren't to be disturbed . . . No . . . She's all right . . . What am I going to do about it? I can't even consider it—what?

On the screen, below, while at first we hear a remote gibbering from Baby, the condensed telegram as subtitle is now visible simply as: WOULD YOU CONSIDER MY BUYING CLINIC FOR YOU?

This by a process of subtraction undergoes a change, becomes: WOULD YOU CONSIDER MY BUYING YOU?

Suddenly the whole condensed telegram as subtitle becomes subject to a sea-change of meanings caused by subtracted words, and the above becomes, the question mark having added itself in each case: WOULD YOU CONSIDER MY BUYING YOUR LIFE?

This becomes: HAVE BOUGHT FORTY EIGHT HOUR OPTION to which is added:

PLEASE REPLY IMMEDIATELY

Dick: (beginning to speak at about the middle of "would you consider my buying you?") No . . . I couldn't consider it. Anyhow I couldn't give you an answer on such short notice, but if I must it's no . . . The truth is—never mind, you wouldn't understand . . . I said I couldn't make you understand at such long distance, Baby, and if I could I—

Simultaneously, on the screen below, by the same process of subtraction has appeared or is appearing:

WOULD YOU CONSIDER . . . GREGOROVIOUS? (becoming)
WOULD YOU CONSIDER . . . ALL CONCERNED? (becoming)
WOULD YOU CONSIDER . . . NICOLE'S POSSIBLE BENEFIT? (becoming)
WOULD YOU CONSIDER . . . BABY WARREN? (becoming)
PLEASE REPLY IMMEDIATELY

Dick: (meantime) Yes, I did . . . Yes, Gregers was . . . very plain, all too plain . . . (Dick fishes with one hand in his pocket for the other telegram, apparently gets it mixed up with Baby's, though we don't see them save at a distance) Wait a minute. (We hear mumbling on the phone to the effect that he is being very foolish, perhaps we hear also the words "foolish pride") Look here . . . If it's really for Nicole's benefit, invest it in Consols or munitions or something . . . Well, if you have to, buy it for Gregorovious then. What? . . . Come, come, Baby—it's a very odd sort of pride that puts the fall before itself—which is what it would be on your terms—

Simultaneously on the screen, below, from the first uncondensed telegram, a fragment by subtraction:

HAVE BOUGHT MYSELF WITH MYSELF TRUSTEE. Then, from Gregorovious' telegram:

FOR THREE HUNDRED THOUSAND DOLLARS

Dick: What?—on the contrary, it's an outrageous idea. Doctors have no right to think of their profession in terms of gold mines . . . He must think he's back in his student days . . . If he wants to do that he can play the stock market . . . I know it, but you asked for a decision—

On the screen, simultaneously below, by subtraction from Baby's condensed telegram again:

SUCH INVESTMENT CANNOT FAIL. By subtraction from that:
INVESTMENT CANNOT FAIL. And from that:
FAIL replaced by:
PLEASE REPLY IMMEDIATELY

Dick: Hullo—tell me, how is Dohmler? . . . Next year? . . . Yes? Where? Oh, Austria, but he's in Zurich *now* . . . For another year . . . (Dick reaches for his drink, which he had not finished when he was contemplating the contents of Gregorovious' telegram the first time, and which he has placed in reach at the beginning of this scene, with his other hand he is trying to look at both telegrams, though he does not stop talking for more than a moment)

On the screen, simultaneously below, as subtitle, by subtraction from Gregorovious' telegram: DOHMLER IS RETIRING

Replaced by: YOU TOO TIGHT. Replaced by:
WOULD YOU STOP

Dick: Well, we might be driving down your way anyway . . . I said, we'd—I'd—been thinking of driving us down to Zurich anyway . . . In two or three days . . . With the children (he takes his drink). Yes . . . In fact—I want to see Dohmler anyhow—No, I've told you Nicole's all right . . .

Now we see that, upon tiptoe, Nicole has approached silently and is listening; her mien is timorous, she seems indeed half scared to death, yet when she speaks she is rebellious too: and this element of rebellion is important here.

Nicole: (suddenly) What's this about my being all right? I'm not all right. What are you doing to me behind my back? What's all this about Dohmler? (takes Dick's wrist) *What's all this about Dohmler!*

Dick: (merely puts his other hand over the mouthpiece, and smiles calmly and gently at her and points back with raised eyebrows to the bedroom, speaks almost reflectively) Please Nicole, I'll explain later. (Nicole obeys him, even with a sudden trusting smile, and goes back. Dick speaks into the phone) Hello . . . oh, hello Baby . . . Yeah . . . No, don't, it won't be any good buying an extended option . . . If we come to Zurich at all it will be simply because I want to see Dohmler.

On the screen, simultaneously below, the last part of the uncondensed telegram begins to travel crazily across the bottom of the screen like news, though not of course illuminated, travelling round the Times Building, and also like a last chance:

STOP BELIEVE THIS MAY BE CHANCE YOU HAVE AWAITED ALL YOUR LIFE AND GREGOROVIOUS AGREES (the word "agrees" now becomes smitten with a stasis and stays where it is while the other words add themselves to it swiftly) STRONGLY ADVISE YOU CONSIDER FOR NICOLE'S POSSIBLE BENEFIT LETTER FOLLOWS BABY WARREN

Dick: . . . no doubt . . . Yeah . . . But that's final.

Meantime, on the screen, almost before we have finished with the word "Warren," all the words save the word "agrees" vanish, against which word other single words continually changing and approaching in the same manner, keep sliding up as if trying to get past, while "agrees" refuses to move, so that the effect, though it is horizontal and not vertical, is as below, the word "reason" having been taken from Baby's uncondensed telegram:

BANKER AGREES
GREGOROVIOUS AGREES
REASON AGREES
LIFE AGREES (to which is added now)
FOR NICOLE'S POSSIBLE BENEFIT

On the screen now a DIS suddenly inserts itself between the AGREES and LIFE and the POSSIBLE disappears so that it reads:

LIFE DISAGREES FOR NICOLE'S BENEFIT then, the life turning into love

LOVE DISAGREES FOR NICOLE'S BENEFIT then, the first two words disappearing:

FOR NICOLE'S BENEFIT then, the last word disappearing:

FOR NICOLE which is replaced by, suddenly:

CHANCE YOU HAVE AWAITED ALL YOUR LIFE to which is added:

FOLLOWS condensed to:

LIFE FOLLOWS

Dick: (on the phone as this last is appearing below, though he has not stopped talking more than a necessary moment or two here) Absolutely final . . . We'll be glad to see you. No, I said glad. G for Grand Guignol, L for Lanier, A for abracadabra, D for damnation. Glad. (Dick hangs up, throwing away the last words in the act.)

Close up of the two telegrams: they are torn up. In Switzerland we see Baby Warren hang up: she looks half angry, half baffled. Cut back to Dick. He is going to throw the telegrams in the wastepaper basket. He can't find it so he throws them in the laundry basket—but the blood-stained blankets, unincriminatingly restowed by Dick, have of course not been removed and we have a glimpse of them. But now the decision is doubly final. (Lowry, pp. 216-31)

29

Dick explains to Nicole that it might be good for them to travel up to Switzerland, and he assures her he has no intention of putting her back in the clinic. Retracing some of the steps that brought them here, he says, might prove medicinal for both of them. He adds that there are no such things as scars that heal; there are only wounds, shrunk sometimes to the size of pinpricks, but still wounds nonetheless. He loves her, he says, and wants to help her. Nicole is pacified and tells Dick that if he loves her, that is all that matters. She asks whether they will be happy again, and Dick replies yes, she will. Dick goes to tell Topsy and Lanier that they are going on a trip. Lanier is playing the game of "Forfeits" with another child, who grabs a toy automobile and holds it over Lanier's head. (See Lowry, pp. 231-34 and Fitzgerald, 2, xi.)

The Child: (intoning seriously and intently) *Heavy, heavy hangs over thy head. What shall the owner do to redeem it?*

Cut directly to the Isotta drawing up beside the statue of Diderot, Dick driving, Nicole beside him, the children together in the back; then a lovely shot of the huge statue of Diderot seated thoughtfully on his pedestal, with the spire of St. Germain des Prés, and Les Deux Magots beyond. It is a beautiful day and Paris at its best.

Dick: Say goodbye to Monsieur Diderot, children.

Lanier and Topsy in chorus: Au'voir M'sieu Diderot.

Nicole: (as the car drives away) Au'voir, Paris . . . Au'voir, Café des Deux Magots . . . Au'voir, Montparnasse . . .

We see that Nicole is, on the surface, bearing up and trying to be gay, pretending it's a holiday, but an occasional sourceless smile betrays her great strain.

Lanier: Au'voir Tour Eiffel (we see the Eiffel Tower in the background) Daddy, will you help me build the Tour Eiffel when I get my number six meccano?

Dick: (chuckling) Sure will. But what gave you the idea I was an engineer?

Lanier: You helped me build the bridge . . . You need forty angle brackets, I don't know how many pulleys—and 500 nuts and bolts. And you make the elevator too. (loses interest as they are passing a zoo—perhaps the Jardin des Plantes) Au'voir, élefant.

Topsy: (thinks this is silly or funny and laughs) Lanier said Au'voir élefant—*he* said—(they scuffle in the back seat)

We see, in passing, have been seeing, fragmentarily, a few of the advertisements we are now familiar with: *Maurice Chevalier en Paris en Fleures. Les 10 Fratellinis. Grand Guignol: La Fosse Aux Filles, de Alexandre Kuprin*: while ZURICH SUISSE appears sinisterly, as a sign in a travel agent's window. They pass a cinema with the electric bell already ringing. Instantly they are driving through one of the numerous lovely avenues of Paris, an avenue of trees, with a blowing fountain, where the road is fairly clear for a moment and Dick puts one arm round Nicole's shoulder tenderly. Nicole rests her head on his shoulder gladly, as if almost wistfully hoping for she knows not what.

Topsy: Look—a blackbird—(we see a blackbird)

Topsy and Lanier: (sing in chorus, to the tune of *Au Claire de la Lune*)

> When you see one blackbird
> Then they come in flocks
> When—

Dick: Hey, stop being anagogical, you two back there.

Lanier: What's anagogical, Daddy?

Dick: (as we see a flock of blackbirds) Metaphysically speaking, a darn nuisance. That's too near the knuckle, after Marie *and* Rainford ... And since when have I lost my status as Dick?

Lanier: (scornfully) All right—*Dick* then—but I call it bloody silly myself.

Nicole and Dick look at each other, laughing; Nicole—showing strain—laughs rather cruelly, Dick is possibly preparing to reprove Lanier. (What hurts him is not the phrase Lanier has picked up, but the implied reflection upon the advanced "psychological" method of bringing up the children, while the tone of Nicole's laughter might be contemptuous of psychology itself, and hence his amour propre.)

Suddenly the screen becomes a flashing moving wall of advertisements, pertinent and otherwise, almost instantaneously gone, but among which we glimpse: Théâtre des Arts, *Le Dilemme du Médecin* (*The Doctor's Dilemma*) de Bernard Shaw:[47] Vieux Colombier, *S.S. Tenacité*:[48] Théâtre des Arts, *Oedipe le Roi*, de Sophocle: Opera, *Elektra*, de Richard Strauss: Casino de Paris, *Paris en Fleures*: Rex, (an old, peeling advertisement) Rosemary Hoyt en *Fillette de Papa* (*Daddy's Girl*):[49] Vincennes, Emil Jannings en *Le Dernier Rire*.[50]

Cut to the Divers driving swiftly through the outskirts of Paris, past factory chimneys, glass factories, debris, whole vacant lots of rubbish, gasworks, millions of box-like structures precisely the same and everywhere ugly, ugly, ugly—a desolation beyond desolation.

Nicole: (suddenly) It seemed too bad to leave Rosemary like that—do you suppose she'll be all right?

Dick: Of course. Rosemary could take care of herself anywhere.

Nicole: She's very attractive.

Dick: She's not as intelligent as I thought ... She's an infant.

Nicole: She's exactly the same age I was when we were married. (suddenly referring to their surroundings which are getting worse) Nom de Dieu! this is ugly ... Do you suppose there's anything beautiful in life that isn't spoiled like this around the edges. (On an isolated blank building a toothpaste advertisement appears: a grinning negro. Nicole groans abruptly) Oh!

Dick: Oh what? (we see the negro again; Dick glances back anxiously over his shoulder lest anything be said before the children, then even more anxiously at Nicole) Better not think of it, darling.

Nicole: Do you think we did right?

Dick: (slowly shaking his head, almost in a murmur, and keeping his eyes on the road) From the standpoint of our responsibility to Rosemary—

Nicole: (cynically) Our responsibility to Rosemary!

Cut to the Divers driving through the country; it is exquisite countryside, trees, rolling fields with flowers, wheatfields with poppies, the long, beautiful, empty road ahead; milestones pass; a signpost: Paris—Bar-sur-Aube. They are on the Troyes—Bar-sur-Aube road, heading for Belfort and the Swiss border at Basle or Vallorbe. Behind them the children are quiet, half asleep. Through the fields the diminished Seine dreamily wanders after them.

Nicole: (remotely but savagely, self-withdrawn) How much we pass by, how much we lose. (Dick looks at her anxiously) Perhaps forever . . .

Cut to a long shot of the road ahead from the car: dissolve to the road under a starry night sky with a waning moon.

Dick: Lanier—are you awake back there? (Lanier does not reply—Topsy is asleep, but Lanier isn't) We all know it's long past your bedtime, but I asked were you awake?

Lanier: No, I'm in one of my difficult moods.

Dick: When I was about your age, Lanier, my old man liked to teach me the stars . . .

Cut to the car climbing a hill into the starry sky.

Cut back to a close up of Dick. Lanier is kneeling on the floor of the car behind him, his head close to Dick's and listening intently now.

Dick: (pointing) All right, you've got Andromeda. Now there, to the north, see those stars that look like an arrow? That's Perseus.—See, Lanier?

Lanier:—mmn—well, sort of. Who was Perseus, Dick?

Dick: According to the ancient legend, he saved Andromeda from a monster of the sea . . . well, this business is rather complicated. . .[51]

Cut to a close up of Nicole, her head thrown back, resting against the seat, she is not listening to Dick and Lanier, she is staring up into the night sky with a remote, strange, secret smile.

Dick's Voice: (during the close up of Nicole) But first he had to slay the Medusa . . .

Cut from Nicole's face to another long shot of the road and the sky. Lap dissolve to the car speeding along another road in morning sunlight. It is a glorious summer morning, and the little family, now by themselves without nurse or chauffeur, seem almost truly gay, for an instant we can almost forget the tragic goal they are approaching. In the back seat the children are singing and as we dissolve all of them, even Nicole, take their parts in the beautiful, gay, ancient canon:

Frère Jacques
Frère Jacques
Dormez-vous?
Dormez-vous?
Sonnez les matines
Sonnez les matines
Ding dang dong
Ding dang dong—

Dick blows his horn in time with the last: Bam! Bam! Bam!

But while they are singing we see that the country is wilder, and the road that stretches on ahead leads straight into the distant mountains, appearing now on the horizon. And looking closer at the little family as they sing, we can see that although the children, of course, have a wonderful feeling of holiday, Nicole and Dick are actually making a gallant effort.

Dissolve to the car speeding along the same road, later in the day, towards these mountains, closer now, and more ominous as we approach the French Alps and the Swiss border. Cut to a close shot, in the car. Dick and Nicole are silent, the children are giggling, scuffling and half arguing, in the back seat, trying to sing *Sur le Pont d'Avignon*. We see signs pointing back the way they have come: Bar-sur-Aube, Paris. Signs pointing straight ahead: Strasbourg, Belfort, Basle. Dick looks at Nicole anxiously for she is gazing straight ahead at the mountains with a set drawn face.

Dick: Pipe down, you kids, give that a rest.

The children start in again on *Frère Jacques*, and Dick tries to put a stop to this by blowing a long note on his horn.

Nicole suddenly puts her hands over her ears, flinging a look almost of hatred at Dick and the children.

Dick: (to the children, glancing at Nicole with anxious love) Better give that one a rest too.

The children stop, subdued for the moment by Dick's tone of voice. Nicole is staring ahead at the mountains, rearing up their walls and cliffs ahead. It is not merely that we feel from her expression that she can no longer keep up the deception of a "holiday," nor that as Switzerland and the mountains get nearer and nearer she becomes more despairing; we sense now an active hatred of the children, of their normality, their ability to be normal and gay, of their unity with Dick, and his with them, partly pretense though she knows that to be.

Dick: (sensing this mood in Nicole and attempting to divert the children) How about this one? (He begins to sing in the middle of the *Kerry Dancers*, the Irish song we heard Abe sing, a song so joyous one always forgets it ends by being heartbreaking.)

> When the clans began to gather
> In the glen of a summer's night
> And the Kerry piper's tuning
> Filled our hearts with a wild delight—

As Dick is singing we see they are approaching a crossroads—the right signpost points toward Besançon and Dijon, the left towards Strasbourg; Dick slows, his song becomes diminuendo.

> Oh, to think of it, Oh, to dream of it
> Fills the heart with tears—
> Oh, the thought of the Kerry dancers
> Oh, the ring of the piper's tune—

We observe again, from Nicole's standpoint, the sign pointing straight ahead: Belfort, Basle, Zug—ZURICH—

> Oh, the sound of the Kerry music
> Gone, alas, like our youth, too soon—

Nicole: (abruptly—we know from the way she speaks it is a ruse, yet it is also sincere, nor shall we ever know if it would have saved them) Dick, why don't we turn off right and go back to Antibes? We could be in Besançon tonight, spend tomorrow night at Grenoble, and be home day after tomorrow.

All at once a mountain mist swoops down upon them, obscuring the road before us and the signposts, and as Dick, intent on driving peers forward through the mist, suddenly right across the screen appears a huge sign in three languages:

STOP!   PAY TOLL![52]

The centre part of this between the two injunctions forms the roofed entrance to a toll bridge above which the vertical clearance is indicated. Beneath the Stop! and the Pay Toll! are ticket offices. There are other signs also of Achtung! Notice! Avis! but the impact of the main sign has quickly devolved into English as it came toward us. (A materialized officer has raised his hand to stop the Divers' car: the next moment we see Dick paying their money into the guichet through the car window—the border is actually perhaps a little further on, but there is a technicality of at least showing their passports here.) Cut to Dick groping his way in their car across the bridge in the mist.

Cut to the Divers' car approaching the town of Zug—in the near distance we see a Ferris Wheel, other appurtenances of a fair, what looks like a menagerie, etc. The mist has lifted, the sky is clear, and we see a signpost: Zug 1/2 km. Zurich 5 km.

Dick: Well, we seem to have a fair.

Lanier: Oh, *do* let's stop, Daddy.

Topsy: (almost jumping up and down) He bonjour élefant, que vous me semblez beau. Bonjour élefant! Bonjour élefant!

Nicole: Oh yes, Dick *do* let's stop and see the fair. (this too we suspect may be a ruse)

Dick: (smiling) All right.

Cut to the Divers approaching the fair, through the menace of a shot of mammoth steam rollers that make way for them, upon each the legend: *Ich Dien*.

Nicole: (suddenly and with vicious rancour) She's quite smart.

Dick: (driving, and paying most of his attention to the car) Who? Topsy? Sure she's smart.

Nicole: Rosemary. Your ickle durl.

Dick: Oh, her . . . not very—there's a persistent aroma of the nursery.

Nicole: (in a voice that might mean danger) She's very *very* pretty. I can see how she'd be very attractive to men.

Cut to the Divers in the car approaching the edge of the fair.

Nicole: (looking to one side, and showing she is losing contact) See the little house—it looks like a painting that hasn't dried.

Instantly the house we are passing blurs, as through Nicole's eyes; it looks something like the blurs we have seen in the psychological moments of Nicole's "absence" in the flashback. (This gives us a knowledge of Nicole's state that exceeds Dick's, preoccupied as he is to some extent with the car and the children, and we feel a mounting tension about, and with, Nicole, and a growing apprehension quite on our own behalf as to what this may precipitate.)

Cut to Dick parking the Isotta. Nicole gets swiftly out of the car immediately it stops, without waiting for Dick to help her, on her face a secret strange smile which we see but which Dick, busy lifting the children out, does not. Meantime we hear the music of the fair and see the fairground—what we notice at first being not its kaleidoscopic quality, but simply its poetic beauty (escape). The camera follows the family walking through the outriders of the fair. On Nicole's face the smile still flickers, derisive and remote. It becomes more remote, more derisive, as we realize that somewhere the mechanical steam music of the fair is churning out raucously the, by now, old tune *Smiles*. Beneath this we can hear the whining and tinkling of a hootchy kootchy show. Cut to a sidewise near close up of a screeching Punch and Judy show, with the word Guignol above it. Slantwise the four appear, each half-turned to us on the screen, Topsy, nearest, then Dick, who has both children by the hand, then Lanier, then Nicole, furthest away.

Lanier: (to Nicole) Look! A Punch and Judy! (as through Lanier's and Topsy's eyes, we see it first as possessing some of the magic of our first Punch and Judy shows.)

Nicole: Yes, a Punch and Judy show—(Nicole seems orienting herself by anchoring to it, and the held sidewise shot of the Punch and Judy show wavers between magic and blurs. Not blurred, however, is the face of a small dark girl of about fifteen, who, happening to bump into them, smiles politely up at Dick. The churning tune *Smiles* becomes suddenly louder and more awful.)

Cut into an almost head on rowdy shot of the Punch and Judy show so that we are looking into it ourselves over their shoulders, with the family in the same order, though it is slightly angled and tilted. Cut into a shot of the whole fair, seen as a blur through Nicole's mind, ghostly merry-go-rounds, ghostly steam rollers, in the distance a ghostly Ferris Wheel, the ghostly Punch and Judy show now comes back into its rowdy aspect, as through Dick's mind, to which we have temporarily transferred, so that it appears simply hideous. While these transformations have been going on we have scarcely had time to notice that Nicole is no longer by Topsy's side.

Topsy: Daddy, is this the same Punch we saw last year in Cannes?

Dick: (as Punch starts belabouring Judy) Couldn't be quite the same one if he is a year older.

Topsy: He *could*, Daddy! He could, he's the very same one, I'm sure of it—isn't he. Lanier? (Judy now belabours Punch, squealing and scolding) Lanier wouldn't know, but *I* do—

Dick: (as the camera holds the word "Guignol" above the show a moment we feel he might be thinking it should be Grand Guignol—then returns to Punch) No—I think he's got a few more grey hairs, this fellow—he's a sadder, if not wiser, man altogether.

While Dick and the children are still watching the show, the squealing of Punch and Judy, the tinkling of the hootchy kootchy, the steam music churning out *Smiles*, seem to reach a climax together.

Cut to Nicole, twisting swiftly and secretly, running through the crowd. Cut to Dick, at the Punch and Judy show. He realizes she has gone, sees her, and runs after her. Suddenly, as he remembers he has forgotten the children, he wheels and runs back to them, drawing them this way and that way by the arms, as his eyes jump from booth to booth looking for Nicole.

Cut to a lottery wheel spinning seen at such an angle that we are sure what it is, then to the young woman in the booth behind it.

Dick: Madame. Est-ce que je peux laisser ces petits avec vous deux minutes? C'est très urgent—je vous donnerai dix francs.

The Woman: Mais oui.

Cut to Dick leading the children hastily into the booth.

Dick: (to the children, quickly) Alors—restez avec cette gentille dame.

Dick darts off again, but he has lost her. Cut to a circling merry-go-round—the source of *Smiles*—blasting its steam music through its whorled pipes, with Dick keeping up with it till he seems to realize he is running beside it, and always staring at the same horse.

Cut to a terrifying shot of an absolutely deserted flying machine, whose gondolas while travelling at enormous speed execute slow rolls, whizzing round empty—but with one cylindrical gondola broken and spinning crazily at a frightening rhythm different to the others, and making a dreadful broken grating sound.

Cut to a buvette, with Dick elbowing through the crowd, then, while in the background, we see a suggestion of a sledge-hammer, plunging, circular, motion of the loop-the-loop machine, to the apparition, ahead of him of the words over a fortune teller's tent: Votre Destin, Astrologie, even, ironically, Psychologie, Clairvoyant, Palmiste; cut to the fortune teller at the opening of the tent.

The Fortune Teller: La septième fille d'une septième fille née sur les rives du Nil—entrez, Monsieur—

Dick snatches up the flap, peers in. Inside we see a round horoscope, even as in a fragment of a nightmare, something about Les Gémeaux célèbres Astrologiques, Robert Edwin Peary, Sigmund Freud, nés le 6 Mai 1856. Close up of the horoscope. The horoscope begins to spin, instantly becoming a Ferris Wheel, but seen in the distance beyond the crazily spinning empty flying machine with the broken, grating gondola; below this machine gazing up, its owner is now hopelessly standing. Dick begins to run past the flying machine towards the Ferris Wheel. The Ferris Wheel fills the screen an instant, then we see it slowly revolving against the sky, beyond it, the lake.

Cut to a shot of the Ferris Wheel motionless for a moment: in the gondola at the top we distinguish Nicole. The camera bears up upon her, and we see she is laughing hysterically, and then we hear her. The Ferris Wheel begins to descend, and we are in the gondola with Nicole, seeing the mountains, the lake, blurred, and the fairground, with Dick approaching now below, revolve, but in the peculiar fashion that is produced by the unique motion—jerk, swing, straighten out—of the Ferris Wheel itself. As the wheel revolves Nicole's laughter grows louder. Cut to a shot of the crowd taken from below looking up, among which we see Dick who, on observing the spectacle Nicole is making of herself, has slunk back into it a little, a movement which exactly coincides with our reaction to Nicole's behavior in so far as we too are with Dick and still standing outside it.

First Spectator: Regardez-moi, ça!
Second Spectator: Regarde donc cette Anglaise!

The two points of view now begin to alternate rapidly. At one moment we are with Nicole in the Ferris Wheel steadily increasing speed past the revolving blurred mountains, while her laughter becomes ever more and more diabolical: the next we are in the crowd with Dick, watching the wheel. Finally we are in the wheel with Nicole as her gondola, slowing, approaches the ground and she catches sight of Dick, at which moment her laughter dies. Quickly she gets out and as Dick comes toward her she makes a gesture of slipping away. He catches her arm as she does and holds it as they walk away. They walk swiftly enough but the rapidity is accentuated by the now kaleidoscopic and nightmare vision of the various revolving mechanisms in the fairground. The confused dissonance of steam music still dominantly playing *Smiles* also adds to the speed, but beneath this, though we cannot notice it, a slower music in the score is acting as a kind of emergency brake upon both our emotions and the tempo, stating and restating a theme, at a much slower yet steadily mounting tempo, for in spite of the drama here, the climax is not yet.

Dick: Why did you lose control of yourself?

Cut to the same terrifying shot, though from the opposite side, of the unpopular empty flying machine with the revolving horizontal gondolas still whizzing round by itself with the owner standing there as if hopelessly smoking a cigarette below, and recurringly the one gondola gone crazy and gratingly spinning and spinning at a disproportionate speed to the others.

Nicole: You know very well why.
Dick: No, I don't.
Nicole: That's just preposterous—let me loose—that's an insult to

my intelligence. Don't you think I saw that girl look at you—that little dark girl—oh this is farcical—a child—not more than fifteen—

Dick: Stop here a minute and quiet down.

Nicole: (they have reached the buvette, she sits down, her hand moving across her line of sight as though it were obstructed) I want a drink—I want a brandy.

Dick: You can't have a brandy—you can have a bock if you want it. (to the woman in the buvette) Puis-avoir un bock, s'il vous plaît.

Nicole: Why can't I have a brandy?

Dick: We won't go into that. Listen to me—this business about a girl is a delusion, do you understand that word? (The reiterated theme in the score now begins to act slightly as an accelerator rather than a brake on the tempo, the effect it has is as if it were part of the fair version of *Smiles*, which, actually recorded from fair music, it is trying to catch up.)

Simultaneously the woman brings the bock—she brings two but Dick waves his aside, declining it, takes the other and hands it to Nicole. Dick lights a cigarette.

Cut to Nicole: almost finishing the bock.

Nicole: It's always a delusion when I see what you don't want me to see. (she drinks)

Cut back to the Punch and Judy show again, as through Dick's eyes, and from the same angle, with the girl smiling up at Dick: cut to Dick at the buvette: his eyes waver from Nicole's; instantly cut back to the Punch and Judy show and we share Dick's indirect guilt as we see Nicole's delusion imply a psychological truth, for this time the girl smiling turns swiftly first into Nicole as we have seen her in the sanatorium, then into Rosemary, all this happening so fast that it too seems slightly to accelerate the action.

Cut back to Dick and Nicole in the buvette, beyond them we see the words over the astrologer's tent: Clairvoyant, Astrologie, Psychologie, Palmiste, etc., and above that, Votre Destin, and the old woman standing there.

Nicole: (finishes the bock) Who do you think you are, Svengali?

Dick: (standing up) Come on—we're going home. I mean we're going to Zurich.

Nicole: (roaring in a voice so abandoned that its louder tones waver and crack) Home. So home is the sanatorium, eh? And sit and think that we're all rotting and the children's ashes are rotting in every box I open. That filth!

Dissolve, as *Smiles* begins again endlessly to repeat itself once more, to Nicole and Dick standing under the words Votre Destin. Her words have seemed to sterilize her and we see a sort of relief in

Dick's face, a withdrawal of anger which is a withdrawal into pity on our part as Nicole's face softens, the effect being that it has immediately softened after her dreadful words.

Nicole: Help me, help me, Dick . . . You *can* help me!

While Dick seems to waver, as if through his mind—though the image is in fact objective—we see a muddy swirling on-rushing flood, half submerged trees, then a dam: one sandbag is thrown against the dam, the water begins to leak through, first on one side, then the other.

Nicole: You've helped me before—you can help me now.

Dick: I can only help you in the same old way.

Nicole: Someone can help me. (Another sandbag is thrown against the dam.)

Dick: Maybe so. You can help yourself most. Let's find the children. I left them with a gypsy woman in a booth. (The water leaks through past the second sandbag, both sandbags are swept away, they sink, though the dam still stands.)

Cut to the lottery wheel spinning, sloping away from the screen, vaguely we notice Lanier and Topsy beyond it with several women and children, then Dick and Nicole advancing swiftly through the revolving and plunging machines to see the children in the booth surrounded by women, examining them with delight like fine goods, and by peasant children staring at them. Cut to Dick giving the young lottery woman her ten francs, simultaneously the camera passes from the faces of the children who, deprived of their fun, look very unhappy and probably by now sense something of what has happened, to Nicole, standing apart, evil-eyed, as if resenting the children, both as a real responsibility of the real world she would deny, and also as the cause of Dick's turning from her, and telling her to help herself.

The Woman: (to Dick) Merci, Monsieur—Madame. Au'voir, mes petits.

The camera travels past the seemingly eternal screaming Punch and Judy show again to the car with the steamrollers beyond, returns to the children's faces, grave with disappointment as they trudge back and get into the car, Dick and Nicole silent beside them—they had been a little family, now each is weighted with their mutual, yet terribly separate, apprehensions and anguish.

Cut to an objective shot of the car as it moves off, threading its way through the steamrollers again; then we see Dick's face at the wheel, tense and unsmiling, the children's faces, disappointed and half fearful, and Nicole's face, hard and distant, though she seems trying to control herself. But as we see a signpost: Zurich 4 km. her face becomes hard again. We now immediately shift our standpoint to a feeling of ourselves being in the car, which is climbing a hill through the mountainous country. We are with Nicole, but we share her consciousness with that of the camera, and that of the film itself. Cut to a sign Zurich 3 1/2 km. Nicole's face gives way to the sourceless smile that already frightens us.

Dick cannot be, and is not, driving swiftly, but nonetheless we have the same or a similar sense of tension that we had first upon witnessing *Daddy's Girl*; then in Baby's configured account of the accident, but so far it is the tension alone that is similar. As we drive up the hill the sounds of the fair, the sound of the mechanical *Smiles*, now begin to drop away and the continually reiterated theme we had been scarcely conscious of in the score begins to disengage itself from these, becoming ever more and more rapid, and acting here something like a literal accelerator, instead of a brake. Still in the car we come now to a straightaway run parallel to the hillside and we actually do accelerate to gather speed for the circling hill beyond. Since there is no fence to the road, signs appear in French and German reminding us of Danger, of Dangerous Corner Ahead, a cross too appears by the side of the road, but this in no way suggests that Dick is driving dangerously: the danger on the contrary, is in the situation, ahead in the film, and to ourselves. The camera remains fixed on the ever unwinding road, and this accelerated run is just long enough for us to experience three combined sensations, that of increasing exhilaration we had when watching *Daddy's Girl*, combined with the feeling of certain but retrospective fatalistic disaster we possessed when watching the accident in the clinic sequence, to which is now added the unbearably horrendous anticipation of something imminently disastrous that is at the moment threatening, but exacerbated by the element of free will not present before, which leads us to hope against hope that accident may be prevented. Simultaneously the theme with its ever accelerating music disengages itself entirely from the fair sounds and music and mounts by itself: the effect is of incredible rapidity, and time becomes simply filmic. Cut to a flash of a signpost: Zurich 3 1/4 km. Cut in again the flood—and we see the dam once more. The flood beats against the dam, leaking through it at every point and rising behind it. Cut from this to the similar scene of the car in *Daddy's Girl*. Cut into this a brief flash of the scene of Nicole driving with her father just before the accident. Cut into this a huge close up of Abe's face, drunk, succeeded the next instant by Peterson's face, the blood dripping. Cut into this a close up of the bloodstained sheets, those first of Peterson, then those used to wrap Nicole's father, from this to the actual car we are in proceeding along the straightaway run: on one side of the road the cliffs rise like walls, on the other an immediate declivity falls away into an almost perpendicular drop into an abyss, with a few trees and underbrush clinging to its sides. Cut in a flash of a signpost: Zurich 3 km. Cut back to the dam. It crumbles and is washed downstream in sinking fragments by the overpowering onrush of the flood and of a rising turbulent racing river that sweeps all before it. At the next moment, cut into the point in *Daddy's Girl* where Rosemary puts her hand on the wheel. There was a moon in that scene, which had been at night: it reappears here, for a split second as an isolated symbol of madness. Cut to a flash of a signpost: Zurich 2 1/2 km. and back into our car going down the straightaway and at the same moment to Nicole leaning over and screaming as she clutches the steering wheel from Dick, Dick's hand trying to crush her mad hand down; then we are with the car for a final instant, as it swerves, rights itself, swerves once more, and plunges off the road, tearing through low underbrush, but as it falls and tips twice, in rhythm with this, and as quickly as it takes to play five emphatic chords on a piano, we have a close up of Peterson's face, a close up of Rosemary, a close up of the sheets at the Roi George, a close up of the crash of the Warren accident, and finally, emerging from a shot of the flood in headlong and complete possession, the car settling slowly at an angle of ninety degrees against a tree, as the children scream and Nicole screams and curses and tries to tear at Dick's face.

Close up of Dick: he seems to be thinking first of the list of the car; he pushes Nicole's hand away, climbs over the side and lifts out the children; then he ascertains the car is in a stable position. Now, looking at Nicole, he stands there shaking and panting while Nicole is laughing hilariously, unashamed, unafraid, unconcerned, as after some mild escapade of childhood, so that no one coming on the scene would imagine she has caused it.

We see a swift shot looking straight up the hill, showing the tearing destructive path the car has made through the trees and underbrush as it plunged downward, another swift shot of the abyss below, where they might have gone.

Nicole jumps out of the car, falling to her knees, she picks herself up and turns on Dick.

Nicole: Ha! (accusing and grinning, her face a grinning mask) You were scared, weren't you? You wanted to live!

They confront each other, over the wreckage of their lives and the silent terrified children, as Dick's expression turns from shock to comprehension, to horror at her attempt on the children's lives, to anger, then to speechless anguished fury (in which we can see his sense of his own guilt in being even partly responsible for having brought her to this) yet finally, absolute fury.

Dick: You—!

Cut—slash—instantly and savagely to a shot of blazing windows facing each other across a court, these windows confronting each other so violently that they seem flaming, almost quivering with a fire within, so that it is both an extension and a symbolization of that blazing anger and hatred. As, on one window, we see bars begin to form and become real bars, we realize that they are the windows of a court in the Sanatorium Zurichsee, whose name we see the next moment over the door: cut to the name, Dr. Frederich Dohmler upon his door, then we go into his office.

In Dohmler's office Dick and Dohmler are standing by the desk, Dohmler with the air of having paused while walking about with his hand on Dick's shoulder: Dohmler looks sad, deeply compassionate, and stern. But so much older does he appear than before we scarcely need the calendar to remind us yet again it is August, 1926. Dohmler gives the same impression of absolute integrity, but in some way also of representing an older order, an order that is not so much giving way to new, as being replaced by something totally different, yet allied to it—like—to borrow a seemingly casual visual image from the next scene—some dignified and magnificent old locomotive about to be supplanted by an automatic electric trolley system. But if Dohmler is stern, we feel that age, and perhaps not merely age, has made him take a more human view of this situation than he would have taken six years ago. Dick, completely humble, has never appeared more dignified, but sleepless, harassed and haggard he too seems to have aged in the brief time since we last saw him. Dick is holding a packet of letters he has opened and a telegram. Dohmler speaks quite swiftly and fluently in his German manner, yet in an old and tired way: when he sighs, the feeling is it is not only for himself.

Dohmler: (sighs heavily) But she is intelligent, little Miss Nicole. When she is better she will understand. If she—

Dick: Yes—if she—

Dohmler: (walking up and down, looking at the floor as he speaks, once he gazes sadly out of the window) *You* understand, of course, it will be necessary to read your letters—and any she may write to you later. (Dick nods) But in fact, little Miss—your wife will understand, after a while that that is being done. (Dick nods his head in assent) I'm an old man, or I wouldn't have asked you, presumed to ask you, something you already know. In fact, Frau Diver may understand much that we do not. *Now* the decision lies, not in the angle of the tree, but in the root. Whether it wants to wash away to sea. And I can promise nothing. (Dick nods again, half staring at his telegram. Dohmler grips his shoulder, then lets his hand fall) First I shall give her case to Griffaton, with Gregorovious there is too much underground bleeding. That will be wiser for a while . . . Where will you go, Dick, my boy?

Dick: (hands Dohmler the telegram he has been staring at) If Nicole should ask—Herr Doktor, if you need an explanation—

Cut to the telegram held in Dohmler's hand: it is a cable from America, from Norfolk Virginia, and reads simply: YOUR FATHER VERY ILL CAN YOU COME AT ONCE THURSTON

Cut back to Dick and Dohmler as Dick takes back the telegram and puts it in his pocket with the letters.

Dick: It was forwarded from Paris with the other mail. Here's my father's address. (He writes it for Dohmler) I'll be there until further notice, though the Yale Club in New York will always find me.

Dohmler: I hope you will find it not so serious.

Dick: (begins to move toward the door, William James looks at him from the wall, Dohmler walking beside him, during the following they go out of the office door, and down the hall, stopping at the front door we will remember) Thank you, I hope so . . . Well, I must be on my way, I'm catching the night train for Paris, and I must see Baby—Miss Warren—before I go. But I expect you know, Franz will have told you about the sanatorium. (Dohmler nods) I'm afraid it was a disappointment to Franz, Herr Dohmler, my refusal, I mean.

Dohmler: (still nodding, has already begun to speak) But don't worry about Franz. He is a good clinician, but he is also ambitious, something will be arranged. Something is always arranged, for the ambitious. It is a pity, in one way, a great pity, for *you* . . . But I suppose *I* am not presumed to be suffering from Stekel's psychoanalytic scotoma in the matter?

Dick: I didn't think you didn't understand. Or were blind to it. I meant, simply, was I right—it would have been condemning Nicole. That it would be condemning her now?

Dohmler: (half to himself, and scarcely stemming the flow of Dick's remarks) You have said it. Surely it's unnecessary to talk about the mountain scenery.

Dick: To let her sister buy Franz and me the sanatorium on Nicole's money—even though it's my—because there I would be— even if Nicole and I—

Dohmler: (made impatient by all this, interrupting; they have reached the front door and stop) In spite of all that, you are a good man, Dick, and what is more a man of character.

Dick: Danke sehr . . . And of bad judgement.

Dohmler: (as the two men shake hands with a strong hand-clasp) But where that bad judgement lies—? Aber. This time, when you go, Dick, there will be no funicular at Glion. Nor shall I be in Berlin—

Dick: I—

Dohmler: By which I mean there will be no happy coincidences, apparently produced by forces beyond our ken, to bring you right back where you started, even if in charge of Gregorovious' sanatorium, bought with your wife's sister's money, your wife—you—it's immaterial. This time, Dick, mein Kapitan Dick, you will do what is *right*—

Dick: I was going to say—

Dohmler: The ship sails out with the tide; homeward bound, against the gale. All too much time to reverse decisions, or to forget them—So, remember that, on your night journey across the sea.

Dick: I promise.

Cut straight into a tremendous concatenation of station noises in Zurich railway station, a brief suggestion of *Frère Jacques* on the sound track beneath the pulsations and blasts of steam. Somehow we are reminded of Abe's recent departure from Gare St. Lazare, only instead of being midday it is nearly midnight. The station, gloomily lighted otherwise, is illumined by sudden blares of light and steam. Gregorovious and Dick are pacing up and down the platform just outside Dick's Wagon-Lit compartment of the already panting midnight Paris express. This is drawn by a great black hissing steam locomotive, but a few late electric trains are seen coming in during the scene at other platforms. Other people are running up the platform, etc. Franz looks slightly flashier and fatter than before, as though his profession had proved lucrative. His mien is sympathetic, even compassionate, but he gestures excitedly as he talks, sometimes as if pulling the air down with his hands. We feel he is still half thinking of the sanatorium and with one part of his mind has not quite given up hope. The camera takes in advertisements: a large panoramic view of Marseilles and the harbour, smaller ones for Paris, Cannes, Nice, etc., as they speak; the signs Abfahrt nach, Départ pour, Partenza per, etc. and most important the eternal signs of interdiction: *Das Ueberschreiten der Geleise ist Verboten*: *Défense de traverser les voies*: *E Proibito Traversare i banari*. The large station placard ZURICH is seen in the background: and a clock says two minutes to midnight.

Dick: (sighing wearily)—I haven't slept for forty-eight hours, Franz, and if I get to sleep tonight it will be one of Zwingli's miracles—

Franz: I cannot understand. If what happened with the motor car was merely an intensification—verstehen sie?—of the situation that already existed when you sent your refusal from Paris I would see all the more reason to reconsider letting your wife's money be invested in the sanatorium. Look here—I'm not going to say, "I told you so," "I warned you," "once I thought never to speak to you again." Now your marriage is a *fact*. You have to look after yourself too, and Mrs. Diver. I would see all the more reason now, and in fact, unless you never have accepted your real situation, I don't really see why you ever refused. (A late electric train is seen coming in at another platform) For I know it wasn't just pride.

Dick: I've got to get on board.

Franz: (as Dick gets into the corridor of the express) See those electric trains, more every year, pretty soon all this will be electrification and these old dirty steam engines will be a back number. (The guard shuts the door on Dick. The electric train is revealed lettered in front: *Glion-Zurich* the train Nicole and Dick once took.)

Dick: (through the open window) But I'm terribly sorry if I've let you down, Franz.

Franz: Well, one was disappointed, but it wasn't just the money, you know—

Dick: I know it, but it's too late now, I've just told Baby personally I wouldn't even consider it.

Franz: See—I shall have my clinic, if not this one, then another. But I'd always hoped we might have our up to date establishment, if not for billionaires. (He hands Dick a cigarette through the window; there are further indications that the express is about to start)

Dick: That was just student's talk.

Franz: Velleicht—but we would have made a great team. For I know my limitations—and you have something I shall never have—true, you have not been practising, but do you know this, of all the men who took their degrees at your time, Dick, in neuropathology, here in Zurich, you are still remembered as the most brilliant, more brilliant than I could ever be—

Dick: Schade—

Franz: It's the truth. I still turn to your old work when cases are highly involved—you were ahead of your time—some of your publications are still standard in their line—ask in any medical library—

Dick: (laughing) I did, and couldn't find one.

Franz:—most students think you're an Englishman. (As Dick win-ces at this unfortunate intended compliment or flattery, closing his eyes for a moment) They don't believe such thoroughness could come out of America.

Dick: I wrote my last symphony seven years ago.
Franz: *Was?*
Dick: Nichts. I was just thinking of a friend of mine who sailed for America three days ago.

There is a prolonged whistle, shouts in German of All Aboard, Dick and Franz shake hands swiftly through the window, as the train moves.

Franz: (walking along the platform beside the train) Gute Reise!
Dick: So long, Franz, old man, good luck!
Franz: Good luck. (as the train gathers speed, becomes the psychiatrist) And get down to work again at another book. I don't mind—even generalities. Now really is time to work—You hear me? Arbeit—serious w—(Franz, outdistanced, stops, watching a moment.)

Cut to the corridor with Dick standing by the window. The train falls into its stride pulling out of Zurich: isolated lights flash by, signs: a signal box, Zurich 7. Dick stares blindly out of the window, then swiftly brings a flask out of his pocket and drinks. The train goes faster and faster, we see the merging gantlets, lit by flying sparks, the noises of the train grow faster and louder in the mounting tempo as Dick raises his flask again and, almost exactly as we remember Abe doing, drinks deeply and wildly. Lap dissolve through Dick drinking to the wash of the *Oedipus Tyrannus* crashing on the cliffs before the Villa Diana: the wash becomes the league-long rollers thundering on a beach in Virginia. The camera follows the spray of the rollers past a few gnarled trees growing in the bank bowed low over the beach by offshore winds, into a church yard beyond where Dick is seen standing by a grave, before a newly erected tombstone, his head bowed, praying. A little church, from which a bell is tolling, stands near. Sea spray and spume skim across the churchyard, mingling with blowing autumn leaves. The camera moves closer to Dick standing in front of the grave, his father's, on which is inscribed: Here lies the Reverend John Ezekiel Diver, 1846-1926, for forty years beloved rector of this parish of Chestertown, Pensby County, Virginia. Erected by his grateful parishioners. *How can ye believe, which receive honour of one another, and seek not the honour that comes from God only? St. John [5.44]*. The camera follows Dick's eyes to his mother's grave next to his father's: Here lies Mary Catherine, ever beloved wife of John Ezekiel Diver: 1850-1918, then returns to the inscription on the grave.

Dick: Goodbye, my father . . . Goodbye all my fathers.

As he says this the camera moves away to a few other graves, on which we make out such names as Elihu Diver-Hunter, Jason Dorsey Diver, Anthony Diver Wayne, the camera lingers an instant on this last name, then looks through the church door into the beautiful and simple little Protestant church, where a few people are praying, with the roar of the sea always in the background.

The bell is still tolling as the scene dissolves through the spray into a shot of a small but imposing old Southern house with Greek Corinthian pillars. It stands, with the sombre evening sky behind it, and the blinds are drawn. Dick looks up at the house, then sadly turns away. The scene merges into a train coming into New York with Dick seated alone in a corner Pullman seat by the window. It is sunset, and through the window gantries are standing against the sky, the El can be seen in motion, with skyscrapers between, a ship standing out in the harbour with tugs. New York looks magical, remote, nostalgic, fantastic as a vision of Troy. We see Dick's familiar briefcase on the seat beside him. Dick is wearing a mourning band on his arm.[53]

Under the usual noise of the train, the train itself is saying: Ashes to ashes, dust to dust . . . Dust-to-dust. Dust-to-dust.

In the window Dick's reflection is replaced by Nicole's reflection.

Nicole's Voice: (very quietly, under the noise of the train) And sit and think we're all rotting and the children's ashes are rotting in every box I open! That filth!

Nicole's Voice: (in supplication) Save me, help me.

The Train: Save me, help me . . . Help . . . Help . . . Ashes to ashes, Dust-to-dust. Dust-to-dust.

The train gives a mournful, wailing whistle: cut to Dick, but without his briefcase, standing down on the step by the exit door, the train is slowing as it nears the environs of Grand Central, the negro pullman porter approaches and with a smile of deep politeness, which has more meaning for us than for Dick, hands Dick his briefcase which he has forgotten: dissolve into the traffic noises of Broadway, music, etc. Dick walking, already all the illuminated signs of the Great White Way are in full swing. As before we are walking with Dick and behind or beside him for the most part so that we see what he sees. At the cinemas, mingling the thematically significant with the insignificant, are playing Flaherty's *Moana*, Rex Ingram's *Mare Nostrum*, Pabst's *Secrets of the Soul*, and Greta Garbo and John Gilbert in *The Flesh and the Devil*. At the theatres we notice, scintillatingly and momently, *Hit the Deck*, *The Hairy Ape*, *Pinwheel*, *A Bill of Divorcement*, Karel Kapek's *R.U.R.*, the *Doctor's Dilemma*, and *Macbeth* by

William Shakespeare.⁵⁴ We feel, in addition to Dick's lone nostalgia, his sense of homecoming, one of our own, looking upon it from a vantage point of twenty or so years, on the other hand how little things have really changed, in spite of prohibition, and whatever ourselves periodically say upon the subject. Moreover, because the camera is haunting Dick, we ourselves feel, with him, a certain sense of haunting the city. The feeling of unchangingness, or recurrence, in history however has been heightened by the appearance at a distance of the illuminated news travelling way up round the Times Building on Times Square. This news goes on recurringly, in a manner that will be indicated, whenever the time of day or geography permits for the greater part of this short New York sequence. Whether the actual existence of the Times Building News itself at this precise time is quite historically accurate is thoroughly immaterial—that is, there was such an illuminated news in Oslo for the Aftenbladet and in other European capitals at this time, or within a year or so, perhaps the Times Building did not have one till a little later—more likely it was the other way round: what is of the utmost importance however—not merely for the purpose of relating the film imaginatively to history but—as will later be explained, for psychological reasons too—is that it should, in one way or another, be *there*. It also serves a double purpose of humour, occasionally somewhat irreverent, but which one will attempt to keep in the highest American tradition, while the news itself—if inventive of juxtaposition—will be so far as possible accurate, bearing in mind too the news' habit of interrupting itself to adjust itself to some immediate incidence, leaving an interesting confusion. Meantime as Dick has been walking we have learned from it:

SHANGHAI—INFORMED SOURCES BELIEVE CIVIL WAR ON MAJOR SCALE IN CHINA IS IMMINENT . . . MANILA—GOVERNOR WOOD WAS REPORTED SERIOUSLY ILL HERE . . . BOSTON—COLLAPSE OF COMMODITY EXCHANGE WAS PREDICTED HERE BY SENATOR . . . OSLO—THE FIRST ROTOR SHIP ARRIVED HERE TODAY SHIPOWNERS SAY THIS MAY REVOLUTIONIZE . . . WASHINGTON—PRESIDENT COOLIDGE RETURNED TO THE WHITE HOUSE TODAY AFTER HIS FISHING TRIP HE DECLARED HIS CATCH WAS A MILITARY SECRET . . . LONDON—DEAN INGE BLAMED GODLESSNESS FOR WORLD CRISIS AT . . . ROME—THE POPE MADE TODAY A PLEA FOR CHARITY IN WORLD AFFAIRS AND AMONG ALL MEN . . . WILKES-BARRE—MINERS STRIKE HERE IS HELD WORK OF REDS BY . . . (a black-out, then) SATURDAY'S SLAYING OF COM-

POSER IT WAS REVEALED TODAY . . . ALL THE NEWS THAT'S FIT TO PRINT (sailing past in a body) PORTLAND—THE GREEK FREIGHTER PERSEUS BOUND FOR SEATTLE WAS REPORTED SINKING TONIGHT OFF THE OREGON COAST THIS IS THE THIRD GREEK MERCHANT SHIPPING DISASTER THIS YEAR . . . LONDON—KING GEORGE PASSED A QUIET NIGHT AFTER HIS RECENT COLD . . .

As Dick passes the Astor the News begins again at: WILKES-BARRE—MINERS STRIKE HERE IS HELD WORK OF REDS BY LABOUR LEADERS . . . NEW YORK—TWO PERSONS WERE HELD IN CONNECTION WITH SATURDAY'S SLAYING OF ABRAHAM NORTH (it pauses a little) WELL KNOWN AMERICAN COMPOSER BUT LATER RELEASED . . . NORTH WAS FOUND BEATEN TO DEATH . . . (the news is held, blacks out, then) ALL THE NEWS THAT'S FIT TO PRINT (sailing past in a body) IT IS NOW REVEALED THAT ABRAHAM NORTH THE AMERICAN COMPOSER DIED WITHOUT NAMING HIS ASSAILANTS.

While this last has been going on, we have been aware that Dick, who has been reading the news like ourselves, has been standing perfectly still. We do not see Dick's face, just his back, as he stands there like a man who has been struck by lightning and the next moment will fall forward. Then as the news goes on—PORTLAND OREGON—THE GREEK FREIGHTER PERSEUS BOUND FOR SEATTLE WAS REPORTED SINKING TONIGHT OFF THE OREGON COAST . . . THIS IS THE THIRD GREEK MERCHANT SHIPPING DISASTER THIS YEAR . . . LONDON—KING GEORGE PASSED A QUIET NIGHT AFTER HIS RECENT COLD . . . and then begins again its eternal recurrence . . . SHANGHAI—INFORMED SOURCES BELIEVE CIVIL WAR ON MAJOR SCALE IS IMMINENT—he seems galvanized into activity, snatches an evening paper, scans the headlines, turns over a few pages hastily, apparently finds nothing satisfactory, (all this while the news is repeating itself) we see his hand on the door of a taxi, we fade through the news and the next instant the words *Yale Club* on a brass tablet loom up before us: Dick has melted through the door as if he were a ghost: simultaneously we hear *In a Mist* being played on the piano . . . The club room is heavy with tobacco smoke, we see the piano player, however, while the camera is still looking as it were over Dick's shoulder, almost we *are* the camera, scanning the faces, and finding them all unfamiliar.

Dick, who has his overcoat over his arm so that we see his mourning band, says nothing, but the group of people about the piano happen to be talking about Abe's death: the first seems standing up for him, the pianist running him down, yet another is indifferently reading a newspaper.

The First Man: Oh, they know who killed him all right. But his cousin didn't want it in the papers because it happened in a speakeasy. What do you think of that?

The Second Man: (barely raising his eyes from his newspaper) It's what's known as family pride.

The Pianist: (playing a loud chord of *In a Mist* on the piano to attract attention to himself) I don't believe his first stuff holds up. Even barring the Europeans there are a dozen Americans can do what North did.

The First Man: The only difference is that Abe did it first.

The Pianist: (playing) I don't agree . . . He got the reputation for being a good musician because he drank so much his friends had to explain him away somehow.

Dick: (speaking quietly, standing at the edge of the group with his back still turned to us) What happened to Abe North?

The Pianist: Didn't you read the papers over the weekend?

Dick: No.

The Second Man: He's dead. He was beaten to death in a speakeasy. He just managed to crawl home to the Racquet Club to die—

Dick: *Abe North*—but he was only just back from Europe—

The Pianist: (still playing) Yes, sure, they—

Dick: *Abe North*. Are you sure he's dead?

The Pianist: It wasn't the Racquet Club he crawled to—I'm sure he didn't belong to the Racquet.

The First Man: The paper said so.

We move, with Dick and behind him, past the group to the door beyond. There is an ashtray, like Abe's, overflowing with stubs on the table.

The Pianist: (behind us now) But I happen to know most of the members of the Racquet Club . . .

We go out with Dick, and begin to descend some steps, all the while keeping behind him: it looks as though he is going down to the locker room.

Dick: (to himself) *Abe North beaten to death* . . .

As he goes down the steps, still hearing *In a Mist* behind him, we feel gradually a mysterious identity of Dick again with Abe, as we had on the train, and the fate of Abe, and ourselves with both, and its obvious relation, now, to this descent. Dick takes a flask out of his pocket and drinks, which heightens the identity. Dissolve savagely into a brief but appalling, confused, and bloody fight and din in the hinterland of a speakeasy in which Abe, very tight, is visible, first as giving, then taking, the most dreadful punishment—some negroes seem trying to help him—finally recovering, and dragging himself, dropping inch by sanguinary inch, down some more steps along a wall in the early dawn, groaning and bleeding: as he rests one awful moment, we emerge through the music of a three piece orchestra—piano, saxophone, drums—playing the *Darktown Strutter's Ball*[55] to find Dick at the bar of a speakeasy, and the fight the account of it the negro bartender has been giving him. Since this speakeasy is assumed to be in the neighbourhood of Times Square, and in a basement, the illuminated news—which had ceased in the Yale Club which is remote from it—now reappears at a distance, tilted, and high up through a grim-looking window, the luminous fiery words about Abe being beaten to death now seeming literally to be going through Dick's brain, even though some way off.

Dick: Don't. I can't stand any more.

The negro bartender pours a drink for Dick from a bottle on the counter. A tart edges toward Dick along the counter. At the other end of the bar a cop who has been talking to another bartender downs his drink and goes out. A detachable sign hung behind the bar observes: *Work is the curse of the drinking classes*.

The Negro: (who seems a very decent simpatico fellow) But I'm telling you, it all began right where you're sitting, sir. Now Mistah North, he hasn't come back from abroad very long, but I'd say he was hitting the juice pretty steady and he was pretty high Saturday night, all right all right. But I'm telling you I can see it all again right now, just as if you was him sitting there (the negro pours himself a drink) and it all started on account of me. That's why I feels so bad.

Dick: (who is pretty tight, but aghast) How do you mean, started on account of you?

The Negro: Well, Mistah North has a lady with him, and three fellows; and another coloured fellow, all of them pretty high, and all at once I don't know how it starts exactly, someone is accusing me of insulting this lady, and someone else is calling me a damn nigger, and Mistah North stands up and knocks him down. I thought that was the end of the fight—in fact I stopped it myself there, but it all breaks out in the washroom again, and—

The Tart: (edging nearer to Dick) Come on, honey. Let's have a li'l drink. Have *fun*—

The negro is going on speaking but for a moment the band playing *Darktown Strutter's Ball* obliterates what he is saying, and there is a quiet again for a moment, with just the hushed cymbal playing—a remote mnemonic of the Eden in Paris, as for that matter the washroom had been perhaps to Dick a remote mnemonic of the bathroom in the Roi George.

The Negro: (with true sincerity, while wiping the bar) But I want you to know if you were a friend of Mistah North's, sir, he always acted like a true gentleman to me. I can't say I knew him very good, but he always come and change words with me when he come back to America—maybe two, maybe lessen three times, and when we moved the speak here from 3rd and 57th this time when he come back, he found me here. I guess he thought what bar I was at was home like, and all I can say is I've lost a true friend. A better, kinderhearted gentleman never breathed than Mistah North. (The negro is visibly moved.)

The Tart: (simultaneously) Won't you have *fun*, honey? What about a li'l drink? (Dick shakes his head) Come on, let's have *fun*.

Cut through the *Darktown Strutter's Ball* to more steps leading down, and Dick going down them.

Dick: Beaten to death in a speakeasy. (he takes another drink from his flask)

As we dissolve into Dick's lonely hotel bedroom there is a confused sound of music emerging out of the *Darktown Strutter's Ball* into *In a Mist* which immediately begins to change gear, so to speak, and sounds something like *Frère Jacques* and as the sequence proceeds, on the score there is from time to time a faint suggestion, without the words, sometimes even in a deep toned jazz rhythm, of *Frère Jacques* at the bottom, as though it wanted to free itself from it and carry on upon its own. In Dick's bedroom his clothes are standing half unpacked, his briefcase is on a table. He takes off his coat, he seems to be about to undress, but instead he takes his flask out of his pocket and pours himself a long drink in a toothglass. Then he takes another bottle out of another pocket and sets it on the table by the briefcase.

He takes his drink and drinks half of it. Then he finishes it. Then he takes another and drinks half of that. No sooner has he done that than he begins to open the new bottle. Then he finds a bundle of newspapers in his pocket, mostly late tabloids, and throws them by his suitcase. That done he takes another little drink and looks at himself in the mirror.

Dick: Where has tenderness gone, he asked the mirror? (after a while he speaks, uttering his words sincerely and quietly, he is not acting, he does not sound tight, even while perhaps he is monumentally so, he is purely and simply talking to himself) It is here, Nicole, I would ask *you* to help *me*—never have I needed you so—but it's I who must—Nicole, do you hear me—with all my heart I pray you will be made well, even if—(while saying this he knocks over his manuscripts in his briefcase)—you are my girl, my love, my sweetheart—do you hear me? May God, may you—

Exhausted, he lies down on the bed, burying his face in his hands. Instantly dissolve into a terrible nightmare that lasts about five seconds, during which we hear a snatch of the whiffenpoof song,[56] and in which a coffin is being borne down a road by mourners, Abe's bleeding face is superimposed on it, then Nicole's, but Nicole's face is tender and appealing and sweet and loving. Dick, who has turned on his back, smiles, almost like a child, then his expression changes to one of horror: he wakes up with a start, sweating.

Dick: Beaten to death in a speakeasy.

Dick rises, pours himself a drink, drinks some of it, and goes to the window. Outside his hotel window can be seen—and it can also be seen in the mirror, reversed and travelling backwards—the silent, sinister news, ceaselessly travelling round the Times Building. He watches a moment.

CIVIL WAR ON A MAJOR SCALE IN CHINA IS IMMINENT . . . ROME—THE POPE MADE TODAY A PLEA FOR CHARITY IN WORLD AFFAIRS AND AMONG ALL MEN . . . ALL THE NEWS THAT'S FIT TO PRINT (sailing past in a body) NEW YORK—TWO PERSONS HELD

Dick picks up one of the tabloids, we see a huge picture of Abe at his best, sitting at the piano. Meantime, the news outside goes on through the window, beyond the close up of Dick and the papers: IN CONNECTION WITH SATURDAY'S SLAYING OF ABRAHAM NORTH WELL KNOWN AMERICAN COMPOSER . . . so that we see the news and the pictures simultaneously. All this time we hear *In a Mist*, as if played by Abe, on the sound track. Dick turns to another large picture in the tabloid, this time taken with himself and Nicole some years back, all of them smiling, in swimming suits: then another picture, Abe, bloodstained, is lying in a similar position on a bed, or in the morgue, as that in which we have seen Peterson; cut back to Peterson lying on the bed, then to the picture of Abe again. All this time also we have seen the illuminated news relentlessly going on, which is now at this point: PORTLAND . . . THE GREEK FREIGHTER PERSEUS IS REPORTED SINKING TONIGHT OFF THE OREGON COAST . . . LONDON—KING GEORGE PASSED A QUIET NIGHT AFTER HIS RECENT COLD . . .

Cut into a howling, screaming blizzard: again we are behind Dick in the swirling snow; he is on 6th or 7th Avenue going toward 14th Street. On the right we can make out St. Vincent's Hospital. We can see lamp-posts, a few cars with chains, another car whose wheel spins, unable to obtain traction. Skyscrapers like phantoms loom out of the snow, which occasionally blows off the snowbanks like spray. Dick is wearing goloshes and a heavy overcoat, with the collar turned up, and beside him appears another muffled figure. The storm is abating as we walk along with them, and we find they are deep in conversation, the other figure is that of a Mexican doctor, whom we see making a few gestures before we hear them speak.

Dick: . . . so it's bad all round, José—I expected to be back in Switzerland now, but they cabled me it would be wiser not to return before spring at the earliest.

José: (who speaks with a slight Spanish accent) But hombre, you can't go on like this. . . If you can't work on your book, can't you practise? No, but after all, you're a doctor of medicine, even if Facultad de Zurich, why not get a license and work at one of our clinics here—

Dick: I don't see how . . . Have a drink. The circulating nurse won't see you.

José: (takes his arm) Well then, amigo, go on a ship—get a job as a ship's doctor on a slow freighter going to Europe—Gracias, salud—ouch! Tequila is the purest music compared to that. (they walk on, José talking rapidly, earnestly, gesturing)—Or write, but try another idea, I have some material for you, though I'm only an obstetrician. I have always held the theory that the relatively slight incidence of psychosis in Mexico is due to the regular occurrence of the religious festivals . . . And instead of the poor priest being told he belongs to the Dark Ages, he should be rewarded with the gold medal at the Psychiatrists' Congress in Berlin—Of course the two points of view are largely irreconcileable!

The two men laugh together in friendly understanding.

José: But I ask you, it is worth thinking about. We have our fiestas and dancing. *You* dance—verdad—you Charleston. But you do not know *why* you dance, or perhaps—Well, (he stops) I must leave you.

They have now reached 14th and 7th Streets and we meantime see a little church come out of the snow with the words: Church of our Lady of Guadalupe. Some lovely singing is coming out of the church: it is *Las Mañanitas*.[57]

Dick: What are you going to do now, José, you can't dance in there.

José: It is the birthday of our Lady of Guadalupe—hear them sing *Las Mañanitas*: the Little Mornings, they are saying: the little birds are singing, and the moon has set. (He takes Dick by the arm) I will say a prayer for you.

Dick: Not for me . . . (half going, then) But José—you might say a prayer for my wife.

The camera shoots momentarily straight into the church with candles burning and people singing: *Las Mañanitas* rises and mingles with the renewed howling of the wind and storm. As it continues, dissolve to Dick walking alone through the snow.

Dissolve to a shot of snow falling over the illuminated news on the Times Building. Dick's head is just visible in the screen, moving toward it, from the direction of the library.

MOSCOW . . . IT IS REPORTED THAT JOSEPH STALIN CELEBRATED HIS BIRTHDAY HERE QUIETLY . . . CHICAGO—NO FLOWERS BY REQUEST WAS THE WATCHWORD TODAY AT SYMBOLIC ENTOMBMENT OF THE EIGHTEENTH AMENDMENT . . . ALL THE NEWS THAT'S FIT TO PRINT (sailing past in a body)

About half way through this *Las Mañanitas*, which has been continuing, is infiltrated with and merges into the tremendous pealing of the terrific choral chant *The Carol of the Bells*[58]—unless, and we do not know, and on second thoughts do not care either, this is a too modern carol and hence an unlikely anachronism—if so, just with a beautiful peal of church bells chiming—as we dissolve into the dark, sinister East River with the snow falling into it and Dick still walking through the snow, his back still half turned to us. While the *Carol of the Bells*, if or if not an anachronism, still continues, he comes to a place where the presses of a newspaper are shaking the building. In the snow, in a doorway, a bum is lying, apparently drunk. Someone steps over him, evidently going into a speak, for a burst of jazz music comes out of it. *The Carol of the Bells* changes into *God Rest Ye Merry Gentlemen*,[59] voices taking up the chorus as we see Dick bending over the body of the bum. Dick kneels to his heart, produces his flask. The bum is dead. Dick drinks from the flask himself, then discovers that his flask is empty, shakes out the last drop, then that the dead bum has a nearly full bottle beside him. Dissolve out of this unsolved ethical dilemma to Dick, evidently having just got up, unshaven, at a more elaborate speakeasy than the first one. *God Rest Ye Merry Gentlemen*, continuing, has now reached the part about tidings of comfort and joy as Dick is gazing down at a Christmas card from Switzerland.

Dick: (reading aloud from the card) Fröhliche Weinachten, Franz Gregorovious. (then, looking up, to the man behind the counter) Two hangovers, please.

The Man: Hamburgers, sir?

Dick: Two hangovers, please.

The Man: (once having grasped the possibility of this sublime mistake it is impossible to say hamburger) Yes, sir, two hang—

Dissolve to Dick, plastered, by himself, in the first speakeasy of the negro, reading another card, though this time instead of Dick reading it, we hear, quietly, the voices of Lanier and Topsy: Happy New Year and love to our dear Daddy.

Overlapping the children's voices, ships' sirens are heard blasting from the river in different keys: the sound of sixteen bells being struck (as is the custom on shipboard at midnight on New Year's Eve) and sailors' voices shouting Happy New Year in different languages. Through the cacophony of horns, shouts, whistles, bells, etc. *Frère Jacques* is heard on the sound track as we dissolve through the falling snow to Dick, half tight, approaching the Times Building with people performing the usual New Year's Eve's antics: blowing horns, throwing confetti, drinking furtively out of bottles, etc. The Times Building is flashing: CHIANG KAI-SHEK . . . CONCERNING THE WAR IN CHINA . . . WASHINGTON—PRESIDENT COOLIDGE IN SENDING GREETINGS TO THE NATION TODAY EXPRESSED HIS HOPE THAT THE NEW YEAR WOULD BRING A NEW ERA OF PEACE AND PROSPERITY TO ALL . . . STAVANGER NORWAY—THE ROTOR SHIP IS REPORTED AGROUND HERE . . . A HAPPY NEW YEAR TO ALL OUR READERS (sailing past in a body) ALL THE NEWS THAT'S FIT TO PRINT while through all this a clock is booming midnight: it is still booming through more ships' sirens when the scene changes to Central Park in the snow in the afternoon with Dick walking through it: people are skating, there are many happy faces and beautiful shadows and the scene looks like a Breughel: this dissolves into Dick seated in his hotel room at his desk, his head on his arm, staring at a letter, in German, which turns into English, of which we see a few words, while we hear Dohmler's voice saying it in German, as the snow falls outside: Dohmler himself repeats the last words in English.

. . . is doing well, or better than can be expected. We now think summer at the earliest would be wiser for your return. I scarcely need to say you should still try as far as possible to exclude all emotional element from your letters. She has the children with her sometimes now, and at present . . .

Then we see the signature: Frederich Dohmler: it is in Gothic handwriting. Then we see Nicole in Switzerland as Dick visualizes her. We do not see the children, just Nicole gazing stonily out of the cunningly disguised barred windows, with the snow drifting down outside.

Immediately the camera picks out another piece of notepaper on Dick's desk on which Dick has written: Dearest Nicole, my girl, my sweetheart—

Dick draws a line through it, then he crumples the paper up and throws it on the floor, and goes to the bottle to take a drink. He looks at his watch—it says 4 p.m. as if to say, "not yet." He sits down again without his drink and writes, this time on a typewriter, but his hand is trembling and it is difficult for him to type.

As he types we see what he is writing:

—As in Mexico— and also perhaps in Haiti—as the labourers are often able to oxidise what would seem vast amounts of alcohol with comparatively little ill effect, simply by virtue of the work they do, (he x's this out, tries again as from "effect") so perhaps it is not too much to say that in the case of these obscure psychoses it is actually the secession from—He doesn't like this, substitutes supersession of, x's this out too, contemplates "vast amounts of alcohol with comparatively little ill effect"—looks at his watch, puts it on to five, apparently is actually satisfied with his self-deception, pours and drinks a long drink, takes a pencil, adds, "and other countries" after "Haiti," looks sidewise through cigarette smoke at a photograph of Nicole, Lanier and Topsy that is on the dresser—but as if he deliberately did not wish to be reminded of them, is not on the desk or beside his bed—rips what he has written out of the typewriter and throws that in the wastepaper basket.

Almost simultaneously as he regards the contents of the basket, the note to Nicole on the floor, which he picks up with a gesture of love as if to undesecrate it, we see Central Park again, changed from winter to spring and almost into another kind of Breughel, with bushes and trees in bloom, and young lovers wandering through it, children playing, little ducks swim, as church bells ring, which dissolves to Dick sitting on the deck of an old sidewheeler, going down the river. The sidewheeler, which is fortuitously named the *Providence*, and belongs to the Fall River Line, so that Dick has probably been taking a short trip, is passing (as it does) Bellevue Hospital, close in, and we see the words (which in fact are there) Bellevue Hospital Psychiatric Ward, in large letters, facing us.[60] We are close enough to see hands grasping the bars, a woman's mad face: Dick turns gloomily from this, as in the ship's engine we detect a note of *Frère Jacques*, opens a huge Sunday paper that has been lying beside him, turns to the book page, when suddenly we see McKisco's face looming at him from the second page: above it we read, in varying type, while Dick begins to laugh.

ALBERT MCKISCO PENS FINE NOVEL OF SOCIAL CONFLICT
Duel in Dinard may be Great American Novel
Like Joyce, only Different.

Clarity highlights the stirring pages of this . . .
The sound of the engine turns from its faint suggestion of *Frère Jacques* and we hear drums again, as at the real duel at the beginning.
Dick turns to another page of literary gossip and begins to laugh again, meantime we have seen the headlines:

ACTUAL DUEL MAY HAVE MOTIVATED CURRENTLY FASHIONABLE NOVEL
Hints now famed writer. Changed title, climax, at last moment, yet "everything seemed mysteriously to fit in."

This, and what follows below is what appears on the screen, though we only have time to get the general drift of it:

—A real duel that writer Albert McKisco was called upon to fight in Antibes in order to defend his honour on a recent visit to France, may have in part inspired the latest American best-seller, called by many the long awaited Great American Novel, the author himself hinted in an interview here today—

Cut to Dick, still laughing, standing looking in at a window of, say, Scribner's: the window is completely full of copies of the novel *Duel in Dinard*, by Albert McKisco, which are arranged in artistic heaps, and on each can be seen a flamboyant cover depicting the duel, the duellists and seconds being disposed much as we have seen them in the actual duel scene, although where it is taking place can scarcely be identified as a golf course. As he looks in the window, Dick's own reflection appears in considerable depth within it, changes to himself sitting at the head of the table at the dinner party at the Villa Diana, with McKisco, tight, on the left (in the window) Mrs. McKisco on the right, seen in a shadowy fashion as if from over Nicole's shoulder, but at the same time as between two pyramids of *Duel in Dinard*, among which, nearer in the foreground, is a large and important and incredibly sober portrait of McKisco himself. In this way Nicole is geometrically almost out of the picture—though at the same time nearest to Dick looking in the window, though her back is turned to him: the other Dick however, at the table, is facing the Nicole whom we can scarcely make out so that the whole thing, though it goes too fast to be stressed, actually symbolizes by its grouping the fact that Dick is deliberately trying to put Nicole out of his mind at this moment, only to be confronted even then by the memory of himself looking straight at her. The following excerpted flashback now takes place in the window at nearly twice its original speed, save for Dick's second remark.

McK: (catercorner to Dick) Aren't you a friend of Van Buren Denby's?

Dick: I don't believe I know him.

Mrs. Abrams: (rapturously) Tender is the night—how does it go on, anybody?

Dick: (as the moon goes under a cloud) But here there is no light.

Abe: (taking a drink) Where youth grows pale and spectre thin and dies.

McK: (rather more drunk) Poor old Oedipus, that's all he's become now, a complex.

Barban: (right across the table) Dick, who was the Greek that smelled?

The real Dick, standing outside the window, and whom we see all the time, has not ceased to laugh while this has been going on, even when we have heard a few chords of *In a Mist* again at the appearance of Abe; the window now instantly re-establishes itself, though we have seen its edges, or frame, all the time, with Dick still laughing at the copies of *Duel in Dinard*.

Dissolve to Dick at another, drab, shop window probably further uptown; it is not exactly to be classified as a second hand book store, or even magazine store, though dusty old copies of the *Dial* and the *Smart Set*, the old *Life* and *Judge* and the *Literary Digest*[61] are to be seen strewn in the window, and many western magazines: what takes the eye is a notice placed to advantage in the window which announces, arraying these items in a list one below the other: Lucky Books, Magic Books, Cook Books, Meccano, How to be a Carpenter, Psychological Books, How to Tell Fortunes, Palmistry, Works of Aristotle, etc., in the middle of the window, in the place of honour is indeed a book entitled *Works of Aristotle*, with some physiological and incomprehensible drawings or diagrams. Dick begins to laugh again: next to this, above, is a copy of a magazine entitled SEXOLOGY, next to this is an Astrology Magazine, open at a headline: FAMOUS ASTROLOGICAL TWINS, ROBERT EDWIN PEARY, THE DISCOVERER OF THE NORTH POLE, AND SIGMUND FREUD, THE FIRST MAN TO EXPLORE THE SCIENTIFICALLY DARK RECESSES OF THE UNCONSCIOUS MIND, MAY 6, 1856. The camera moves up to this and we read: Peary was 29 years of age when Destiny took him by the hand . . . Sigmund Freud was born at Freiburg, Moravia. The father did not die early in his life, as did Peary's father . . . The family moved to Vienna . . . This would have been about the time when his progressed Moon reaches his natal fourth cusp and made the square to his natal Neptune . . .

Next to this, placed in a position of such little honour as scarcely to be placed at all, is a dirty little book: *The Psychological Value of Ventriloquy and Puppets in City Hospitals*, by Richard Diver, M.D.—10¢

Dissolve to Dick in the subway: above the swinging straps opposite him, an advertisement: Have you read *Duel in Dinard*, by Albert McKisco, with a sort of silhouetted Fairbanks-like McKisco[62] brandishing a sword.

Standing under it, hanging on the straps, are a young couple, they do not speak, but they are smiling at each other and seem to be in love. A little to their right, in a corner seat, is a young student who might be a medical student, deeply absorbed in a book. Dick is staring sideways into the blank, black window.

The Train: Nicole . . . Nicole . . . Ashes to Ashes. Dust-to-dust. Ashes-to-ashes. Dust-to-dust.

The noise becomes louder, growing into a sort of delirium, just as the train stops. Dick and the young couple get out and as they do the girl throws Dick a look which shows she finds him attractive. Just before this the young student was so absorbed in his book his companion had to shake him three times before he realised it was his station. He makes a dash for the door, and just barely makes it, just behind Dick. We see the book he was reading. It is called: *A New Approach to Occupational Therapy for the Ordinary Practitioner*, by Richard Diver. Dick does not see this, or notice him, and they depart in different directions.

We follow the student an instant, then the camera wanders up the façade of Bellevue Hospital and looks into a window where two psychiatrists are talking. Sirens are heard from the East River.

The First Psychiatrist: I never could have handled that borderline case if it hadn't been for Diver's early work.

The Second Psychiatrist: You mean his stuff about puppets. Yeah.

A frightful, fiendish, though muffled scream is heard from outside. Neither doctor pays any attention to this.

The First: After that marriage of his, they say—(a nurse knocks, then opens the door and stands there; the first psychiatrist nods, and, just going out the door, throws the remark over his shoulder) I wonder where Diver is now?

Cut to Dick, in his hotel room, typing. The news can be seen through the window as usual, travelling around the Times Building, though Dick pays no attention to it.

WASHINGTON—PRESIDENT COOLIDGE RETURNED TO THE WHITE HOUSE TODAY AFTER HIS FIRST FISHING TRIP OF THIS YEAR ON BEING ASKED ABOUT HIS CATCH HE REPLIED THE FISH DO NOT CHOOSE TO RUN . . . ALL THE NEWS THAT'S FIT TO PRINT (sailing past in a body) ST. LOUIS . . . REPORTS THAT AN ATTEMPT WOULD BE MADE TO FLY THE ATLANTIC BY CHARLES LINDBERGH ARE REPORTED UNFOUNDED . . .

Dick, typing, sighs, notices it is two minutes to seven, puts his watch on the last two minutes, sighs again, has a quick drink, looks at his manuscript, reads it, smiles, but shakes his head, rips it out of the machine, puts it down, then tears it up, hopelessly, looks out of the window. Cut to Nicole, as she appeared by the window during the flashback in Zurich, watching the one tree in bloom in spring: dissolve back to Dick looking out the window at the news upon which now appears:

TRAGIC LINK WITH THE PAST (this is held, then) CARLOTTA ONCE EMPRESS OF MEXICO WIFE OF MAXIMILIAN DIED IN TRIESTE TODAY AGED 87. (the camera begins to move up on the Times Building news, it appears very much closer, so that it now seems to be seen from the angle of somebody walking along and reading it) SHANGHAI—AN UNSUCCESSFUL ATTEMPT HAS BEEN MADE ON THE LIFE OF CHIANG KAI-SHEK LEADER OF THE KUOMINTANG . . . IT IS PREDICTED THAT CHAOS MAY REIGN IN CHINA FOR THE NEXT TEN YEARS . . . LONDON—SHIPPING CIRCLES HERE SAID THAT RECENT EVENTS IN CHINA HAVE MADE NO APPRECIABLE DIFFERENCE IN TRADE (the person reading this is revealed as Dick in evening dress, walking up Broadway again: whether this is in his mind or not the news is now behaving oddly, as follows:) CATASTROPHE (blackout) BOSTON SACCO AND VANZETTI (blackout) DISASTER (blackout) CHAOS MAY REIGN (blackout) ALL THE NEWS THAT'S FIT TO PRINT (sailing past in a body) ATHENS—GEORGIA—MURDER OF . . .

Cut to an illuminated theatre front with the sign: *Season of Greek Tragedy*. OEDIPUS REX, by Sophocles—In Modern Dress.

We are behind Dick in evening dress going in. Cut to Dick behind his programme in the theatre.

On the stage, but in close up, Oedipus appears blinded, and also in evening dress.

The Chorus: (we don't see the Chorus because we have already cut) Count no man happy until he's dead.

It almost seems to apply to Dick, smoking a cigarette in the foyer in an interval. We think it is the interval of the same play but we see, by his programme, that it is the *Antigone*—it may be the next week. Dick is about to go back in when the electric bell starts ringing to summon the spectators back to their seats: we cut back a moment to the electric bell ringing outside the Eden, and the taxi circling away out of the screen.

Abe: It's a device they have so that Americans won't look at their change.

Cut to Dick, standing alone at the back of the theatre; he takes a drink from his flask. On the stage we see the Chorus.

The Chorus:

> Wonders are many and none is more
>   wonderful than man . . .
> The power that crosses the White
>   Sea . . .
> Yea, he hath resource for all.
> But from baffling maladies, hath
>   he devised escapes.[63]

Cut to Dick going down into the street, into the Great White Way again, pursued by the voices of the Chorus endlessly repeating the first and last lines, so that it sounds above the traffic, as he walks once more down Broadway, always seen from behind, or in glittering reflection, while the Times Building reiterates visually—this time we are not so much focussed upon it but every time the camera looks up at it we seem to see: CHIANG KAI-SHEK . . . CATASTROPHE . . . DISASTER . . . TERROR . . . MENACE . . . FLOOD . . . ALL THE NEWS THAT'S FIT TO PRINT (sailing past in a body) DEATH . . . MADNESS . . . CARLOTTA . . . TRAGIC LINK WITH THE PAST . . . Meantime we hear the words:

> Wonders are many and none is more wonderful than man . . .
> But from baffling maladies hath he devised escapes . . .

as if they were pursuing Dick in relentless counterpoint. Dissolve to a cinema front with the illuminated words: PABST'S SECRETS OF THE SOUL, with Dick still pursued by the first and last lines of the Chorus. Dissolve to Dick looking with amusement at the ballyhoo about this in the outside lobby on either side of the box office, as follows: *Freud's Sensational Exposures brought to you in smashing form for the first time on the American screen!* SECRETS OF THE SOUL! *What should a doctor feel? How should a doctor behave—with a human soul at stake?* FIND OUT INSIDE. SEX—DRAMA—THRILLS

It might be a good film, nevertheless, and Dick would like to go in: suddenly he sees a three sheet: "On the Same Program: Rosemary Hoyt in *Daddy's Girl*."

Dissolve to Dick walking down the street again. Opposite is a recurrent jittery animated advertisement for a tailor's or haberdasher's shop figuring a little man transforming himself eternally and jerkily into a bowler-hatted and bechecked fashion plate with quick bright wide frightful illuminated grins. "But from baffling maladies hath he devised escapes," is heard for the last time. On his right he is passing a taxi dance hall, outside which, though he does not stop walking, a girl tries to pick him up; Dick half hesitates, goes on. Following him, from high up in the taxi dance place, widely echoing and discordant, and mingled with the sound of dancing feet, we hear the strains of *The Japanese Sandman*.

Dick now pauses in front of a full length mirror or shop window which reflects the frenetic illuminated signs. Eliminating word signs this time we see, reflected, a man riding a bicycle, an automobile apparently going at terrific speed, a repeated zig-zag of lightning, and a wheel: Dick, staring at these reflections, takes a drink from his flask and steps forward, as it were into the reflections, (like Alice going through the looking glass) but at the instant he steps through and into them they become simply flashing blazing lights so that he steps through into unreality and phantasmagoria: but, in another more important way, he steps through into the expressionism of the period, or even into the schizophrenia of the period (nearly, even, of this period) itself.

Dick is walking through the lights, the people, the noise: a sort of archetypical electric Great White Way cum 42nd Street; all is movement and swiftness. While the Times Building keeps up its endless contradictions of news: good, evil, disastrous and humorous, an endless succession of sandwichmen drift past Dick, saying on their boards: THE LIBERATOR, GOD IS LOVE, HOW TO PREVENT WARS IN TEN EASY LESSONS, ALL MEN ARE BROTHERS, FREE SACCO AND VANZETTI, SACCO AND VANZETTI ARE MURDERERS,[64] FEET ACHE? TRY FITZ U MART CORNER OF 4TH AND 47TH FITZ U FITZ U. Cut to a huge hammer in a shop window descending upon a huge skeleton foot, and we see the sandwichmen coming the other way in this window, preceded this time by a bearded sandwichman with a board saying: I AM THE WAY THE TRUTH THE LIFE, this man, as does the man with the board saying GOD IS LOVE, having such beautiful and charitable faces that we feel they mean precisely what they represent; this window we also enter with Dick, only here we are in 42nd Street approaching the building from the side remote from the library—two more sandwichmen now bring up the rear, one dressed as a gorilla, advertising *The Gorilla*,[65] the last dressed as a robot, advertising, at the Morosco, Karel Kapek's *Rostrum's Universal Robots*.

The Gorilla: (amiably, to Dick) Got a light, buddy?

Dick gives him a light. The gorilla passes by Dick, followed by the robot.

The Gorilla: Ashes to ashes and dust to dust.

The Robot: (also smoking) If the Camels don't get you the Fatimas must . . . H'ya pal?

Following the robot we now see a pair of Siamese Twins: they advertise Pabst's SECRETS OF THE SOUL, *Sigmund Freud's Sensational Revelations, for the first time on the American Screen: Sex! Drama! Thrills!*

All this while we hear jazz music through the roar of the traffic, not bad or banal, but on the contrary wildly good, chiefly of the Venuti-Beiderbecke-Ed Lang type, with the accent on violin and guitar or hot piano, it expresses a marvellous yet furious sense of freedom, and what is strange, is completely asexual—sometimes also we hear a lone piano playing *In a Mist*, sometimes even fractionally, *Tea for Two*:[66] while the same electric signs express the energy and final saving grace of humour of America, whether sardonic or kindly.

A little lost child, not knowing it is lost, gazes up at it all, in front of Dick, in obvious awe and wonder of its sheer magic. The child sees it as an expression of it knows not what. At this point, while we continue to see and feel Dick as protagonist, he becomes objective, like someone we are watching from a little way off. Cut to an obvious socialist or anarchist near Dick, gazing at the lights: he shakes his fist at the lights, muttering to himself, obviously seeing in it all an expression of the horror of the world. Then immediately, as the sandwichmen drift eternally past, we see a kindly priest, with his prayer book—he looks up at the lights, smiling and shaking his head—he, too, in his compassionate way, seems to think that it expresses outwardly a quality in man that demands salvation, of another sort. Then a youth with his books under his arm (who might be played by the actor playing Dick) runs past them, not looking one way or the other, even though it is night. Suddenly Dick—though we still see him from a little distance—seems to realise the presence of the lost child, who is almost Topsy herself, and stoops to ask her, perhaps, where her mother is—there is too much noise for us to hear what he would say anyhow—in a comforting kindly tender fashion. Almost at the same moment, the priest sees the child's plight, and

Dick's bewilderment. The priest and Dick seem to consult together as to what to do with the child. Simultaneously a soldier passes them, smoking a pipe, in uniform, among the sandwichmen. He too seems to be drawn into the discussion as to what to do with the child, but has to pass on. Dick and the priest scratch their heads, the child is weary and Dick picks her up and carries her while the priest confers with them both in a kindly and sympathetic way. Cut to a policeman conducting traffic. Cut to another policeman, down a back alley shooting it out with gangsters who have crashing submachine guns. Cut back as we hear a fragment of another lyrical Beiderbecke piano piece, *In the Dark*—a sort of ghost of *In a Mist*, which will play a part later—to the policeman conducting traffic, he takes the child by the hand, holds up the traffic, and walks across the street with her, meantime his place is taken by another policeman who blows his whistle and waves the traffic on. Cut to the priest and Dick: they smile, shake hands and part, going in opposite directions. Lovers pass Dick, holding hands, with happy faces, wrapped in the magic of their love of which the bright lights seem part. Dissolve into more lovers skating hand-in-hand under arc lamps in a rink. Cut into a head on shot of the apron lights of a cinema: it is playing de Mille's *King of Kings*.[67] The screen slides by and we see the film playing next door: it is Eisenstein's *Battleship Potemkin*.[68] Dissolve to Dick, drinking alone and covertly in a doorway, watching the scene, the same sandwichmen drift past. Dissolve into Dick walking again through suddenly religious music, and past the cinema playing *King of Kings*: it is the hymn: *Fierce Raged the Tempest O'er the Deep*, sung by the Salvation Army at the street corner. Dissolve into a beggar with one leg, through Dick's eyes, sitting on the sidewalk. A beggar with no legs then appears, dragging himself the other way. While this is going on someone is preaching at a street corner, saying "Neither he nor this man's parents have sinned but he was brought into the world that he might demonstrate the word of the Lord."

Cut in a shot of the night sky, with a rising moon, which can scarcely be seen for the lights. Cut back to the first beggar who, with compassion, gives the second a coin. Dick gives them each a coin. Cut to another Salvation Army man saying: "How can ye believe which receive honour in one another, and seek not the honour which comes from God only?" Dissolve to Dick's face watching the scene alone. Cut to the same Salvation Army man shouting: "And Christ walks in this garden too!" His voice is drowned in the rattle and foam of lights and jazz music, this time raucous, *The Darktown Strutter's Ball*. We see the sandwichmen: *I Am the Way, the Truth, the Life*, followed by *Love One Another* then a confused noisy superimposed shot of electric lights merges into Dick entering a cinema—again a head-on shot of its electric lighted apron front—playing Rex Ingram's *Mare Nostrum*: immediately on the screen in this cinema a man is seen drowning beneath the sea: the scene of drowning now fills our screen so that we feel ourselves almost to be drowning in this sea through which now appear other electric apron fronts of other theatres which we feel Dick still walking into, saying *Hoppla Wir Leben*, by Ernst Toller,[69] *From Morn to Midnight*, by Georg Kaiser, the *Hairy Ape*, by Eugene O'Neill—we drift swiftly with Dick through these—then *A Bill of Divorcement*; then *Macbeth*.

A Sudden Voice: Macbeth hath murdered sleep.

The confusion very swiftly now arranges itself as follows. There is a tremendous roaring growling awe-inspiring din. Then, on either side of the screen, as if the bottom of the screen were the stage and the whole a sort of Donald Oenslager[70] constructivist set, (though the intention is the opposite of ridicule, this was one of the most exciting periods of the modern theatre, the point is, it depended on the dynamic of the unconscious for its effect, see notes)[71] appear two men with enormous megaphones. In the centre is a cage with a gorilla in it, in front of the cage a man as if talking to the gorilla. Behind that, a little higher, is a Salvation Army man beating a drum but in increasing voodoo rhythm and with unbelievable percussive intensity, he being a parody of a figure in a scene in *From Morn till Midnight*. Both the men with the megaphones in unison on either side of the screen, holding their instruments up almost perpendicularly like trumpets, and the Salvation Army drummer, are shouting with enormous rapidity above the mounting rhythm of the drumming, this parodying Toller and Kaiser respectively—but not for that reason but because it brings the age itself, of which they were the shadowy spokesmen—and incidentally this age—into telescoped focus.

The men through the megaphones:

> Nineteen eighteen! People go mad!
> Nineteen nineteen! People go mad!

The Salvation Army drummer:

> Come to the penitent chair!

The men through the megaphones:

> Nineteen twenty! People go mad!

"Tender Is the Night"

Nineteen twenty one! People go mad!

The Salvation Army drummer:

Come to the penitent chair!

The men through the megaphones:

Nineteen twenty five! People go mad!
Nineteen twenty seven! People go mad!

The Salvation Army drummer:

Come to the penitent chair-air!

The man in the centre opens the cage and gets in: the gorilla (or the Hairy Ape) gets out and stands there: cut back to the flood and the dam of the fair sequence: the dam crumbles and the flood sweeps it down stream: cut back to the gorilla: he hurtles out of the screen as if into the audience: suddenly the megaphone men and the Salvation Army drummer begin to go round like a Catherine Wheel, which makes a ringing noise like an electric bell, in the middle of which and through which Dick emerges from the window and we are walking with him down Broadway again, approaching the Times Building, over which is dimly seen a full moon; the way he had first come when he got the news of Abe's death: the theatre lights are somewhat the same as at the opening: we see A BILL OF DIVORCEMENT again, somewhere, REVIVAL OF THE CHOCOLATE SOLDIER[72] and Elmer Rice's THE ADDING MACHINE[73] and we are approaching a theatre, on the right wing of whose front is illumined: HIT THE DECK. On the Times Building the following words flash round: CHARLES LINDBERGH TOOK OFF IN HIS PLANE THE SPIRIT OF ST LOUIS TODAY IN A DARING ATTEMPT TO FLY THE ATLANTIC ALONE . . . THE WHOLE NATION AWAITS BREATHLESSLY TONIGHT THE OUTCOME OF THIS COURAGEOUS ADVENTURE WHICH MAY REVOLUTIONISE AVIATION AND TRAVEL . . . LIVERPOOL ENGLAND—THE ROTOR SHIP PUT IN HERE TODAY FOR EXTENSIVE REPAIRS TO HER ROTOR . . . ALL THE NEWS THAT'S FIT TO PRINT (sailing past in a body) . . . BALTIMORE MARYLAND—IN ORDER TO STUDY CONDITIONS IN OUR DECLINING MERCANTILE MARINE SENATOR WILLIAMS OF BOISE IDAHO TODAY COMPLETED A TRIP UPON THE FREIGHTER ROBERT LINCOLN AS SUPERCARGO . . . CANTON

CHINA... FULL SCALE REVOLUTION IS LIKELY TO BREAK OUT HERE ANY DAY INFORMED SOURCES SAID...

Meantime, in about the middle of this, Dick has reached a place outside the theatre where they are selling newspapers which everyone is buying, and on the hoardings we see:

Flying Fool reported nearing Ireland.

The Newsboys: Flying Fool nears Ireland! Read all about it!

Dick, caught up in the enthusiasm, buys a paper, automatically looks up at the news to see if there is any more news about Lindbergh: meantime to the above news about China has been added: IDEOLOGICAL DIFFERENCES MAY... (the news can't make up its mind, adds incongruously) OSWEGO NEW BRUNSWICK... OUTBREAKS OF... It is standing like this when Dick looks up from his newspaper; everything suddenly blacks out save the ID of ideological at the very beginning and the EGO of Oswego: then, for a few seconds, either the Times Building goes mad or Dick has a delusion: while the EGO stays where it is, the ID swoops up to it in a trice to try and get past: another ID comes swooping round the other side of the Times Building in the reverse direction—and at this moment it ceases to behave like the news at all, and behaves in the flashing dancing manner of a frenetic frenzied illuminated advertisement in perpetual metamorphosis, and for a moment the EGO is caught between the two IDS but still holding its ground: not merely that, but coming up on the left the sentence about the senator from Idaho has repeated itself in a flash, then blacked out leaving only the ID of Idaho and SUPERCARGO, which instantly changes to SUPEREGO; simultaneously yet another ego has been coming round from the right so that the EGO is caught between the SUPEREGO as well, so that the hammering lightning dispersal of the words is something like:

ID—SUPEREGO—EGO—SUPEREGO—ID

Yet the EGO still holds.

Dissolve to the theatre front of HIT THE DECK with Dick going in: dissolve to the show itself, the chorus are singing:

The Chorus:

> Hallelujah! Hallelujah!
> And you'll shoo the
> Blues away

Cut back to the outside with papers being bought like wildfire.

Someone: He's made it! He's made it!

The news ripples into the theatre: The Flying Fool's made it! The Flying Fool's made it!

People go crazy in the auditorium. They stand up and cheer. They go wild. Even Dick cheers—why not, isn't he the Flying Fool too?

The chorus on the stage catch the enthusiasm, change the chorus to:

> Yuh Flying *Fool*, yuh!
> Yuh Flying *Fool*, yuh!
> And you *shoo* the
> Blues away—[74]

Then in a terrific roar:

> Oh Satan lies a'waitin'—

Cut, muting it off at that point, it may be the next morning, though Yuh flying fool, yuh, is going on quietly on the sound track for a while, perhaps in Dick's head. He is sitting down some place in the park, or in Washington Square, upon a bench, smoking a cigar, with an obvious hangover. He has a letter he has been reading and we read, or hear in Franz' voice:

... that Nicole is very much better and she now seems much more interested in the children, even to the exclusion of her interest in her convalescence. So we think, Dick, it would be all right for you to come back by summer, though the advice is if possible by easy stages. For the rest, we can only say ...

Dick looks wistfully happy at first, a matter which is entrusted here largely to music. Then his expression becomes almost hopeless as he "remembers." Simultaneously his eye is attracted by a flagpole on a neighbouring roof. His eye travels up it: someone is sitting on top of the flagpole. Then we see that the man up on the flagpole is also smoking a cigar. Dick smiles, then seems to be wondering for a moment whether the man up the flagpole is himself or not. He looks round, takes out his flask and, raising it, drinks the man's health.

Cut to a travel agent: in the window the words ATLANTIC CROSSINGS FRENCH LINES; we can also make out the enigmatic phrase, Quest for Beauty, and other suitable advice such as Zurich, Switzerland—spend your holidays in Switzerland, winter or summer. Cannes, where the days go by in a golden haze, etc. The camera goes through the window to find Dick talking in one of the offices.

Dick: No, I want to go by a slower boat, a freighter if possible.

The Man: We have a French boat loading now that takes two passengers—but she's going to Naples.

Dick: That's fine. (nervously) Incidentally, do you know if any of these freighters carry doctors? (laughs) I don't mean I'm ill—I'm a doctor, and I've often thought of—

The Man: Well, that's hardly my department. Wait—here's the Captain—you can ask him. Captain Gregoire, Mr.—Doctor—Diver. (he addresses someone else)—Yes sir?

Captain Gregoire: (he looks a prince of good fellows, in appearance something like Pinza, and is cheerful and urbane.) What did you want to ask, Doctor?

Dick: I was wondering if—no, your ship now, Captain Gregoire, I wondered how you are fixed for refreshments, drinks and so on, if it's going to be a long voyage. Our laws are none too happy here now, and—

The Captain: (heartily and understandingly) Aaa!— Well, we have wine for the crew at meals, but we carry just enough other liquor for the officers. The engineers and firemen get more wine than the sailors by law, so if you are sensible you will eat with the engineers. Ha! Ha! Ha! (the sound track begins to lap dissolve and we hear the ship's engine while they are talking) But, (with a gesture) we are a ship très bien chargé—our steward will not let you run short. A good friendly ship, though we have to beauty her up somewhat this trip.

Dick: (smiling) What's her name?

The Captain: The *Diderot* . . . Yes, the *Diderot*. (laughs)

Cut back to the brooding statue of Diderot, with the Isotta drawing up beside it.

The Children: Au'voir, M'sieu Diderot!

Cut to the Isotta on the road, with the children, Dick, and Nicole singing:

> Frère Jacques
> Frère Jacques
> Dormez-vous?
> Dormez-vous?

Cut to a close shot of the engines of the *Diderot*, a tremendous crashing confused bass noise of machinery, but it is singing, and carrying on the song:

> Sonnez les matines
> Sonnez les matines
> Ding dang dong!
> Ding dang dong!
> Frère Jacques

> Frère Jacques
> Dormez-vous?
> Dormez-vous?

a song that relentlessly and unceasingly—if not always the words the tune, though with variations that will be occasionally indicated—accompanies us all the way to Naples.[75]

Cut from the ship's engines to Dick standing on deck watching the ship cast off, beginning gradually to back out from the wharf: it is night, and we can see only the wharf, and a shed under arc lamps: on the wharf is a sinister sign: WATCH THE HOOK! IT CAN'T WATCH YOU! Standing on the wharf is the sole person seeing Dick off: José, the Mexican obstetrician. Whistles, bells, sound from the bridge, beneath which the engine, more muted, remotely tuned to the lilt of *Frère Jacques*, is heard. Ropes are being cast off, one by one, as if they were ties cast off in Dick's life.

José: (on the wharf) And I will pray to the Virgin of the Soledad for you. She is the saint too of mariners on the deep.

Dick: (he is somewhat unshaven, but speaks soberly) I'm not going to be soledad. I have a cabin mate.

José: (as the ship draws a little further away) And also to the saint of Desperate and Dangerous Causes. And—Dick—diablo! I almost forgot. Can you catch? (he looks round covertly, then throws a bottle which Dick catches neatly) Habañero—(barely phrases the word) Mexican brandy.

Dick: Thanks! (he puts it in his overcoat pocket) It shall be used strictly to comfort the dying.

Orders are heard from above—whistles—the engine telegraph.

José: God bless you.

Dick: Adios!—Say, José! (shouting) I'm going to dance the Santiago every morning at 3 A.M. and get rid of my neuroses!

José: Adios, mi amigo.

Further orders are heard from above: we see José faintly as he turns away, and just the large sign WATCH THE HOOK! IT CAN'T WATCH YOU! is still visible. Then we hear a voice behind Dick, familiar, but much quieter than we remember it.

The Voice: Well, we all have to go back to go forward, as someone said. (it is Albert McKisco, he looks a hundred percent better, and in enormous contrast to Dick)

Dick: (without looking round) Before taking a leap, wasn't it? Nietzsche said—

McK: It can't watch you, eh? Now have you ever read *Moby*— (McKisco shouts as Dick turns round) *Dick* Div—!

At this instant there is a terrific deafening shattering reverberating roar from the siren. McKisco is trying to shake hands, add "Diver! by all that's holy!" etc. with the sudden familiarity (though it is not overdone) bred from the fact they are two Americans who have met on foreign soil, while McKisco's former sense of inferiority seems almost non-existent. Both, at the same time, have to put their hands to their ears.

Cut to the two men beginning to walk aft in the wind, spray blowing in their faces. And as the ship starts to feel the sea for the first time, scending slightly, they stop, standing by the rail. Near them the carpenter is knocking wedges into the cleats of the hatches: in passing they bow and smile: Bon soir, M'sieu, etc. The wind is blowing with a harsh shrilling and their dialogue is almost thrown away, tossed by the wind. In the background we see the moving lights of a big liner coming in.[76]

McK: Someone said—Ouspensky, one of those philosophers—that if you wanted the right image for the soul of a man, you should think of a liner at night. (he points to the moving lights of the vessel) What do you say, Diver?

Dick: It depends on what you mean by soul.

McK: It's a thought I'd like to use . . . A ship at night with all its lighted ports, its different factions, with its vast moving body, its multiple—yet single—goal, but each little room with its special light, its capacity for rest, its separate activity. (the liner blows her siren)

Dick: Why not bring in bulkheads that give way, and the bridge with no one at the wheel, (they begin to walk aft again, a siren mourns faintly somewhere) or if someone, the order to starboard taken as port: collisions and shipwreck: messages for help, and the ship that retracts her S.O.S.

As they go aft, sailors pass going forward: they all seem decent and cheerful, they say "Bon soir, M'sieu, bon soir, M'sieu," Dick and McKisco bow, their words of greeting blown away by the wind.

Dick: (scarcely without pausing, though he, like McKisco, turns, holding his hat) Not to speak of the privity of the owner, that is not yet the privity of the master. And icebergs that change the symbol, being three-quarters under water, and not half seas over, like me. Come and have a drink.

McK: On me, Diver. I have some French cognac.

The wind whines as they reach amidships. A shot of the mainmast and the reeling stars, then an engineer descending the engine room with a long-beaked oil-can. The ship's engine is beating to the tune of *Frère Jacques*.

(Note: We feel a note is necessary here on the use of *Frère Jacques*, since the idea may have proved rather puzzling. We have had a suggestion of it at the very opening of the picture, then we heard the children, joined by Dick and Nicole, singing it, now we have it blended with and sometimes as if sung by the ship's engine. Thus it is established as a symbol of nostalgia, the use of which during the following scenes, whether with words or without and simply as the rhythm of the ship's engine, reminds us that Dick is thinking of Nicole and the children. But since at the very opening it was used as the rhythm of the universe, so to speak, it binds the whole picture to eternity, on the acoustical side that is, while the visual parallels it. And since it is a canon, or roundelay, with everyone taking up his part, dropping out, new voices joining in, and dropping out, without beginning or ending and capable of infinite variations, it relates us to humanity. We might ask ourselves what the words to *Frère Jacques* mean in terms of the song's own naive self. We don't know who brother John is, emphatically he is not *Big* Brother! It might be a buried appeal to ourselves, however, to wake up and ring some bells, and redeem from the corruption with which Stalinism has invested it the idea of the brotherhood of all mankind under God. As to its purely musical use, once the rhythm, and the rising and falling of the tune has set itself to the ship's engine, the possibilities which may suggest themselves to the musical director are almost infinite. But it should be pointed out that we have discovered and put to the test the fact that this canon could not be mechanically a more exact arrangement, not only of the rhythm of a ship's engine, but of its polyphony, its reverberating and continually recaught echoes and reechoes, while the engine is the arch-realistic expression of the ship itself—cinematically speaking, more important than the ship. However for the total effect which we suggest might be obtained from this minor invention, we are perhaps relying on something more profound still, namely upon Schopenhauer's dictum that, on looking back over our past, we see at once that our life consists of mere variations on one and the same theme, and that the same fundamental bass sounds through it all.—If this is not reducing art altogether to black magic, it is something like an evocation of the universal experience that we feel it ought to call forth in the audience, which doubtless explains the awful fascination of ship's engines in the first place.[77]

But this section at the same time on the visual plane is also intended to be a cinematic expression of the Night Journey Across the Sea, mentioned by Dohmler—specified by Jung—of myth, and within the racial unconscious, etc. This, very remotely too, is a parallel of an analysis itself, an analysis being a night journey through the unconscious: consequently it can stand for—formally—in so far as this is relative, what Nicole is going through also. There is no need to explain about this night journey: the idea is that people watching and listening will be gripped without necessarily being equipped to say why: the appeal *is* to the unconscious. But in its higher meaning it is a journey of purification for Dick, towards a sort of rebirth: he ascends to a kind of inchoate yet final knowledge of his true purpose.—But his ordeal does not end with the voyage: in Rome he has to meet the configurations of his conscience. Here are a few further notes we set down in the course of writing it—not to be taken literally but placed here simply as suggestions, or as a possible inspiration to the director.

One principle commodity needed is noise: continual and unrelentless from the *Frère Jacques* point of view, varying according to the others. Most of this Atlantic part should be at night, to symbolise both Dick's state of mind and the theme, or it is nearly dark: long dark swells of wilderness of water—seabirds—at evening no sense of brightness, unless very occasionally, on the sea: dark shadows in alleyways cast by ceiling lights: ladders and ventilators: the funnel: the swaying masts, the confined space of alleyways, of cabins: harsh cries of shearwaters, or the lone eternal albatross following the ship: always the engine and the ship's bells: the confined space of the bunk: crash of crockery in the galley: kerang-kerang of shovels in the stokehold: in the few scenes during twilight the eternally twirling log from the stern of the ship: huge lit galleries of the engine room, glistening emery papered rails every bit like those of a prison: the lights on in the rooms at night or during the day with the doors on the hook: the whole thing considered like the various factions of the soul. The strange night life of a ship—the firemen down below on watch, Dick, sleepless, haunting these strange prison galleries of the night: remembering too the terrifying deeps of the unconscious, the mind that has its flights of jaegers and shearwaters, its sharks, its eternal albatross, its stokehold: while all this is going on, we have a little glimpse of a society which, if anything but ideal economically, is at least as well adjusted as may be under the abnormal conditions posed; casting, from our own experience, a frightening and salutary doubt upon the nature of those matters which are said to occupy men's minds in isolation, to the exclusion of all else.

All this, together with most of the dialogue, should everywhere be subserved to what the director may make visually and aurally out of whatever cinematic poetry he may consider negotiable in the chaos of the sea and the night and the engine, with some hope of rebirth not out of sight. One justification for attempting it at all is to be found in a buried ambition of Fitzgerald's own—"But I couldn't find another form to put it in—the Conradian legend that the sea exists"—while he was writing *Tender Is the Night* itself, which we did not discover until after completing the whole thing.)

We have cut from Dick and McKisco on deck into their cabin and well on into their conversation. McKisco's cognac, because of the motion of the ship, has been placed in the hole reserved for a caraffe, over the washbasin.—June can be a bad time in the Western Ocean and it looks as though they are in for a storm already.—The cabin is on the lee side, at present, so that the porthole is open, and we hear the sea, can even see it darkly below as it rises up to us. (Nonetheless the sea apparently sounds more muted with the closing of the door. This is a general rule, not to be lost sight of, or we shall lose the sense of the ship—every time conversely the men are seen in an alley the noise of the sea and the engine is terrific.) There are various notices in French on the cabin wall, concerning boat drill, life belts, etc., as follows: *Alarme*: le signal d'alarme consiste en 5 coups long donnés par sonnerie et sifflet. A ce signal: Allez dans votre cabine, Couvrez vous chaudement. Mettez votre gilet de sauvetage. Laissez vous guider par le personnel et rendez vous au Pont de Embarcations. Cote à l'abri du vent. *Abandon*: Le signal d'abandon est donné par 6 coups *brefs suivis* d'un coup long. A ce signal vous embarquerez dans le canot No. 1 Tribord: No. 2 Babord: Selon la direction du vent. The camera takes in these sinister instructions for abandoning ship as the men speak. They are half unpacked, and we notice a picture of Nicole and the children beside Dick's bunk, where he is reclining, glass in hand. McKisco is unpacking while he speaks.

McK:—so that's how it was. (puts down a hairbrush and picks up his drink) I just didn't take to success.

Dick: Too good for it?

McK: It wasn't that . . .

Dick: Yet it's improved you—you seem to have become informed on more subjects than Goethe since I last saw you.

McK: I wasn't so dumb before . . . But I had to get away, to avoid the publicity. You know—"The *Berengaria's* most precious cargo," and all that. So I grabbed this freighter. Violet lapped it up, but I couldn't take it. (Bells are heard) Well, I know I've no real genius, but if I keep on working hard I may do something good someday.

Dick: High dives have been made from flimsier springboards.— What about trying to promote a snack?

Cut to the messroom. It is a small room, forward on the main deck, under the bridge, giving on alleyways on both sides. There is a large nautical map of the Atlantic on one side, and a place where notices are pinned on the other. There are two or three tables and something like a sideboard-cum-icebox against the opposite wall. Unlike ships of most nationalities the officers and engineers mess together, this being modified by the difference in the duration of their watches. But the Commandant (that is, the Captain) and the Chief Officer dine alone on the bridge, never in this messroom. This does not always apply to the Chief Engineer because of the proximity of the messroom to the engine room. A machiniste and a deck officer have come off watch about midnight and are just finishing a snack of paté, bread and wine; they get up to leave as we cut. Dick and McKisco are already seated and the officers stop to shake hands with them as they leave. The ship is still rolling, more formidably in one way, though not so sharply, now they are further beyond the confluences of the estuary of the Hudson. But the caraffes of wine and glasses on the tables slowly chase each other down the tablecloth. We see McKisco's cognac in a safe place.

The Officers: (as Dick and McKisco say the same) Bon soir, Messieurs.

The steward brings Dick and McKisco a plate of paté, ham, and sardines, bread and butter, and fills up their wine glasses, then busies himself over by the sideboard putting water in another caraffe of wine.

McK: (to the steward in halting French) Merci beaucoup, nous sommes très tard—nous avons faim.

The Steward: C'est égal, messieurs. (he laughs) A steward's life, n'est fini jamais.—This is for the chief engineer, not for you. (he finishes filling some of the caraffe with water.) He likes it like that. Not for me. Eh, bien, c'est l'habitude.

McK: Combien d'heures travaillez-vous?

The Steward: Quatorze, quinze . . . Mieux, comme vous êtes loin de votre famille; better so when you are far from home, your family. (he places another caraffe of good, unwatered wine on the table for the two Americans, Dick seems profoundly interested in the whole procedure) A steward works even in his sleep. Still, she is a good ship. A ship bien chargé.

Dick: (with his mouth full) She rolls a bit—il a un grande roule—your ship.

The Steward: (sprinkles water on the tablecloth to prevent the slide of their glasses and crockery, laughing) Even in dry dock—the chief engineer told the Commandant last voyage, he found her still rolling in dry dock. (they laugh) But still, she is a good ship, the *Diderot*. She is what sailors call a happy ship.

The *Diderot* rolls and the glasses, etc., begin to slide down the other way, partially impeded by the wet tablecloth.

McK: Do you mean you are contented?

The Steward: (who should not "act" too much either—he speaks English quite fluently) Ah no, monsieur. No sailor is ever contented . . . But a happy ship, that is a different thing.—And we are all glad to be homeward bound. (eight bells strikes, the steward begins to go out, as it were uphill, he smiles at them; as he opens the door a burst of very muffled concertina music and singing comes from the alleyway. It is the first night homeward bound and routine is slightly disarranged. McKisco is going to say something, but simultaneously, climbing "uphill" from the other side, comes apparently the chief engineer, in dungarees, but with some suggestion of a uniform, and absolutely covered with sweat: he is an enormously fat, red-faced man, with handlebar moustaches, but not in the least ludicrous: he has just come off watch also, because of leaving the harbour.)

The Chief: (blindly, removing his spectacles)—M'sieurs . . . (he takes the caraffe of wine left by the steward, drinks it off at a long gulp, goes off at the other side) Bon soir, M'sieurs.

Cut to Dick and McKisco returning to their room down the alleyway, McKisco carrying the depleted bottle of cognac. We see the separate cabins of some of the officers, their doors on the hook, the lights on in some rooms, and we are reminded, perhaps, from inside, of the former image of the soul. Both McKisco and Dick are pretty tight, but their staggering down the alley and their difficult progress up a companion ladder is less due to this than the rolling of the vessel.

McK: Look here, when I first met you, I wouldn't have dared talk like that to you—not even when I was drunk—not to you, whatever I may have said to some other people—but all I'm doing now is giving you back what you've given me the last few hours. You said I never was a practising writer—I say you never were a practising doctor—

Dick: I told you as much.

McK: (unabashed) You say I wanted all kinds of experience first—I say you wanted all kinds of experience first before you became the kind of doctor whatever kind of doctor it was you wanted to be.

The two men, teetering back and forth, are now struggling up their own alleyway.

McK: You say I get aggressive when I'm tight because I wanted to be in the war. I say what you mean is you're sorry *you* weren't in the war, or not in it enough, maybe.

They have reached their door and try to get in: it is difficult to open it against the careening angle of the ship.

Cut to their cabin a little later, the porthole still open, the sea a fringe of foam below it, the ship slanting down to their porthole rather like a windjammer, down to their side, still a'lee. The wind is still rising.

Dick:—Certain experiences?—But you've only had one experience yourself, haven't you—hadn't you?

McK: What was that?

Dick: The duel.

Cut to Barban firing his pistol straight into the screen: the ship's engine in huge closeup: back to the cabin.

On the sound track underneath the dialogue, *Frère Jacques*:

McK: How did you hear about that?

Dick: Did you know you'd lost your second?

Ding dang dong!
Ding dang dong!

McK: Abe North asked me—and I did my best to shush Violet about it. Sure I told the reporters about it later, but I didn't mention any names, and I put the duel in Dinard, not Antibes—so—

Beaten to death!
Beaten to death!

Sonnez les matines!

Sonnez les matines!

Dick: So it was Abe who told me. Abe North's dead.

Poor Abe North!

Cut to Abe smiling and nodding on the duelling ground, then back to McK.

Poor Abe North!

McK: *Dead?*

Beaten to death!
Beaten to death!

Dick: Didn't you read it in the papers? He was beaten to death in a speakeasy.

Poor old Abe!
Poor old Abe!

McK: (after a pause) Beaten—I'm sorry—I—my gosh—but *dead*.

Sonnez les matines!
Sonnez les matines!

Dick: How did it happen, the duel?

McK: Hap—But dead, I can't figure—the duel?—well, now I remember—I—the last thing I heard him say, I guess, we're all in about equal danger—the duel—

Ding dang dong!
Ding dang dong!
Poor Nicole!
Poor Nicole!
Sonnez les matines!
Sonnez les matines!

"Tender Is the Night"

Dick: Yeah, how did it happen?
McK: Well, your friend Barban and I went on with that crazy argument about politics.
Dick: It's all right Albert. You're a good fellow. I know what the real reason was. (Dick gets up and takes a drink) I seem to be all right now. But it's not going to be all right later tonight.

Poor Nicole!
Poor Nicole!

Sonnez les matines!

Sonnez les matines!

Ding dang dong!
Ding dang dong!

Cut to the wireless operator's cabin next door and the spitting spurting typing hammering noise from in there. He too has to be up late.

Cut to the night: the unholy racket from the wireless operator's cabin fades in Dick's cabin. McK. is asleep, his light turned off in his bunk. Dick has left his light on, gone to sleep reading, or trying to read, three books: McKisco's own, *Duel in Dinard*, *Fantasia of the Unconscious*, by D.H. Lawrence, and *Moby Dick*. Dick's face is sweating.

A Deep Voice: Heavy, heavy hangs over thy head! What shall the owner do to redeem it?
Dohmler's Voice: Remember that, on your night journey across the sea!
Dick wakes up with a stifled groan.

Frère Jacques, but just the tune first, then the words:

Why not live?
Why not *die*?

Do you wish
To survive?

Poor Nicole!
Poor Nicole!
Poor Nicole!
Poor Nicole!

Ding dang doom!
Ding dang doom!

McK: (waking, puts on his light) What is it, Diver? You all right?
Dick: (laughing) No.
McK: Can I help? (he gets up) My gosh, you're sweating. Have a drink. (he pours drinks for them both)

Cut to later in the conversation; Dick, drinking, picks up the copy of *Duel in Dinard*. They are now both, if still tight, intelligently wakeful and *conscious* for a brief while.

McK: You read it?

Dick: Yeah, that is, professionally—psychiatrists are usually lousy judges of art, because by and large they are impressed by success—that is—

McK: That's very unusual!

Dick: I mean they look for the faculty of communication seen as a faculty of social adjustment, measured in dollars and cents; unless the author happens to be dead, an intimate friend, or otherwise useful to the psychiatrist himself, a great work of art that was at the same time a commercial flop would be identified with its author from the point of view of that author's maladjustment rather than as art, unless of course someone like Freud had already taken it up—

McK: Too bad your friend Barban didn't polish me off at that rate—(taps lightly the picture of the duel on the cover) Maybe he didn't have any intention of killing me, at that?

Dick: (interested) Did you try to kill Tommy?

McK: I hope I never know for sure either way, so I can go on feeling good about it.

Dick: If you had been killed, the guilt would have been mine—indirectly.

McK: I don't know about the guilt, but the corpse would sure as heck (they begin to laugh) have been Albert A. McKisco's.

Cut to a close shot of the engine: *Frère Jacques*: the night watch down below: flickering dials, the chief engineer, moustachioed, on the fiddley, then the sea sweeping by with spume blowing off the long dark swells. Cut back to the cabin, later in the conversation.

Dick: (pretty tight again) So many things in America get cheapened by our enthusiasm . . . How about it, Albert, how would you like to feel the ethics of your profession dissolving into a lifeless mass?

McK: (similarly tight and laughing)—mine never had any—

Dick: What began as an understatement, a sort of corrective in man's overstatement of his soul, could end at this rate by depriving him of his soul altogether—

McK: Soul!—But what about the economic problem, Dick, the relation of man to—

Dick: (tight, serious, getting sleepy) I'm beginning to feel it's what man suffers alone— On the sound track *Frère Jacques* becomes,

McK: Did you ever know Van for a moment, *Au*
Buren Denby? *Claire de la Lune*.

Dick:—what he *thinks* he suffers alone, in his own unredeemed loneliness with his, with his, whatever—the man who's lost his—yeah, by what he *thinks* he suffers alone in his terrible separate guilt—blindness—at three, four in the morning. That alone is what relates him to other human beings.—See you later. I'm going to catch a little delirium.

Cut to Dick's wristwatch at 4 A.M. Simultaneously 8 bells are being struck, then echoed from the engine-room.

A Voice: (deep, terrible, and tragic) Heavy, heavy hangs over thy head! What shall the owner do to redeem it?

Dick wakes up again, takes a small drink, is careful not to wake McKisco. He walks out into the engine room alley. The firemen are changing shifts. The firemen coming off watch go to get the black pan from the galley (food left warm for them). Though we hear no clear dialogue, Dick is seen talking to people, curious, nodding his head. The engines go on with their noise and song.

Cut to Dick's wristwatch: it says four A.M. again. The same scene is repeated, except for the voice "Heavy, heavy hangs," etc., and this time Dick walks out on deck, stands by a mast. There are heavy seas all round, the mast is swaying against the night, and the eternal engines are going on.

Dissolve to Dick standing in the same place at dawn—a shattering stormy dawn at sea with rifts of wild light near the horizon. The screen lightens, and darkens immediately, becoming a tremendous glowering sunset, with silhouettes of sea birds blowing, and Dick in the same place, though staring in the opposite direction. During this *Frère Jacques* says sometimes: Please go on; why not die; sonnez les matines: the tune is taken up from the ventilators; sings in harmony, one would swear one could hear aerial infernal choirs.

Cut to the ship's engine in huge close up. Then all the noises of the engines set themselves to the tune of *Frère Jacques* taken up by the ventilators.

Cut to the ship's bell: it comes up toward us and is struck by hand.

Cut to the ship's run being posted on the notice board in the messroom, more or less as follows:

> W.R. Chamberlain & Co. New York
> POSITION REPORT
> Cie. Gle. Transatlantique.
> *S.S. Diderot.*
> Date: 5 Juin, 1927
> Latitude: 43.01.N.
> Longitude: 30.47.W.
> Course: 48
> Distance: 213 m.

> To Go: 1087 m.
> Length of Day: 23h. 40m.
> Average Speed: 10kn.
> Wind: N. F 18
> Sea: Grosse roule de N.N.W.
> Current . . .
>   Signed: 1st Lieut. Charles Guichet.
> Arrival Gibraltar le 14 Juin vers 8 hr.
> A Marseilles—Genoa—Napoli—?

(Note: if other position reports are used they should be used swiftly in this manner, half seen, varying with latitude, longitude, wind, etc. This is guesswork, but places the *Diderot* as roughly approaching the Azores.)

Cut to McKisco and Dick at the bow. The camera takes in a grey wilderness of heaving water all round, with skimming sea birds: shearwaters, a long searching albatross, with sabre-like wings. (The *Diderot* is a ship with a deep well for a foredeck, and no foc's'le head, and with the men's foc's'le right aft—but it would be adapted to almost any deep sea freighter to today or yesterday, with the exception of a Hog Islander.) Right at the bow the iron bulwarks slope out quite high on either side, and the ship sinks deep in the trough, so that at times the sea seems almost over their heads, rising high about the two men: occasionally there is a noise of it bursting up through the scuppers or even the hawseholes, to discommode the carpenter who is oiling the windlass just abaft of them. McKisco and Dick, wearing sweaters, are looking up at a sailor aloft on the crosstrees of the foremast adjusting the topping lift of a derrick.

McK: (reminiscently, gazing up at the sailor) Not like the old windjammer days.

Dick: (smiling) I never heard about your old windjammer days—tell me about them.

McK: I mean it doesn't look so dangerous up there.

Dick: The deck below is just as hard.

The camera suddenly descends on the bulwarks by them, where there is a little bird lying dead, that has evidently collided with the ship.

Dick: (as he picks it up and they examine it) Poor little thing. It's got little feet like a bat. Yet it's a bit like a swallow. It must have flown into the ship.

The Carpenter: (who has come up) C'est un petit petrel de tempête, Messieurs . . . Pauvre . . .

McK: A stormy petrel, eh?

As Dick holds the little bird in his hand, before throwing it overboard, the bird becomes the other bird in Dick's hand when he was on his bicycle tour, just before he fatefully met Nicole again: that bird had flown up in the direction of the Glion funicular, and we see it again as it flies happily out of his hand. Then we watch the dead stormy petrel as it falls overboard into the sea. On either quarter we see the shearwaters and the lone albatross glide ceaselessly about the ship, following it, skimming the rough sea, scarcely moving their wings.

McK: (turning round and leaning against the V of the rising bow, looking back astern) What reason would you give for the good feeling on board this ship, Dick. It interests me.

Cut to a long shot of the Commandant up on the bridge; he waves blithely from behind his window and we see the man at the wheel. The ship's bell strikes: seven bells. *Frère Jacques*—not the words, just the tune, scarcely the tune, of the engines—is very muted here. We can scarcely hear anything save the sea gurgling in the hawseholes. The carpenter goes on oiling his windlass. The two men move aft toward the alleyway under the bridge. As they move away they exchange "Bon jour, Messieurs, Bon jour," with the carpenter.

Cut to the two men climbing up on the poop aft: *Diderot-Le Havre*—on a lifeboat. The French flag flies and the log twirls endlessly astern. The shearwaters and the lone albatross circle and follow the ship.

Dick: (as if continuing to speak)—the explanation is they quarrel all the time, but we just don't hear them. I'll bet you they quarrel about the conditions, the food, do nothing but talk about each other's women, rob each other—and in order not to give the two American passengers a bad impression, since they mean to rob us too, the dead are thrown overboard at night.

McK: How much you bet me they're fighting right now?

Dick: Five bucks. And I'll lay double or quits the subject is women.

McK: O.K. You're on. It's a dirty trick, but let's take a look. No, I'll bet the subject is politics.

Dick: You can pay me in lira.

Cut to a shot looking down through the open skylight—as if the lid of a box of toys had been lifted—into the firemen's foc's'le. As we look the engine's tune of *Frère Jacques*, though without the words, grows louder and immediately a confused rapid conversation rises in French, meantime the camera is showing us that while some of them indeed are having an argument, everything is said in a friendly and cheerful manner. The quarters themselves are cheerful and clean too, however cramped. We see two firemen finishing their dinner with a caraffe of wine, one fellow washing his dungarees in a bucket, someone else whittling away at a piece of wood, another repairing a concertina, a guitar lies on a bunk, other firemen sprawling around their bunks, in among which and on the bulkheads may be glimpsed several pin up girls from French magazine covers, Greta Garbo, the hammer and sickle, the Dolly sisters, the Virgin Mary, a head of Christ, an old Christmas card, souvenir photographs of New York, many pictures of French cyclists, a magazine cover on which we see "Tour de France," French rugby football players, many family groups, even a bunch of faded flowers—the treasures of the firemen. The following dialogue is spoken rapidly, often overlapping, and in *French*: out of what follows should be chosen sufficient subtitles in English to give its gist, which run below across the screen during the scene.

"I say the best concertinas are made in Saxony." "No, Jaraguay was the best right wing three quarter France ever had." As the camera takes in the picture of the bicyclist in the Tour de France: "Geraud's a dead certainty for the Tour de France!" Evidently from the number one fireman: "Sacré! You're only a lazy trimmer! But if you ask me would I rather be on one of these Russian packets and be pushed around by a lousy Judy for a chief engineer, I'd say no." The man washing his clothes: "Come off it, Andre, you'd be able to play billiards in your watch below and have running hot and cold water." Number One: "Sure, we all want better conditions. But the only way to better firemen's conditions is to abolish coal burning ships—and then we'd all be out of a job." Another voice: "It's a good idea for the second engineer anyhow." Another: "What is, Bolshevism?" The other: "No, to have a woman chief engineer."

They all laugh. Another fireman makes a friendly but incomprehensible gesture on his face, as if he were pretending to ride a bicycle on a pair of handlebar moustaches—then we remember the chief engineer we have seen, who has a pair of handlebar moustaches. The man plays a chord on his concertina, is not satisfied, though it is a beautiful chord. As from this man: "Well, I still say they're made in Saxony." A tattooed man reading a Bible on his bunk and smoking a pipe: "Now there's this place where it says every hair of our head is numbered." A bald fireman: "That counts me out for a start." Another: "Yeah, except for firemen. God counts all his children, but not stokers and firemen, he leaves that to the Board of Trade." An old sailor has wandered in from the other foc's'le. As from him: "Well, they say God looks after sea-faring men with a special grace, like. After fifty years at sea I'm beginning to think there must be some truth in that." Other voices: "Maybe on your side of the foc's'le, but there isn't a man over fifty years old on this side." "No,

"Tender Is the Night"

we don't live that long here." "But the old *Diderot*'s a good ship, and I've seen some—" "She's a good feeding ship." "She's a terrible firing ship!" "The only one as good I was ever on was a Greek, and we had ten different nationalities on board her coming back from Santos." A negro: "A Greek—I had a friend on the *Ariadne N. Pandelis*." "They're fine sailors and good hearted men." "But for me, I'm just

looking forward to getting me a job ashore this time home." "Just me and the wife—" "Yeah, it's too long at sea, but we'll soon be home now." The number one: "Well, we'll have to turn to—where are we, men?"	On the sound track *Frère Jacques* rises to a pitch, and now we hear it in English as the bells seem to chime in: Are you sleeping? Are you sleeping?
Eight bells begin to strike, and some of the men begin to go forward to watch. The camera now moves through, without coming up on deck, to the seamen's foc's'le on the other side of the poop: there is only the watch below asleep down there, and a deckboy and an ordinary seaman swinging ropes between them, as if to unravel them,	Brother John, Brother John, Morning bells are ringing! Morning bells are ringing! Ding dong ding! Ding dong ding!

but at the same time tying them into even more complicated and wonderful knots that seem as swiftly to be untied, the camera moves up through the port skylight to reveal McKisco and Dick there, as we hear two lines of dialogue in French which do not appear in English subtitles: the sailor: "Well, she's a good ship." The deck boy: "We've even got a couple of decent passengers."

Dick: (turning away from the skylight) McKisco, we have received a compliment. They said we were decent. That's what we get for eavesdropping.

McK: (as they walk forward again) Well, so we are, aren't we?

Dick: All I know is, to be so once seemed a worthy object.

McK:—and neither of us gets ten smackers.

Cut to the Commandant's stateroom, where McKisco and Dick have been invited to an apéritif, with the chief officer and the wireless operator. The wind howls and through the door forward the bridge is visible, with the quartermaster at the wheel and the officer on watch. As the cut is made, a little cat jumps off the Commandant's lap, and the chief officer is mixing drinks at a sideboard. He is a red-faced, jolly, slow, sleepy man.

Dick:—And her name, le petit chat, Commandant?

The Chief Officer: (chuckling and coming up with drinks) Grisette.

The Commandant: Yes, when I am on the Pacific run, I get a ton of sand for her at Le Havre. (Grisette runs away—we see that the skipper's stateroom, as well as his office, the main sanctum of which is inner, is well lined with books.) And this is my Chief Officer, Monsieur Sachs—if you have not met him socially before it is because when he is not on watch he is nearly always asleep.

They all laugh. The Chief Officer sits down and they drink. (The Frenchmen try sometimes, courteously, to speak English for the Americans, and the Americans courteously likewise French for the French, though it is thought too cumbersome to indicate always precisely where) Cut to later on in the conversation: all five are seated around the Commandant's table, except the Commandant himself, who is moving along his bookshelves, searching for a book. McKisco has the cat on his lap.

McK: (to the chief officer) No, they *weren't*. Someone else was talking about concertinas, and another about your French rugby football—

Dick: And the rest seemed to be talking about God.

The Com: (in the background, at his bookshelves, to himself) Buller, *Voyage du Cachalot*, Jack London, Pierre Loti, *Moby Dick*, oui, mais je cherche—(then, to Dick, but without turning round) That's nothing unusual. The men have exhausted talking about women and politics and food on the outward trip.

The Wireless Operator: (in broken English) Sure, homeward bound, with our sins to keep us company, is time to think about God again.

The C.O.: In another few days everyone will be talking about home.

The W.O.: (in French) My experience is, outward bound, it's one topic at a time.

The Com: (still at his bookshelves, to the wireless operator in French, without turning round) How many have been shipwrecked on board, Max-Pol?

The W.O.: Je ne sais pas ... Eh bien, vous, Commandant, moi, René ...

McK: (simultaneously) But I wondered how you manage to keep so cheerful, why the monotony doesn't sometimes get you down?

The Com: (simultaneously, returning, with several books) As it happens, four of our men: the bosun, steward, our number one firemen—we rescued ourselves from a sister ship nearly three years ago—adrift in an open boat. At Le Havre they were able to join the *Diderot* together. Since then we have had remarkably few changes in the crew, except among the junior seamen and trimmers. That is quite unusual, so we have some chance to become a family. That is no explanation, but it is something for so many in these positions to have known the worst.

Dick: You mean they knew what it was to be lost.

The Com: (laughing) Aaaah—they are a good crowd on board the *Diderot*.

Cut to a close shot of the engine as *Frère Jacques* rises again to a pitch.

Cut to the Commandant, who is talking to Dick about the books he has brought from his shelves: *Typhoon*, in French, *Lord Jim*, in English.

The Com:—No, here it is, in *Jim* (Dick examines the book interestedly at the page the Commandant is holding open for him) There may be something for your article even if you have read it . . . Conrad was a man who said nearly everything about the sea it seems, from our point of view, as officers on the bridge.

Cut to the bridge, the man at the wheel, the officer on duty, then back again, a little later in the conversation.

Dick: (with a glance at McKisco, because it reminds him of their first conversation, though he is addressing the Commandant) So I could say—could I?—that such a consciousness was like a good ship. But what you call a bad ship is like a sick mind, where the smallest thing—done more or less happily or effortlessly as, say, on the *Diderot*—becomes an effort.

The Com: But I can see some sense when you say the body is like a machine, and the soul—

Dick: (suddenly reflective) The soul—

The Com: (to McKisco) But the fact is, Monsieur McKisco, there are always more long faces on an outward voyage . . . Besides, it is not always so monotonous—

At this moment the chief engineer appears in the doorway, with half his handlebar moustache shaved off.

The Com: (sotto voce to Dick and McKisco) Don't laugh—let him speak first. He's been threatening to do it for months.

They all try to keep straight faces.

The Chief Engineer: (challengingly) Well! (glares round) Don't you see any difference—you, Messieurs—?

The Com: (keeping a straight face, to Dick and McKisco) Do you see any difference in my chief engineer? (he nods as if to say, please say yes, now. Everybody breaks down and roars with laughter.)

Fade out on their laughter, in on Dick and McKisco after the evening meal in the messroom. It is very much rougher. McKisco has just finished, but is still sitting down: Dick, standing by the notice board on which we read, as Dick reads aloud half of it in French:

—Chacun est prié d'économiser l'eau attendu que nous ne pourrons pas nous en approvisionner avant Marseilles ou Genoa. Au cas ou le gaspillage serait trop grand, nous serions obligés de rationner l'eau . . . Bord, le dix Juin, 1927 *S.S. Diderot*, le 2me Capitaine, etc.

Dick: (breaking off) My gosh, Albert, we're running out of water.

McK: That's a comfort. (he finishes his wine at a gulp, next moment has joined Dick at the notice board.) So what, they're going to ration the water—well, you haven't shot the albatross yet, have you?

Dick looks none too sure. As they turn to go out they see the steward this time pouring wine from a caraffe on to the tablecloth to stop the plates from sliding for the second engineer's dinner. The Americans look aghast.

Cut to the albatross, the shearwaters, following the ship, McKisco and Dick pacing the foredeck.

McK: Water, water, everywhere and—no, I see you haven't—there it is.

The sea with its eternally gliding birds is now a grey heaving mass rising above the ship.

Dick: Imagine this fellow Lindbergh—it's extraordinary to think of someone flying alone over all this.

McK: (who looks not exaggeratedly queasy) It's more extraordinary to think of anyone wanting to do anything else—

They laugh, the carpenter passes, they all exchange friendly and ironic bonjours.

Dick: (to McKisco) Feeling any better? Come along, the fresh air'll do you good.—I wouldn't like to interpret Lindbergh's action psychologically till I've thought it through further. But it was clearly something more for America than just an isolated heroic thing.

McK: Seems to me on a par with everything else cuckoo we do, only it happened to come off.

Dick: Not by a long sight . . . Sure, we'll make it look like that. But it was a pioneer action, you'll see it foreshadows the end of a period, in which America has been ridden entirely by her unconscious . . . The idea is, the sea, like the unconscious, is an enemy. Something you have continually to outwit—(the lamptrimmer passes them, carrying the anchor light) but upon which—look around you—as a sailor you're utterly dependent to get anywhere at all. (McKisco gets the point) Now these seamen, they're not satisfied—who is?—but every day in order to live at all, not merely to live peaceably as friends, or to endure the grinding monotony, but to exist in this dreadful wilderness, their ego has to win a victory every single day, every hour, wrest a little from the Id—their lives (a sudden shot of a blackened young fireman, up from the stokehold for a breath of air, the wind blowing his flimsies, gulping the wind, a sort of exultance in his demeanor, but wistfulness too, even tragedy, in contradistinction to the former optimism; very unlike the Hairy Ape, if muscularly strong, he appears a rather frail man, and we sense the unequalness of the struggle in the face of the howling elements) are a sort of cheerful but bitter and continual warfare against it.

McK: (as the stoker disappears) What in thunder is the Id?

Dick: (points to the grey, heaving Atlantic—suddenly the wind catches the spray from the crest of a wave and begins to blow it across the sea like rain) That, McKisco, is the Id—the unconscious itself—what Conrad called the irrational, and the watery jungle of those dark forces which Melville personified as Moby Dick.

Simultaneously there is a mighty burst of thunder and the gale rises, with huge waves, driving rain and a screaming wind: cut to a brief long shot of seamen with oilskins and souwesters battling against the driving rain and wind, stretching lifelines on the after deck, the terrific seas beyond and astern of them, snow-capped mountains of seas, taken from the top bridge deck looking toward the stern, as it sinks, sways, and ascends: the screen begins gradually to darken to night: cut to a shot of great fleece-lined gowns of sea furling off immensely to leeward, accompanied by a sound of wind rising to a pitch of wailing in the cordage so extreme it sounds almost false, like movie wind about a haunted house: the screen darkens to night in the clangorous alleyways and engine room entrances of the *Diderot*, with the sounds, partly coming up from the engine room, but in heterogeneous addition to that of the engine itself, like an exaggeration of the same thing; from the engine room itself now comes an insane noise of hammerings, inexplicable clankings as of chains, whistling, thumping, unearthly chimes—the noise is probably connected with repairs to the steering gear, ceases after a while, and is continually resumed throughout the following scene but the engine sounds through it all: cut to the men's cabin—the storm is wilder, through the closed porthole we see the sea smashing and battering against the glass; the same noises as before though slightly muted; Dick is lying half asleep on his bunk: McKisco, quite tight, is tying on his lifebelt, as the camera takes in the French Abandon Ship sign on the wall—A ce signal d'Abandon vous embarquerez dans le canot No. 1 Tribord, etc.

McK: (to himself, as if translating some of the instructions, but reciting this matter of factly) Your lifebelt is in the stateroom . . . Put it on as you would an ordinary jacket . . . your arms through the shoulder straps . . . (does so) Never wear the shoulder straps without the lifeboat . . . Pull the two ends of your life together . . . and tie the straps very securely. (does so, unties them, pours himself a drink, evidently from Dick's Mexican habañero bottle)

McK: Somebody told me the albatross was getting in the way of our light, Dick. It's sitting up there on the mast. You can see its tail feathers from the port side. The Captain's furious. I think you ought to shoot it.

Dick: (sleepily) It's an overstatement.

Cut to Dick, asleep, the racket as before: his watch points to midnight. McKisco asleep—*Frère Jacques* with the aid of the wind now seems sung by a hoarse Cossack choir, beneath which can be heard the other insane noises, etc.

A Voice: Heavy, heavy hangs over thy head! What shall the owner do to redeem it?

Dick wakes, takes a short drink, goes out into the alleyway, the operator's door is on the hook.

The W.O.: Entrez, entrez. No is sleeping? (he hands Dick some spare earphones, smiling) Musique.

As through Dick's earphone we hear the radio: This is Nassau, in the Bahamas: Kraft-Ebbing, funeral directors, each evening send soothing transcribed music to you . . . The beginning of *Smiles* is played on an organ.

Cut to Dick looking out to sea from an outer engine room alleyway to leeward: beyond the mountainous waves the moving lights of another freighter passing in the opposite direction may be seen momentarily as lights signal from her bridge.

Cut to the engine room galleries: here the noise of the engine is louder than the storm, but the sound as of hammering almost drowns out the engine, while the ship is rolling so badly it is hard to take hold of the emery-papered rails. Dick leans on a rail and looks down from a place where he can see the stokehold: firemen, leaning on slicebars, every time they rake out the ashes a trimmer throws a bucket of water on the ashes and a cloud of steam goes up with a hiss: at this moment a trimmer, who has either had to do something above decks, or is late on watch, begins to slide down one of the engine room ladders, not immediately above the stokehold, at a great pace: the ship lurches, he misses his footing, recovers himself, trips, yells, and falls about half a flight on his back. Hearing his cry an engineer and a trimmer come to help and start to pick him up.

Dick: (starting down the ladder) Arrêtez-vous, Messieurs! Ne le remuez pas! Je suis médecin!

Cut down to confused shots of machinery, clouds of steam, the recumbent trimmer, as Dick approaches him. Taking off his coat, which one of the others takes, he stoops to the trimmer.

An Engineer: (approaching) Qu'est-ce que c'est . . . Ah, it is you, Doctor.

Dick: Your man's had a bad fall, Monsieur Lapierre. He shouldn't be moved without a hard board of some sort—he may have injured his back.

The Trimmer: (as orders are given, groaning) Merci . . .

Cut to the following day, Dick and McKisco at the rail: we see a strange sea: no wind, but with long, deep, terrifying grey swells.

Dick: (but gazing at the sea with a sort of supplication) My gosh, the wind's gone, it should be calm, but the sea looks worse than ever.

The Commandant: (passing, stops, points) It is what we call La Mer Mort, Messieurs. A sea that comes following a day of high wind, when the wind has dropped, leaving the dead swell of the day before.

Dick: You mean these waves are the result of a storm, hundreds of miles away, that has long been over?

McK: (almost simultaneously) Then what we're looking at here is not a stormy sea, but the result of a stormy sea.

The Com: (smiling) You could put it like that.

McK: (interrupting Dick, who was about to speak) It seems a heck of an idea to have to go through a storm like that only to find it waiting for you at the other end!

The camera takes in the dead swell. Cut to the ship's bell on the bridge: it comes toward us on the screen and is struck by hand, as it has done recurrently. Cut to the messroom: more position reports are being placed on the notice board.

Cut to Dick and McKisco at the port side in day time. Still a grey swell, but much less and little wind. A few sea gulls, the first shore birds in a long while.

McK: (looking through binoculars) I swear it's land . . . Take a look, Dick. (as Dick takes the binoculars, the 4th mate passes and McKisco addresses him) Isn't that land? What land is it?

The 4th Mate: (passing, smiling) Aah, Messieurs . . . no whiskey, no interesting.

The Commandant: (coming up, as Dick looks through the binoculars) Not yet. We are a long way from home still . . . Permettez-moi un moment, Monsieur. (takes the binoculars from Dick) There's no grass on that island—they say that is where the goats wear green spectacles to eat the morning newspapers . . . How is our patient today?

Dick: He should be kept off duty a few days more, Commandant. I feared he had an injury to the back, but he seems to have been lucky.

The Com: I must thank you again, Doctor. (he shakes hands, turning to go, turns back) You mentioned you might like to make a voyage as a doctor on a cargo ship . . . One of my oldest friends is a Greek Commandant—we spoke his ship, the *Aristotelis*, that night of the bad storm, outward bound from Pireaus—Paulos and I were wrecked together once, off Cape Horn, in a Finnish threemaster—

Cut to a shot of the Rock of Gibraltar passing.

Cut to the messroom. A nautical map of the Mediterranean has replaced that of the Atlantic. Hands point to Marseilles, Antibes, Nice—and we gather that the ship is keeping an offing somewhere off the coast of France not far from Marseilles.

Cut to Dick asleep in a deck chair on deck. It is a calm, sunlit day. He has a table before him, with a typewriter. On the table are two books: *Moby Dick*, *Lord Jim* in French, and a French dictionary. In the typewriter, or beside it, we see the title of his projected article: The Conception of the Id in Some pre-and-post-Freudian Writers of the Sea. 1. Herman Melville. 2. Joseph Conrad. In the typewriter we read as much of the following as may be desired or necessary.

—Joseph Conrad, if he may be called a post-Freudian writer, probably knew less of psychology than Melville, who it has been recently pointed out, may have been acquainted with some of the conclusions of Janet. But to hear Joseph Conrad talk one would suppose that he had served his time at the neuropathological institute in Zurich rather than as an apprentice upon sailing vessels. In *Lord Jim* we find the following:

"There was a villainy of circumstance that cut these men off more completely from mankind, whose ideal of conduct had never undergone the trial of a fiendish and appalling joke . . ."

On the sound track the words of *Frère Jacques* begin to emerge in time with the engine as a song.

And again:

"Trust a boat on the high seas to bring out the irrational that lurks at the bottom of every thought, sensation, emotion . . . It was all threats, a terribly effective feint, a sham from beginning to end, planned by the tremendous disdain of the Dark Powers whose real terrors, always on the verge of

"Tender Is the Night"

triumph, are perpetually foiled by the steadfastness of men..."

Through the following Dick is seen asleep in his deck chair in one corner of the screen: he is dreaming: now other, inhabited deck chairs materialize, and Nicole and Dick are seen walking round the deck, the children playing near them: but there is an integrity about the family.	Now we hear *Frère Jacques* as sung by the children: Frère Jacques Frère Jacques Dormez-vous Dormez-vous

Nicole's Voice: Life is fun with Dick—the people in the deck chairs look at us, and a woman is trying to hear what we are saying... This is the blowy corner, and each time we turn it I slant forward against the wind and pull my coat together without losing step with Dick...

While Nicole's voice is saying this we see Dick and Nicole walking, talking and smiling together, we see	Then *Frère Jacques* is sung by the four of them together.

the people in deck chairs looking at them and a woman trying to hear what they are saying, but we don't hear either. They reach the blowy corner and we see, as Nicole turns it, she slants forward against the wind and pulls her coat together without losing step with Dick, but at this point the picture freezes into a static photograph: it is an essence of caught windblown happiness, to which one theme of the music rises.

Nicole's Voice: (as the picture comes to life again) Dick is tired of singing, so go on alone, Dick; you will walk differently alone, dear, through a thicker atmosphere, forcing your way through the shadows of chairs, through the dropping smoke of funnels, you will feel your own reflection sliding along the eyes of those who look at you...

We see Dick, holding his hat against the wind, walking off alone by the funnel.

Nicole's Voice: (we do not see Nicole) Then everything suddenly grew dark again. (We see the sea grow stormy and dark, and hear the menace of the ship's engine) It was because he was afraid it might that he took me travelling... (it grows darker and darker and the engine and storm louder) When I get well, I want to be a fine person, like you, Dick. I would study medicine except it's too late... We must spend my money and have a house, a home...

The scene darkens, momentarily to a suggestion of galleries,	*Frère Jacques* ceases to be a song and

engine room, and the night journey across the sea. Then it comes back to the calm sunny day and becomes the monotonous voice of the engine again.
we see McKisco reading over Dick's shoulder as Dick wakes with an exclamation of disgust.

McK: That's me, old man . . . whose ideal of conduct had never undergone the trial of a fiendish and appalling joke.

Dick: (half shaking himself, rising, as he speaks) Doctors advise sea voyages, Albert, because of a priori ideas on the subject. I prescribed it for myself. Of all the traditional fallacies of medicine this is the worst. If you want to forget, the memory, on the contrary, has all this boundless space (indicating the sea) to fill with memories. To kill time—but here time itself becomes a menace, in itself a nightmare. (the ship's bell sounds) You tell yourself you won't drink—but you take care to fill the cabin with bottles of hooch just the same, so you can enjoy telling yourself the same story, under more comfortable circumstances.

Cut to the upper bridge with the wheelhouse. Everyone there, Dick, McKisco, the Commandant, some of the officers and engineers, (the chief is now clean shaven) are standing to port, looking through binoculars or telescopes at France, the coast of which is clearly in view. On the deck below the crew are looking too, without binoculars. In the background, ferocious and tremendous, the white Alps. We hear the engine as *Frère Jacques* pounding on loudly, and the feeling is that everyone is related to one another through the great power of nostalgia. The engine room telegraph rings from time to time since closer inshore they are picking their way fairly carefully. It is about 11 A.M.

The Com: (to Dick) This is one of the hardest things for all sailors—to have home in sight and have to go sailing past it. Have you found Antibes, Monsieur? They spoke to us from Eden Point just now.

Dick: (looking intently through his binoculars) Mmm . . . Ah! Now I have it!

Through Dick's binoculars, on the screen, we see the coast and the Bay of Angels, but are mainly aware of the savage pinnacles of the white Alps beyond which, we can imagine, in Switzerland, is Nicole.

The Com: (looking through his telescope) Aaaah! Here is Antibes—the tower at the top, like battlements—Zut! I don't remember such a beach with so many people.—Where is your house, Doctor Diver?

Dick: (standing beside the Commandant and pointing) To the left and up—you come to a precipice, and it's above that—

The Com: Wait—yes, I have a house, a villa, very low with walls, a little summer house in the garden, precipice underneath . . . Ah, très joli, très joli . . .

"Tender Is the Night"

Dick: C'est ça.

The Com: Someone is cutting your grass, I think. Take this telescope, Doctor, it is very powerful. (handing the telescope to Dick) But your wife, you say, she is not at home?

Dick: (looking through the telescope) No, she's in Switzerland. Through the telescope we see the Villa Diana: the house, with its walls and precipice. Then, abruptly, Dick's workhouse at the bottom of the garden: as through Dick's mind (but still through the telescope at first) we see Dick himself on the porch looking out to sea through his own telescope, (as in the early Villa Diana sequence) looking, as it were, at himself. Cut to the actual scene of Dick standing on his porch looking through his telescope: we see Nicole standing at the parapet, Barban behind him in the garden, and, as we hear the distant ghostly chords of *In a Mist*, in the background, Abe, playing the piano.

Cut to the bridge of the *Diderot*. Dick puts the telescope down, leaning on the rail. Beside him we see McKisco who is trying to focus Juan les Pins, a little forward of Antibes. As through his binoculars we see first some suggestion of more hotels, the casino nearly completed, then a few golfers playing on the golf course: they dissolve into the configuration of the duel scene, at dawn, Barban with his second, McKisco with Abe, the doctor, and Rosemary. McKisco and Barban raise their pistols and fire and the next instant McKisco sees himself run away into the bushes where he is sick.

Cut to McKisco on the bridge. He puts down his binoculars, slowly, looking down, but as if inward, even feeling slightly sick again, for a moment.

Beside him, the Commandant has another telescope.

The Com: (focussing) It's strange to think this coast was once all Greek—And Antibes now, it was a Greek city too, two thousand years ago.

Dick: (smiling wryly, to the Commandant) They'd forgotten all about it in Antibes, being Greek, until I arrived and had to remind them. It was peaceful then, but after that the merchants came—and they still seem to be coming—

Dick looks through his strong telescope again. Through Dick's telescope we see Gausse's and the beach, with too many people on it. Then we move back to the Villa Diana where, as through Dick's mind, we see the children playing in the	On the sound track: Frère Jacques Frère Jacques Ding dang dong Ding dang dong Beaten to death Beaten to death (changes to, but with

garden, Nicole standing at the parapet, looking down at the sea below. Then Dick's house comes back to reality. The man with the scythe is standing in the garden facing us. Suddenly he begins to come closer to us on the screen. He sweeps his scythe.	the same underlying rhythm and for a moment we hear the children's voices) Au claire de la lune Mon ami Pierrot Prêtez moi ta plume Pour écrire un mot. Beaten to death! Beaten to death! Poor Nicole! Poor Nicole! Ding dang dong! Ding dang dong!

Cut—his scythe seems to execute the cut—to Dick and McKisco on deck that night: the moon has risen, and the Alps are visible. Both men are leaning on the rail smoking: Dick seems profoundly gloomy and reflective, McKisco in a sympathetic mood.

Cut to the engine room galleries, the engine; *Frère Jacques* becomes slower and slower, then stops with a grinding down of the engines. Dissolve from the still engines to a shot of a harbour, at dawn, with factory lights blazing, huge chimneys already smoking, but with the gantries standing deathly still like skeletal giraffes against the dawn sky, beneath which all of the lights of any great seaport city seem to be on, twinkling, moving, active. Cut to the motionless gantries: slowly they begin to move—they are 300 foot high geometrical filagree meccano giraffes moving now automatically, continually, with slow majestic motion—when they are at rest, as sirens faintly mourn, they seem pointing at every angle against the early summer sky. Cut to a view of the harbour from the *Diderot* lying out at anchor—it is a sparkling early summer morning and this time we see Vesuvius and recognize the harbour at Naples.

Dick, at the gangway head, evidently has just received a letter—he looks gloomy (it is from Baby Warren and isn't the one he wanted). A launch below, tossing at the gangway's foot. McKisco comes up, all dressed to go ashore.

Dick: I've got to try and catch my sister-in-law in Rome.

McK: (in a great hurry) I've just had a message from Violet. I'm not coming ashore on this launch after all—she's meeting me later. Look, I've got to hurry and find that purser. Well, with luck we'll be seeing you at Antibes this year. So long, old boy.

Dick: (as the Commandant comes along at this moment) I'll see you at Antipolis.

McKisco hurries off.

The Com: Ah, Doctor—here is the letter to Commandant Aidono-paulos, should you see him, give him all my—

Cut to Dick and the Commandant shaking hands heartily and patting each other on the back. The noise of the winches now drowns out what they say.

Cut to Dick going down the gangway, to the tossing launch below: he glances back: some sailors and firemen in berets on the poop wave happily and cheerfully to him: among them may be seen the injured fireman, with a shirt open down to his waist, so we see his ribs are taped—he lifts his injured arm, makes it wave harder than the rest. Dick waves back, glad in his soul for a moment, but as he goes down the gangway his expression changes. Cut to the launch going away, merging instantly into the moving gantries. (Lowry, pp. 235–342)

30

In Rome, Dick drinks heavily and waits for news from the clinic. Each letter that arrives from Zurich tells him that Nicole is improving, but that he should wait a little longer before seeing her.

At his hotel he suddenly runs into Rosemary, who now looks more poised, more sure of herself than before. In Rome to make a movie, Rosemary cannot help but notice that Dick has deteriorated though she is still attracted to him and invites him to come up to her room later.

The meeting in Rosemary's room does not go well. They kiss but are continuously interrupted by knocks at the door and phone calls for Rosemary. They do not get along as they once did, and Rosemary, crying, wishes that they had never run into each other, that she had been left with only good memories. Dick, claiming he no longer seems capable of bringing happiness to anyone, leaves.

Later, Dick dines with Baby Warren in one of Rome's fashionable restaurants surrounded by posters of Mussolini. In one poster, "one of the rare full length ones, Mussolini looks about six feet high and wears a tender compassionate expression, as if he were Coriolanus about to meet his mother"; in another, "Mussolini, looking about 5 feet high [. . . is] pitching hay with a hayfork" (Lowry, p. 348). (See Lowry, pp. 342–49 and Fitzgerald, 2, xix–xxi.)

Lowry's note follows.

Note: it is suggested that a more original attitude be preserved toward Mussolini insofar as he tangentially manifests himself, than is customary or current which, as conquerors, would seem to me more chivalrous, especially considering his hideous death, this, not least to spare Italians' hidden feelings, but because it would be more true. It would be more in keeping with one's attitude at the *period*, however wrong headed, if one saw him as a kind of monstrous and inimical anachronism, nonetheless to be grudgingly and ironically half respected in a distasteful manner, rather than an obvious tyrannical dictator, with all the modern and banal implications of that. With this in mind a police lieutenant in a later scene should appear, though probably a complete bruto, a fairly reasonable fellow: while the other side will be seen to be charitably and forcefully presented. The identity between psychoanalyst seen as dictator, or dictator seen as hypnotist, can also with obscure profit be borne in mind. (Lowry, p. 349)

31

Baby tells Dick that what Nicole needs is a change of scenery—England, she suggests, much to Dick's somewhat bitter amusement. She says that she is grateful for all he has done for Nicole, but that if he thinks she might be happier with someone else, something could certainly be arranged. Baby seems actually surprised when Dick tells her that he loves Nicole; in anguish during the conversation, Dick laughs at Baby's naive ignorance, but there is a sad strain in his laughter. For Dick, the scene is repeatedly interrupted by his imagining scenes from a very proper cricket match in which the umpire calls him "Out!" when he "suicidally" hits his wicket; "all this," says Lowry, "being as explosive and slashing as one of von Stroheim's late French brainstorms"[78] (Lowry, p. 353). After leaving Baby, Dick walks the streets of Rome alone and ends up in a cabaret. (See Lowry, pp. 349–53 and Fitzgerald, 2, xxi–xxiii.)

Cut to Dick sitting at a table, a bottle of Spumante before him. He eyes with disfavour the steps of the dancers as the camera follows these with just the feet of the dancers visible for a moment. The camera dissolves into an ashtray on the table overflowing with stubs à la Abe as the tango stops, becomes the confusion of tuning instruments. Instantly the negro orchestra starts to play *Whispering*. Quite apart from Dick's identity with Abe, so established again, we feel that *Whispering* makes him think of Abe and Nicole at that time in the Café Chagrin, when Rosemary had gone out to phone, Abe was talking to the orchestra, and Nicole had spoken of Dick's irresistible charm. Cut into a sudden swift flashback of this scene in the Café Chagrin fading into the end of *Whispering* in this Italian cabaret, and the subsequent applause, growing louder. Dick rises and threads his way through the applauding dancers to speak to the orchestra leader. We see that Dick is so confused and disturbed by this memory that he appears drunker and more offensive than he intends to be: which is not at all.

Dick: (to the orchestra leader) Do you speak English?

The Negro: Yes, indeed. I'm from the Bahamas.

Dick: Well, in that case, could you use your English to stop your outfit playing this American song again.

The Negro: What?

Dick: I said—(the negro smilingly inclines his ear) Please don't play *Whispering* again. I have my personal . . .

The Negro: What? (throws away a remark to the effect it is hard to hear in all this noise and applause)

Dick: (as at this moment a horn is thrust under his nose) See—I'll give you fifty lira to sit down and not play *Whispering*!

He gives the orchestra leader fifty lira, who smiles his thanks absently, puts the bill preoccupiedly into the horn, and at the same time, as the applause is now ebbing, signals to his boys to start again, who thereupon do so with gusto. They play *Whispering*. People dance. (Lowry, pp. 353-55)

32

Dick insults almost everyone to whom he speaks, from the orchestra leader to a young woman with whom he dances and who he keeps imagining is Nicole. He leaves the cabaret, decides to catch a taxi, and promptly gets into an argument with the driver over the fare. The argument grows progressively uglier and more violent until it involves other drivers as well as various policemen, who finally take Dick to the police station. At the station a very drunk Dick is told to pay the driver the requested fare, whereupon he walks up to a smirking man standing by (whom he does not suspect is a policeman) and strikes him in the face. At once Dick is attacked from all sides and beaten severely: "We feel [. . .] as if it were our face the blows are raining on" (Lowry, p. 360). *Finally, Dick is thrown into a cell: "Dissolve to Dick, seen through prison bars, in the early light of dawn, sleeping peacefully on the prison floor. On the sound track we hear a snatch of the Whiffenpoof song briefly. The camera's point of view seems to be that of someone peeping into the cell, possibly a carabinieri. [. . .] Dissolve into the same scene from Dick's point of view some hours later. This time someone has covered Dick with a blanket and his own overcoat and he is pillowed on his sodden dress jacket"* (Lowry, pp. 361–62).

Baby, with an American embassy official in tow, rescues Dick the next morning. As Dick and Baby leave the station, a crowd of people gathered outside starts jeering loudly; they have mistaken Dick for the murderer of a fifteen-year-old girl. Dick asks Baby to say nothing of the incident to Nicole because she would not, he says, be strong enough to handle it. (See Lowry, pp. 355–67 and Fitzgerald, 2, xxi–xxiii.)

As the booing continues, we cut (in a peculiar fashion, by a sliding downward movement, so that we obtain the physical feeling that this scene is taking place on a lower level) to Dick in a totally deserted bar. Dick is seen facing us, as from the barman's standpoint. He looks terrible: he is still in his torn and filthy evening clothes, and his eye is bandaged. From outside the booing still continues, or seems to within Dick's mind. The barman places a steaming grog on the counter. Dick glances rather furtively at the door, once or twice. He is shivering. He sneezes.

The Barman: Ponce . . . Grog. Si, signor.

Cut, reversing the standpoint to Dick's. We see the barman smiling sympathetically and tactfully, the bar, a mirror, and above it one of those familiar pictures, ill painted but melodramatically impressive, of a shipwreck at sea: sailors trying to swim away from the ship, drowning men, people in panic, all dim and confused, but with lightning in the sky and a tremendous sense of storm-torn ocean.

The Barman: You Americano? (Dick nods) You have-a the accident?

Dick: (who has made two unsuccessful attempts to pick up his drink, takes a tip from the picture, makes a swimming motion, so far as he can with his injured hands) Nagio, nel Tiber.

Cut to a shot in the mirror of Dick's face, below the shipwreck, but still keeping in one of the drowning struggling men at the bottom of the picture at the top of the screen. First Dick and ourselves take in his own awesome appearance, then we see another figure who might be a plain clothes detective coming through the open door into the bar, as nonchalantly as if he were George Raft in *Scarface*.[79] He vaguely resembles the detective Dick has hit. He sits down in a corner and orders nothing, just apparently watches. Nor does the barman take any notice of him.

Cut now to the detective's standpoint, though a little behind him so we see the back of his head and shoulders, immobile and implacable. The booing ceases, hinting its continuation had been in part subjective, though for that matter, in one way, so may be the detective. It is replaced by tolling bells. From this angle we now see Dick trying to pick up his grog again with one hand. He tries it then with both hands, gets it off the counter but nearly spills it.

Cut back to Dick who now sees the man in the mirror looking at him. Suddenly imaginary handcuffs materialize around his wrists. The handcuffs melt away. The sympathetic barman helps Dick, lifting his drink to Dick's lips.

Dick: (drinks gratefully) Grazia . . . Otro, per favore . . . Make it a straight rum.

The glass is filled with rum. This time Dick manages the rum with both hands, spilling half of it, pays and departs hastily, with a glance at the detective, whom the camera follows rising from his seat and going to the bar and craftily conferring with the barman, both of whom take covert and interested looks in Dick's direction, while above we see the shipwreck with the drowning men, with Dick below, departing in the mirror.

Dissolve to Dick, passing in a deserted cobbled street, a poster of Mussolini. He hisses at it, painful though the effort undoubtedly must be. The bells continue through all the following sections intermittently.

Dissolve to the desk of the Quirinal—Dick getting his mail. He has bathed and shaved and is in clean clothes, but looks ghastly still, though a good deal better. In spite of his bandaged face, and his arm in a sling, he still contrives not to look ridiculous. At the desk he opens one envelope, looks at it obliquely, and we see it is not the one he is waiting for, that he is disappointed, but at the same time he is gravely affected by it. Dick looks round, sees the detective sitting in the lobby, then seems to be looking for some place to read his letter alone; he peeps into the bar but Rosemary and one of her Roman boy friends are in there and he turns away hastily.

Dissolve to Dick in the same café as before facing the picture of the shipwreck, and looking at the letter of which first we see the signature: Frederich Dohmler. He drinks a grappa, orders another. Two workmen go out. The barman is not there, and a woman sits knitting behind the bar. Seen in the mirror, in the street, lovers pass, all happy, the women all Beatrices, with the touching anguishing beauty of Italian women. In the mirror also, seen seated in the corner, is the detective. Dick seems to have trouble reading his letter without recourse to alcoholic refreshment. Now we see on the screen a few words of it: in German but changing to English.

. . . Nonetheless, everything now indicates a conditional recovery in the near future—

Dick lifts his head and smiles wanly. We see into the mirror and see the watching figure of the detective. Now, from behind him, a bearded figure detaches itself from the shadows and comes over to the bar. The bearded figure is Dohmler, who stands behind Dick and puts his hand on Dick's shoulder. Bells toll from time to time and the lovers go past in the mirror as he speaks.

Dohmler: (in English) But do not think that I do not appreciate the agonizing nature of the decision that faces you, when that happens. (We can see the letter, lying on the bar, during all this speech) At the moment it would help us if you would face up to a final period of silence from us. When this silence is broken it will be by Nicole herself. Again I do not need to tell you that it is then that the hardest decision of all comes. You have chosen to make her your wife, and were you not the man I feel you to be I would not speak to you as I do—

Dick buries his face in his hands. Dohmler vanishes. Above we see the shipwreck.

Dissolve to Dick walking down a flight of steps. (He is coming down from Trinite del Monte to the Piazza d'Espagna) Church bells from Trinite del Monte toll spasmodically as he approaches a house near the bottom, by a flower stall, upon which is a notice, in Italian and English, the two versions linked by the drawing of a lyre.[80]

> L'inglese poeta Giovanni Keats mente maravigliosa quanto precoce mori in questa case li 24 Febraio 1821 ventesimoses dell'eta sua.

Then the lyre, beneath which is written:

> The young English poet, John Keats, died in this house on the 24th of February, 1821. aged 26.

As Dick goes down the steps toward the house he brings out his letter again to read it, looks behind him, sees that the detective is still following him.

As Dick enters the house, passing by the flower stall, we hear a clear sombre voice out of nowhere, quietly:

Tender is the Night . . .[81]

Dissolve to Dick within Keats' house; it is gloomy inside, and all we can make out are walls of books. In one room we see Keats' gentle face in a portrait; a guide is showing round two people, speaking in lowered tones; Dick looks at the books, at Keats' portrait, catches a few words by the guide: outside the bells faintly, dolorously, toll.

The Guide: (in good English but with an Italian accent as the two tourists are seen gazing into a glass case) . . . And here is the tragic letter from Severn, begun just before the poet's death. Permit me to read it, for it is a little hard to make out the writing. (reads) Keats has changed somewhat for the worse—at least his mind has, much, but the fatal prospect hangs before his mind yet, and turns everything into despair and wretchedness.

Dick looks up at the picture of Keats' face, he crosses to a small room away from the tourists.

The Guide: (his words following Dick) . . . for his knowledge of internal anatomy and medicine enables him to judge of any change accurately and adds largely to his torture—(the guide interpolates)—as you know, Keats was trained as a doctor of medicine, though he never practised.

Meantime Dick has sat down at a table in the anteroom and has brought out his letter from Dohmler again, of which we have seen a few more words as the last words were spoken by the guide. We now see that Dohmler seems to be sitting opposite Dick, and Dick half reads, half listens to the guide, and also seems to be listening to what this imaginary Dohmler is saying.

Dohmler: But of the terrible unwisdom of that choice, taken in defiance of all professional ethics and reason, you must be prepared to bear the full brunt. You know I must speak frankly to you, Dick. For this very fact of your marriage, at the period of recovery, emerges again as the most important factor. It is now a moral factor; but the psychological one, the turning point, remains the same. But even if you are married in the sight of God, and this whole thing approached through the religious sphere, I must point out that there are such things as momentous causes. I must say that this does not altogether rule out the possibility that a miracle may occur. But alas, I cannot give you much hope that it will be the kind of miracle that were I merely your friend, without the knowledge we both possess, we would both pray for—

Dohmler turns into an old gentleman who has been saying something about Severn's portrait of Keats.

A quiet voice, as from Keats himself, from the portrait, an observation, compassionate and wry at the same time:

Tender is the Night . . .

The Guide: (reading from the letter) And were he to recover he would not write another line—and this is another load . . . But of their high hopes of him, his certain success, his experience, he will not hear another word . . . then the want of some kind of hope (Dick gazes up at the portrait of Keats again) to feed his imagination . . .

As from the portrait of Keats, in Abe's voice (though the portrait does not, of course, move its lips):

Where youth grows pale and spectre thin and dies . . .

Dick gets up abruptly and goes into the other room; as he does so, the guide has gone with his tourists to another case.

The Guide: Many people are surprised to find some relics of the poet Shelley here, but as you know, Shelley lived here in Italy, and also died here, drowned, when his boat was wrecked off the coast near Pisa in the Mediterranean . . . To us, Shelley seems more of an adventurer . . .

Baby's Voice: (in a whisper) I mean, sane, well balanced English people . . . Mad Anthony Wayne—

The Guide: Here, in this case, are some remnants of aromatic gums used by his friend Trelawny while cremating his drowned body—

As he says this the screen becomes suddenly fluid, we see a strong sea and wreckage, much as in the picture in the bar, part of which is half suggested, as if the bottom section of the picture had come to life, with someone making efforts to save himself, which again almost has time to remind us of the moment we saw of *Mare Nostrum* in New York, superimposed upon the guide talking; the screen clears again and we see Dick listening, then turning again to the portrait of Keats.

As from Keats' portrait, ironically, but deeply serious:

Tender is the Night . . .

Cut to Dick going down the stairs: the detective is waiting for him half way down, at the turn, and as Dick descends the stairs, follows him while the screen darkens.

The Voice: (continuing) But here there is no light . . . Save what from heaven—

Cut with a yell of music to a tremendous maniacal shot of moonlight over Rome with the full moon dominant and riding high, merging into a shot of the night sky with which the picture opened. The sky brightens, becomes morning, Dick is still walking.

Cut to the bar with the pictured shipwreck with Dick seated as before, facing the shipwreck, the struggling, drowning men: he is drinking a grappa. Dick looks a bit better so far as his beating up was concerned but still wears an eyeshade, his arm in a sling. He looks in the mirror and we see the detective in the same corner as before. Suddenly, in exactly the same manner that Dohmler had materialized from the shadows behind him, we now see another figure so materialize; this figure has a bandage round his head, though not over his eye: it is Barban, seen as in the funicular sequence, and he approaches and stands beside Dick.

Barban: How can I tell? I'm not the Sacred Penitentiary.

Dick: (in a hallucinatory dissociated voice that does not disturb the barman) And if you were?

Barban: Sacrifice . . .

The bells peal out from St. Peter's.

Cut to the desk of the Quirinal.

Dick: C'e posta per me?

The man behind the desk shakes his head.

Dohmler's Voice: When this silence is broken—sooner or later—it will be by Nicole herself—

Behind Dick the detective comes in and takes his place as before.

Dick: (noticing the detective, now in a lowered tone) La prego far proseguire la mia posta al mio nuovo indirizzo—Is that right?—Yes, Pisa.

Dissolve into the word PISA coming up to us, as a sign upon the station. Through it we see the leaning Tower of Pisa, then another hotel desk, with just Dick's face.

Dick: (anxiously) C'e una lettera al mio nome, Dottore Diver?

The Man Behind the Desk: No, signor.

Dohmler's Voice: At the moment it would help us if you would face up to a final period of silence from us. When this silence is broken—sooner or later—it will be by Nicole herself. Again I do not need to tell you that it is then that the hardest decision of all comes.

Dick's face collapses in despair.

Cut to Dick in a crowded bar. He drinks. Through the window outside a procession of mourners pass. Dissolve to Dick, half tight, approaching the leaning Tower of Pisa, the camera keeping behind Dick as before. Dick stops, regarding the leaning tower from a little distance. Dick too leans against a lamp-post—or a post, the Tower of Pisa being in a field—and looks at the tower. From rather further behind than usual Dick seems to be leaning the same way as the tower. Dick evidently gets the same idea for we now see him leaning on the other side of the post in the contrary direction, as if in rebellion. Cut to Dick in a bar drinking. The word FIRENZE appears, as a sign upon a station, superimposed in the bar, and the bar turns to the desk of another hotel with Dick again inquiring:

Dick: C'e posta per me?

The Voice: No, signor.

Dick shakes his head sadly.

Cut into exactly the same scene repeating itself.

Dick: C'e posta per me?

The Voice: No, signor.

Cut to Dick, walking alone down a steep stony street, then back to the same scene yet again.

Dick: C'e posta per me? Dottore Diver.

The Voice: No, signor.

Dick: Grazia. (He turns away)

Dohmler's Voice: When this silence is broken—sooner or later—it will be by Nicole herself—

Dissolve to Dick entering a bar. He now has no eyeshade, just the remains of a shiner, and his arm is no longer in a sling. The barman pours him a grappa: he evidently has a bad hangover but he manages the drink all right.

Dick: Otro, per favore.

The barman silently obliges, withdraws, while Dick sinks his second at the same time silently raising his head to a picture over the bar, not of Mussolini, but in fact of Dante, looking particularly gloomy.

Dick: (addressing Dante) Hullo, old fellow, where do we go from here?

Cut to a close up of a Hieronymus Bosch in a museum: hideous demons, bears being hung, visions of hell-fire, flaming buildings, corpses drifting down a river, etc., all with a detailed landscape in the background. The camera focuses upon a particularly malevolent demon, and Dick is revealed looking at it quizzically, and ourselves with him, over his shoulder.

Dick: (raising his hat) Good morning. Is Doctor Diver in?

The Demon: (encouragingly) Yes, come in and take a seat.

Cut to Dick at the hotel desk again with a sign Firenze near, and a picture of Mussolini.

Dick: C'e posta per me?

The Voice: No, signor.

Dick shakes his head despairingly.

Dohmler's Voice: When this silence is broken—sooner or later—it will be by Nicole herself . . . But of the terrible unwisdom of that choice, taken in defiance of all professional ethics and reason, you must be prepared to bear the full brunt . . .

Cut to Dick in a bar, looking through the shuttered window through which light shines in such a manner that all the people passing in the street outside appear to be wearing prison clothes.

Cut to Dick, seen from behind, almost running down a long, long empty hill. He stops, staggers, drinks from a bottle. As he does so, a horrible little voice speaks in his ear:

The Voice: But you see, there is such a place as hell. Let no one deceive you with vain words. What men do not like they try hard not to believe. There is such a place as hell. I know, because I run it.

Dick flees down the hill.

At the end of the street, coming toward us, with a great burst of music, as a sign on a station platform is the word WIEN. The film now begins to slide downward on the screen, giving the effect almost that we are being carried down in an elevator: the word WIEN slides down to FRANKFORT, and Frankfort slides down to KOLN, Köln slides down to RHEINISCHER HOF and Rheinischer Hof to WEINLUST, these two having been simply the signs across the front of bars inside which Dick can be seen drinking alone as if one were looking in from the sidewalk. WEINLUST becomes simply BAR, and Bar slides down into RESTAURANT KLIPSTRAAT—STEP INTO ICE COLD BEER, this slides down into BAR again, with Dick in the doorway, with in the foreground a sign warning of danger of death from electricity, flanked with two scrawled flashes of lightning:

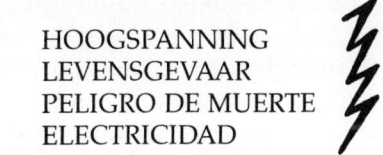

HOOGSPANNING
LEVENSGEVAAR
PELIGRO DE MUERTE
ELECTRICIDAD

We do not however, cease to be carried down, as it were, upon this elevator, the foregoing becomes PARIS, Paris slides down to BUFFET, Buffet slides down to BUVETTE, Buvette to CAFE, after which the screen becomes a solid mass of bistro fronts, into which we see, with Dick taking up an ever more remote position inside, as the cafés become steadily shabbier and shabbier and smaller and smaller: once this downward moving façade moves briefly in the reverse direction, upwards, to take in the words on CAFE DES DEUX MAGOTS, but immediately it starts down faster than ever, moves once upward again momentarily to CAFE CHAGRIN, then the façades slide down in a culminating diminishing rush which dissolves into Dick unshaven, shaking and looking like the wrath of God, standing in a small, sordid hotel bedroom at night, by the wash stand, with a glass of water in one hand, and a pill of some sort which he has just shaken out of a phial, in the other. His suitcase, evidently mostly unpacked, stands near, his brief case has still survived but is on the floor; so has the picture of Nicole and the children, it looks at him from on top of the suitcase. Near him on the wash stand is a Pernod bottle, nearly empty. He decides not to take the pill, and replaces it in the phial. Then he decides the phial—probably containing barbituates of some sort—was not such a good idea and throws it out of the window, down into a long, dark alley of stone steps leading down between houses. Dick throws the bottle after it; he seems to regret his rash action and we dissolve to his going down the gloomy stone steps looking for the phial in vain. Then, overcome with weariness and despair, he sits on the steps and buries his face in his hands.

We are behind Dick starting down the steps again in the gloom, still keeping half an eye out for his phial, though he has evidently given it up as a bad job. Dissolve to Dick walking down an ill lighted street, approaching a small, dark bistro; he puts his hand in his pocket and pulls out a few centimes. We see him having a glass of cheap wine in the bistro. Cut to Dick walking and walking down dark lonely streets. (This is again through the dark night of the soul where, as Fitzgerald puts it, it is always three o'clock in the morning, or even four o'clock in the morning.)

Dissolve to Dick still walking in the dawn, through Les Halles, half dead of despair and fatigue, amid the beautiful bustle of life and energy around him. Dissolve to Dick walking past Notre-Dame, and once more we hear the bells of morning, and shoot inside into a soft blast of candles and people praying. Dissolve to Dick crossing the Seine, then down St. Germain in the dawn mists past the statue of Diderot—at which he can't look, although we see it, and hear for a moment the children singing *Frère Jacques*, and from this into the pigeons breaking over St. Sulpice at sunrise with Dick approaching. Dissolve into the familiar park, with children swinging. Dick stops for a moment, watching the children, and we hear a voice, not a child's voice, but the voice of fate itself: Heavy, heavy hangs over thy head! What shall the owner do to redeem it?

Dissolve into a bank, the clock standing at someway past nine. Dick, still unshaven but cleaned up a bit and looking not too much like a bum, approaches the guichet with a cheque. The cashier is busy for the moment and we see the cheque: a gold cheque on a Chicago or Zurich bank, so that we know the source is Nicole, or Nicole's money; we also see that Dick's hands are trembling, although he is sober (but it is characteristic of this malaise related to the conscience, that they do not tremble so much now, when unregarded, as a little later, when he is observed.) The American cashier now gives Dick his attention.

The Cashier: (tactfully overlooking Dick's dishevellment) Why, good morning, Doctor Diver . . . Long time no see.

Dick: Hi, Bill. (Gives him the cheque under the bars) Will you cash this for me?

The Cashier: Sure . . . Just endorse it here. (He hands Dick the cheque and a pen)

Dick takes the cheque and tries in vain to sign it. Simultaneously a diabolical little commentary begins to accompany the action, seeming to come from just at Dick's elbow, not without compassion perhaps, but mocking and deeply serious: it is an accusing voice, which closely and wickedly follows his inability to sign the cheque.

The Voice:

> Pity the blind and the halt but yet pity
> The man at the bank in the pitiless city

(we see Dick at a little distance standing at the guichet)

> The man at the bank who can't sign his own name

(The cashier smiles encouragingly at Dick, who can scarcely make any impression on the paper)

> The man at the bank, with his shakes far from home

(Dick gets the nib to the paper—no more)

> The man at the bank with his pitiful income
> Arrived now from far, from far sources of shame
> For a man at the bank who can't sign his own name

(we see it is impossible)

> Though he sweat till the Ultimate Manager came

(We see him sweat, the bars look like prison bars)

> Pity the blind, and pity the lame
> But pity the man who can't sign his own name.

Dick: (at the guichet) I think you know me well enough—I can't make any impression on this cheque—will you lend me a couple of hundred francs for ten minutes to correct this?

The Cashier: Le violà . . . (takes money out of his own pocket, peels off a couple of hundred francs and gives it to Dick)

Dick: (attempting to explain) Thanks—I—my wife—er—

Cut to a small bistro, through which a man is carrying a sack of coal. Dick stands helplessly with a cognac before him, can just pick it off the counter with both hands, spilling half of it, but cannot get it to his lips, it being as though a violent horrible magnetic force was drawing the drink down. Handcuffs appear on Dick's wrists. They fade.

Dick: J'ai pris un bain chaud—c'est la réaction.

The Bartender: (interestedly, sympathetically, who knows perfectly well what it is) Ah, oui . . . la réaction.

Absolutely without scorn the barman helps him, lifting the glass to his lips. Some other people, an elderly tart, a workman in dungarees, a poet, a criminal looking type, generously suspecting Dick will be hurt by their glances, simply do not look.

Dick: (paying) Mille remerciments.

The Barman: (smiling) Sans faire rien.

Dissolve into the American Express: Dick, shaved, clean, but exhausted, receiving a telegram. We see the telegram:

DOHMLER SAYS IT MAY BE ALMOST ANY TIME NOW, DICK DARLING. COME TO ZURICH AS SOON AS YOU WISH AFTER THIS FORTNIGHT. THEN OH DARLING LET US START LIFE ANEW. LANIER AND TOPSY SEND LOVE. AS DO I. THY NICOLE.

Dissolve to Dick walking down the street, dazedly, half happily reading the telegram. He is passing an ancient advertisement for Rosemary Hoyt in *Daddy's Girl* with the picture of Rosemary torn in half.

Cut to a sign CULTURE PHYSIQUE. Dissolve to Dick, obviously with a terrible hangover, gamely punching a ball.

Cut to Dick in a pool swimming: once he lies on his back, half sinks, seems to struggle like the drowning man we have seen before: smiles, manages to swim just the same, though he seems in bad shape.

Cut to Les Deux Magots: the waiter, seeing him, brings a cognac automatically.

Dick: Non, Charles, de la bière, s'il vous plaît. (The waiter looks surprised, but tactfully brings the beer.)

Cut to Dick finishing an enormous meal in a terrace restaurant. The waiter approaches and Dick puts one hand over the empty beer tankard. But he indicates he would like to buy drinks for the waiter and all the Americans on the terrace.

Cut to the night—Dick lying in bed—then a nightmare: flames, a burning car, people drowning, Abe being killed, through which we can hear Dohmler's voice saying over and over: But of course a miracle is not impossible. Of course a miracle is not—

Cut to an unopened bottle of whiskey, a glass beside it. Dick rises, opens the bottle, pours himself a large drink, hesitates, then pours it back into the bottle again. His gaze goes out of the window: it is night, he encounters a sign, with a wan light shining upon it: Huitres Fraiches. Fresh Oysters. A tart passes under the light.

Dick: Ugh ... (he takes the still unbroached bottle of whiskey and puts it under his pillow.)

Cut to Dick riding a bike steadily and concentratedly in the country: the spires of Chartres Cathedral rise up over the fields in the background.

Dissolve to Dick at the American Express reading another telegram from Nicole. His hands are fairly steady, he looks well, and wistfully happy at what he reads:

THIS LAST FORTNIGHT WAS A YEAR. STOP. IT CAN BE ANY TIME NOW. STOP. OH BUT LET US GO BACK TO ANTIBES RIGHT OFF I DO NOTHING BUT LOOK FORWARD. HAVE MILLIONS OF PLANS. LOVE. THY NICOLE.

Near Dick in the American Express we see a sign: ZURICH SUISSE.

Cut to a plane, then the plane landing in Zurich.

Cut to Dick's hotel room in Zurich: a smaller, unopened bottle stands on the table: he opens it, pours a drink, pours the drink out of the window. He recorks the bottle, smells it, then goes to bed.

Cut to Dick walking towards the sanatorium again, the same walk as he made after he said "I promise," but in reverse.

It is a beautiful summer morning as we see the sanatorium ahead of us, with its high walls around the garden and the big gate. Dick now observes, ahead of him and just entering the gate, Dr. Gregorovious, talking seriously and animatedly to a younger doctor, about Dick's age when he first came there. Dick starts forward to speak to Franz, then his eye falls on the other, younger man and he hesitates, and drops back so as to avoid them. Dick doesn't look sentimentally or pathetically at this emblem of his lost possibilities or youth, he looks while sternly, sadly, even with a kind of half amused tragic curiosity, but in stepping back to avoid the two, he finds himself half hidden behind, if not quite involved with, a large rose bush in flower. Dissolve from Dick standing amid the roses back for a few seconds to that point in the funicular sequence where Dick and Tommy are not talking but the roses are beginning to drag through the ascending car: this was just before Nicole reappeared and the memory is induced partly because at that moment Dick was still free. Dissolve from this to those moments a bit later where, with the funicular stationary, Nicole and Tommy, embowered in roses, are leaning out of one side of the car with Marmora, and Dick is across the aisle, leaning out of the other side. At this point Dick recognized, and we now recognize it again, that the conductor looked exactly like Dohmler, in fact, turned in his imagination into Dohmler and held up his hand in interdiction. As we see this gesture once more, the imaginary conductor-Dohmler dissolves into and becomes the real Dohmler looking thoughtfully out of the window of his office in the sanatorium now; he turns away just as Dick comes in at the gate, but he was simply looking out of the window into the garden, as was his old habit, and does not see Dick.

Cut to a close shot of Nicole and the children. She is sitting in a garden chair quietly, with her hands in her lap, and we feel at once a poise and self possession about her that we have never seen before. The children are playing near her and they come running toward her, lean lovingly and trustingly against her, asking her to settle some dispute between them about their play. We also realise at once that her attitude toward the children has utterly changed: she now seems to love them dearly, and wisely, and what perhaps is equally important, we have the feeling their love and trust in her is complete. She settles their argument, or gives them advice, and they run off, Nicole giving Topsy an extra kiss as they go. Nicole gazes after the children for a moment, then, looking up, suddenly sees Dick. We do not see him, but we know by the expression of ecstatic joy that comes over her face that she has. She rises to her feet and starts toward the camera, she says nothing, but puts out her arms as she moves, faster and faster.

Cut to a long shot of the garden. Dick, who was standing still, now starts toward Nicole with his arms out as she comes forward to him in a final little rush of love. They meet in the centre of the screen and clasp each other in a close embrace. We have a wild moment of hope, at the same time an agonized dreadful feeling of what might have been.

Leaving Dick and Nicole still locked in each other's arms in the centre of the screen the camera now moves back and back: the little summer house where they played the records comes into view on our right, and on the sound track we hear a few bars of the *Japanese Sandman*, then, still swiftly moving backward, we go out through the walled garden of the sanatorium: as we see the sign, Sanatorium Zurichsee, over the gate the words change to Villa Diana, while the walls become the walls of the Villa Diana, seen from outside its gate. Moving, conversely, forward now, and more swiftly, we travel in through the gate of the Villa Diana and down through the garden, passing Dick's workhouse, as we do so hearing a few bars of a piano solo of Beiderbecke's called *In the Dark*, (a reversal of *In a Mist* that will be explained later) and straight to the precipice where Nicole used to stand: without stopping we take in the Bay of Angels, the lighthouse, the church, the walls and towers of Antibes, and the Alps beyond, clear and awe-inspiring, and from this, precisely as at the beginning of the picture, come almost to a halt before a sign standing in a field beside the railway lines, on which we see in huge Greek capitals again:

ΑΝΤΙΠΟΥΙΣ

Meantime, as the camera moves closer, we see once more what is necessary in French and English of the sign itself:
    Touriste Américaine! Vous vous approchez maintenant de la ville ancienne d'Antibes. Original Greek name: ANTIPOLIS:

ΑΝΤΙΠΟΥΙΣ

Originally Greek, founded by the Greek Phoenicians, in the 3rd century, its latest walls were built by the great Vauban, and up till 1860 marked the Italo-French border.
    HOTEL DES ETRANGERS, ANTIBES, 5 km. Confort Moderne.
    Patron: Charles Gausse. (son delicieux couscous)
    Beach clots—vins—liqueurs—Bar—
    Everything for the American tourist at popular prices!

We now move up on another sign ahead of this:

    Buvez Dr. Popsicoola
    Pour votre santé.

The camera goes beyond this and instantly into Antibes as before travelling once more up the Via Crucis where we see several tourists, and into the narrow and once quiet street, where we see more tourists. But the two ancient square towers are the same, and Antibes reasserts its old dignity for us as a walled city, a fortress, with the solid towers rising above the walls, and the Alps always behind: the stone with its inscription in ancient Greek is still there, and the guide, with a dozen or more tourists. Cut as before to the station: a train has just drawn in, and we see tourists getting out. But we observe the same signs in the Antibes station, in French, Italian, and English: Défense de traverser les voies, E proibito traversare i banari, It is forbidden to cross the lines: also the travel advertisements for Cannes, Nice, and Paris, and lastly Zurich, Suisse, with the pictured Alps once more.

Rapidly the camera descends the road that Rosemary and her mother drove down at the opening, passing four more Buvez Dr. Popsicoola signs, and one for the Hotel Colossal, Nice, though the dusty poplars and the smoke from merchantmen on the horizon seem not to have changed: we enter the Hotel des Etrangers the same way through the garden, pass swiftly through the lobby again where we find the calendar by the desk says Août 4, 1927, and that there are many more people, and an air of bustling activity that contrasts sharply with a year ago, and before we know it are out on the verandah looking down at the beach itself from nearly the same viewpoint as that of Rosemary's at the beginning.

The beach in front of Gausse's has now suddenly become a really popular rendezvous for the International Set: all kinds of new paraphernalia are apparent: swinging rings, trapezes over the water, floating towers, searchlights from last night's fête, and many portable bath houses: there is even a white fatuous modernistic buffet bar with a banal modernistic theme of handlebars: the camera takes in this—even here the Buvez Dr. Popsicoola pour votre santé advertisement is to be seen, whatever the drink is—and the other things, just long enough for us to obtain the dramatic contrast, plus a hint of its philosophic meaning: at first the implication might seem to be: what an ending things conceived in simplicity and rightness seem to have! Or we might feel that all this paraphernalia obscurely parallels the superficial popularization of Freudianism itself that we have caused Dick to mention: but then again the opposite of some of these things might be true too. Had after all, the beginnings, in the former instance, been so simple and right? And further, has not Dick himself a popularizing, cheapening side to his nature, as witness *Psychology for You*, etc.? Moreover is not Dick one mysterious cause of all this spoliation or success, however you look at it, of his own beach? He has said as much. But then a lot of people are being happy, and extroverted, and socialized, or what have you, instead of merely a few in their private selfish worlds, a few who turned out not to be so happy. Perhaps it is the perfect outward expression of something else: the beach, stupid and unbeautiful though it now is, has become "adjusted," to its, and our world. But as now the camera accompanies Dick and Nicole walking down it, together with the children and a nurse, we doubt very much that this is an expression of a Better Thing for Dick, just as we come to feel that Nicole is simply taking it in her stride. The camera subtly takes us into confidence about another happy, or sombre quiddity in the course of the whole scene: we see the Alps again behind, a symbol of the Swiss Alps, feeling that they are indeed in the background but rather as something left behind than threatening. The sea, however, seems more and more as if ahead, or as if representing something ahead of Dick. It is now late summer, 1927, as we have been reminded. Dick is wearing his old jockey cap, and bathing trunks with a shirt over them, and is carrying their umbrellas, etc. over his shoulder.

There are a few glances in the direction of the Divers as we walk with them: nobody notices them very much, but we hear some flying words from one group of people, one of whom might be an equivalent of Mrs. Abrams in the first sequence as they walk past.

First Person: . . . that's Baby Warren's younger sister . . . But she's thrown herself away on some dissipated doctor.

Second Person: Well—that's him, isn't it, the dissipated doctor?— But I thought he was dead.

Third Person: No, you're thinking of that composer, that pal of his we met in Cannes—what was his name? Fellow that was always talking about sawing up a waiter—

Second Person: Oh yes—you mean the guy who was beaten to death in a speakeasy . . .

Close shot of Nicole and Dick—the last words have caught them.

Dick: Beaten to death in a speakeasy. (he does not have to say this aloud, but we know he has heard.)

Yet the camera passes immediately to Nicole. We see her look at Dick with sympathy and sorrow and understanding for his feeling about the loss of Abe, and the change in their old beach. Nicole is now well, and rather resembles it, so to speak with one part of her nature, in that she too is "adjusted," nearly self-sufficient, and has a hard practical viewpoint of the world. But she also has something we have never seen in her before: an ability to identify herself with another person's problems and sufferings. To oversimplify: we can remember that as a child she was sweet natured and good, so had an inherent capacity for this. Since then, for the involved reasons we know, she became self-absorbed to the extent that even at her best, practically to maintain herself in balance, it was a risk to allow herself to become emotionally overwrought. "Nicole mustn't suffer." Now she is shown as a woman capable of compassion and understanding. If we remember she had once tried to do something for Peterson, in fact it was a mere automatism of a sort of innate decency: her proximity to suffering there was in *part* responsible for her later and more serious breakdown. This new quality of compassion must be emphasized, from time to time, from here on, as well as her hardness. This latter is a quality that is not new but which Nicole must have come to recognize as absolutely necessary for her: there is an element of choice or decision even in such a matter as sanity vs insanity. And Nicole has made her decision to be sane, at whatever cost. This might seem to compromise her pity because she won't, even cold-bloodedly, let it go beyond a certain point. But it is very important that we see that it is there, or for one thing, we shall lose sympathy with her and think Dick well rid of her. Her character has hardened, if not into a mould, into an indestructible series of rational responses to certain situations. But the pity is there. What is more, unconsciously she will look to Dick not to weaken her even if that means his humiliation. For if she is well, she is still not *free*. It gives us a chance for a rare enough type of character development on the screen. But we must also bear in mind that, tragically, Dick cannot now allow himself to respond to this understanding part of her nature he must have missed and longed for.

As through Nicole's mind therefore, (and probably Dick's too) we see a shot of the beach as it used to be—themselves and the children, Barban, but particularly Abe, sitting there by themselves in the sun and wind, Abe's beautiful face, Abe swimming, then we come back to the close up of Nicole looking at Dick with compassion, and her attempt to establish a unity, a rapport, between them again. But Dick does not look at her. He sets up the umbrellas then produces a bottle and drinks as they sit down. Despite any familiarity with Dick's former occasions we feel a decided shock. But the shock is not obvious: it inheres less in the drink, for Dick is not essentially a drunk, than in something it tells us and yet does not tell us. Even if taken merely to drown the specific memory just seen expressed through Nicole's mind, the warning bell it rings is of diverse tones. Dick takes off his shirt and we see that he looks rather flabby, fairly tanned again, but in poorish condition.

Nicole glances along the beach to where, a little distance away, a couple are holding court, the centre and focus of a "brilliant" laughing group—the centre, we might say, of the beach, as the Divers used to be. The reversal of the contrast is not overexaggerated but it is patent. The group breaks up as this couple start down the beach in a diagonal direction that will bring them past the Divers; perhaps the final object is the sea, but we get the impression that, under this new regime, the sea is not used for swimming so much any longer, save by the children: we feel its importance now is largely ornamental, either in itself or because people think they appear to advantage against it, though waves breaking against the rocks beyond the safety of the beach remind us it is still the sea. As this couple start their parade we notice that it is the McKiscos. (McKisko himself is riding the crest of success as we know but despite this has become a rather decent fellow: even some of the criticisms that Dick levelled at him on the *Diderot* might equally have been flung against Dick himself. As for his socialist principles, we have scarcely been able to take them otherwise than cum grano salis and anyway his present life scarcely upholds them. Probably he is secretly hugely enjoying his success, whatever he has said, or may say. But whatever the dichotomies of his pose, the effect of his success on his wife is clearly quite different, and McKisco's own attitude is not altogether uninfluenced by it while he is in her company.) As Violet McKisco approaches, she is laughing and whispering something that causes her companion to raise her eyebrows, and glance at Nicole. Dick rises to greet the McKiscos.

Dick: Hi there, so we do meet again.

McK: (embarrassedly) At Antipolis, and how.

Violet: (as McKisco smiles, albeit a bit furtively, and bows to Nicole) Well, so I hear that my husband and yours had the pleasure of each other's company on the trip back over . . . I daresay you find your beach rather changed—but then, it isn't exactly your beach any more, is it?

Nicole shakes hands, obviously burning with indignation and turning to Dick, but McKisco has meantime been signalling violently with his eyes to Dick and we see the two men adjourning to the bar.

Nicole: (rising, absolutely sure of herself, to Violet) Look here, I called at your hotel in Paris twice to apologize for that night. But there's absolutely no reason for your putting on that tone of voice and I won't have it.

Violet: My husband might have got killed, you know.

Nicole: *Killed*? What do you mean, killed?

Violet: My husband was dragged into a ridiculous duel by what was his name, your soldier friend, because I ventured, quite excusably, I may say, to mention the fact that you'd kicked and screamed at me.

Nicole: (boiling with righteous and clearly non-pathological rage at the intolerable Violet, but at the same time nonplussed and also incredulously moved) Do you mean Tommy Barban—!

At this point the camera swings away from Violet and Nicole and though Violet and Nicole do not see him, we see Tommy Barban himself. He is clad in the full panoply of war in the uniform of a captain in the French army, and is standing back by Gausse's hotel on a slight eminence, at the point where the road runs down to the beach and the cars are parked, among which is the Divers' Isotta. He looks tanned and remarkably fit and, having recognized the Isotta, is smoking his pipe and evidently gazing round for its owners.

Cut to McKisco and Dick in the bar with the handlebars motif from which can be seen the beach and the sea. They are drinking pernod and talk rapidly, round, rather than at us; as they do so we can remark certain other symptoms that Antibes is now "on the map"; such as, behind the bar and around the room, advertisements saying: When on the Riviera keep in touch with world events, day by day—read the *Continental Daily Mail*. Antipolis Cabaret, Antibes, présente chaque soir la nouvelle revue à grand spectacle: On Est Nu à Venus, avec les jolies "Black Bottom Girls." 15 artistes, 200 costumes. Buvez Dr. Popsicoola, pour votre santé. Ciné Antipolis, Antibes—Les films en exclusivité chaque soir: *Chang!* (with a picture of stampeding rogue elephants knocking down houses on stilts in the jungle, the elephants being dominated, however, by an extremely pretty, half naked, dark wench)[82] Une jolie femme dans sa jungle, élefants terrifiants et les drames de l'amour et de la mort— Behind the bar: Try our Antipolis Cock-tail! near which is even a sort of college pennant with the Greek lettering: ΑΝΤΙΠΟΤΙΣ. Matching the handlebars are photographs about the wall depicting bicyclists in the forthcoming Tour de France, which remind us almost of the foc's'le of the *Diderot* and competition enters in by way of another advertisement for the Hotel Colossal, Nice, and one for Le "Paris-Hollywood," at Cannes. Le seul cabaret où vous pourrez passer un joyeux Reveillon dans l'ambience traditionelle du "French Riviera," etc.

Dick:—thanks—well, I couldn't help wondering what this "I know thee not, old man," business was about, at least—

McK:—it's just as I said on the ship. If I could feel my—well—my success, you know what I mean—

Dick: (laughing) I don't, as a matter of fact. Your experience exceeds mine there.

McK:—if I could feel it had made her proud of me, it would have been different. But it hasn't. (laughing, to take the sting out) I'm beginning to be afraid that I can't live up to *her*. What's worse, I'm beginning to feel I wasn't cut out to be this kind of success; right at bottom I'm a serious fellow and I ought to be a failure—

Dick laughs loudly and takes a drink.

McK: Now I'm afraid I've done the wrong thing again by luring you over here and she'll upset your wife—

Dick: No—Nicole's all right. Nicole is now made of—of Georgia pine, which is the hardest wood known, except lignum vitae from New Zealand. (They glance momentarily over toward Nicole and Violet, who, strangely enough, seem to be talking quite matter of factly. In the distance we can see Barban slowly filling and lighting his pipe, but neither Dick nor McKisco see him) No—take it for what it's worth, success, or failure, (the camera takes in briefly, beyond the handlebar motif again, the beach with its crowd, and also a motorboat with an aquaplaner cruising quite near; somebody, a girl, dives from the motorboat, swims out to a raft) let your wife get her kind of kick out of it, and if it's led you to evaluate the first in terms of what can be learned from the second, so much the better.

McK: Look at your old beach—look what's happened to it—(the camera is still looking, in such a way that we see some of the advertisements in the foreground in the bar)

Dick: (gazing over it out to sea where there is a very distant freighter, scarcely more than a smudge of smoke on the horizon) So many rituals, so many quiet restful extroversions, toward sea and sun, many inventions, buried deeper than the sand, under a span of a single year—by the way, have you seen Rosemary Hoyt? We had a wire she was coming to Gausse's.

McK: Violet saw her—I think that's her in the motorboat with the aquaplane. No—there she is—out on that raft. (the camera follows his eyes briefly to the raft)

Dick: (he is just slightly, almost imperceptibly, tight) I've got to catch her then, if she hasn't seen we're on the beach—see you later—

Dick leaves McKisco and dives into the water. Cut to a long shot of Barban advancing down the beach; he has seen Nicole and is approaching her. Cut to McKisco—he recognizes Barban suddenly from the bar and we see the shot through his eyes. Nicole has stood up and has seen Barban. McKisco seems aghast at the prospect of encountering Barban, as he will have to do in order to reach his umbrella, turns back to the bar.

McK: Un cognac—

Cut to Barban approaching Nicole.

Nicole: Tommy . . .

Barban laughs his boisterous laugh of delighted welcome, is putting out his hand.

Barban: I heard you were in the Villa Diana again, and I came to see you.

Barban takes her outstretched hand and they greet each other with pleasure. (Lowry, pp. 367-97)

33

Dick joins Rosemary out on the raft, and as they recall their good times of the year before, he is taken aback as he recognizes Barban on the beach with Nicole. Nicole and Barban are enchanted with each other and convey a strong feeling of mutual attachment. Lowry specifies: "In our version he has been away only a year and most of that year Nicole has been in the sanatorium. What we might feel is that Barban, having long loved Nicole, however much or little he knows, surrounds the entire position in an instant, and Nicole mysteriously recognises this" (Lowry, p. 398). *Later they watch from the beach as Dick attempts to carry out a stunt on the water—the same stunt on the aquaplane that Rosemary had watched him perform perfectly the year before. But Dick is not what he was then, and his continuous attempts to perform the stunt fail miserably, to the point where he becomes almost an object of pity for Rosemary and the men pulling him on the boat as well as for Nicole and Barban on the beach.*

Dick and Rosemary join Barban and Nicole, and Dick supplies drinks for them all. Nicole is obviously not pleased to see Rosemary again and is rather curt with her. Rosemary asks Dick and Nicole what they thought about her latest picture, but before a now rather tipsy Dick can finish his rambling and somewhat cryptic reply, which she obviously does not understand, Rosemary asks Topsy if she wants to be an actress when she grows up and adds that she thinks she would make a fine one. Nicole, infuriated by this suggestion, bluntly lets Rosemary know her displeasure. She brusquely informs Dick that she is going to drive home in the Isotta. He grows alarmed and reminds her that she hasn't driven since—but before he can finish, Nicole interrupts to say that she has not forgotten how. She drives home, happy and relaxed in her new self-assurance. "She is almost singing. Firmly, and finally giving us a sense of her near mastery, Nicole goes on driving, always uphill" (Lowry, p. 405). *As she gets out of the car at the Villa Diana, she lets out a small cry of satisfaction: "Ha"* (Lowry, p. 405).

In the villa the next afternoon Nicole is disturbed from her nap by an altercation between Dick and their cook, Augustine. They have squared off against each other in the kitchen—Dick with a heavy cane and the cook with a butcher knife—after Dick has accused Augustine of drinking some of his expensive wine. The Divers threaten to call the police, Augustine calls Dick a drunk, and Nicole wonders aloud where Barban is, for he, she feels, would certainly do something. After much yelling and threatening, Augustine finally leaves the house—with a bottle of wine.

Later, in a restaurant in Nice, Nicole tells Dick that they cannot go on as they have. She says she has ruined him: that Dick, who had once wanted only to create, now wants only to destroy. She asks him what he gets out of his life with her, and Dick answers that he gets the knowledge that Nicole grows stronger every day, and for a moment they seem happy again. Dick spots an acquaintance's yacht out on the water and suggests to Nicole that they attend a party there to which they have been invited. Nicole is hesitant, but Dick tells her that Tommy Barban has been invited too and reminds her that she had missed Barban's tact during the incident with Augustine.

The guests on the yacht are mainly English: "*we realise that we are present, with contrasting and energetic modifications, at that dreariest of functions, an expensive party consisting largely of the kind of doomed scions of Britain that people such plays as Noel Coward's* The Vortex"[83] (Lowry, p. 410); *the host is a genial English Jew named Golding. Nicole and Tommy—she self-assured and he looking very handsome in his captain's uniform—sit together in the lounge of the yacht drinking champagne and observing the other guests. Among these is a Lady Caroline Sibly-Biers, a fragile and exquisite young woman and the current toast of London: "The camera gives us a few close ups of faces, some serious and tragic, some fatuous, some lovely and gay and we hear words from some of these faces; what they say is merely what Englishmen do say, and it should not be exaggerated, and is not meant to be funny (even if it is). [. . .] The camera strays for a moment to the bar, where it discovers the band, all save the pianist, several of whom—guitar, violin, hot clarinet, bass fiddle—are playing* Show Me the Way to Go Home[84] *in the wildest and hottest rhythm, a rhythm that could scarcely be bettered by the best of American hot combinations; these young Englishmen, apart from the fact that they are probably Scotchmen, are on the contrary of the most exuberant and happy go lucky type: they are simply enjoying the music and if they are decadent have not realised it: decadent or not, they are all pretty tight; then we come back to Dick and the Sibly-Biers entourage,* Show Me the Way to Go Home, *muted, comes back with us*" (Lowry, pp. 412–13). *Dick wastes no time in insulting Lady Caroline Sibly-Biers, who humiliates him somewhat by promptly putting him in his place. The whole episode is smoothed over by Golding before Nicole can reach Dick, and the party continues.* Lowry writes: "We move with Tommy and Nicole up to the ladder to the deck, the sea is louder, but then, as they pass the engine room entrance, the engine thrumming seems to express Nicole's further anxiety. A bell strikes eight bells" (Lowry,

p. 414). *Later, as Tommy and Nicole walk along the deck of the yacht, they see Dick talking with Golding.* (See Lowry, pp. 397-415 and Fitzgerald, 3, v, vii.)

The camera leaves Tommy and Nicole and travels up to Dick and Golding talking by the gangway. Dick seems to be in complete control of himself. They are standing by a lifebelt with the name of the ship on it: M. V. MARGIN.[85]

Dick: (speaking quite fast—not as if tight, with the exception of one place) I was wondering why you called your yacht the *Margin*, Golding. Do you mean an amount, as of time or money, which is allowed to meet conditions that cannot be foreseen? The difference between the net sales and cost of merchandise sold, taken as that—ship!—from which expenses must be met or profit derived? Or a customer's equity if his account is terminated . . . at prevailing market prices?—Had you been an American, I would have thought it was the *gin* that had the significance.

Golding: (laughs, patting him on the shoulder and turns away jovially) No, Diver my boy, by calling her the *Margin* I meant the minimum return, or reward, barely covering the costs of production and constituting a limit below which economic conditions cannot be continued. Ha! Ha! Ha![86]

Dick: (laughs and calls after him) Well, I hardly supposed you meant it as collateral—(Dick, released from the tension of pretending to be sober, totters to the bow, talks to himself in a sinister fashion, while the engine becomes slightly dominant again) Or did you mean it as a condition *approximately* marking the limit—(he gazes over the bow and we see the sea rising up at him and the ship's engines sound momentarily more menacing)—the edge. Hullo, Shelley, old boy, down there? Shelley? (at this moment there are cries amidship, Dick looks round, and an English rugby football drops almost in his arms)

From amidships; English cries: Line out there! Right-o! No—Foul! That's a forward pass from where you are, old chap!

Dick hurls the ball back successfully amidships where it is caught amid cries of Tackle him low! Offside! Thank you, old sport, that was nancily done! Twenty-five! Hey-*scrum*! Forward pass! Down with the Academicals!

The camera follows the football back amidships then goes beyond it back to Barban and Nicole alone, leaning over the stern; the Union Jack unfurls itself above them. Near them, right aft, under the awning, is another cottage piano, but covered with a huge black cloth, that might remind us remotely of Abe. The wake stretches away into the distance, and we hear the sea and the propellor. (Lowry, pp. 415-16)

34

Barban and Nicole continue their walk along the deck. They discuss the respective merits of the English and French languages for expressing heroism and gallantry with dignity, and the expression of these same qualities in movies, such as the 1926 American film Beau Geste, *starring Ronald Colman. (See Lowry, pp. 416-17 and Fitzgerald, 3, v.)*

At this point they are near enough to the lounge with the piano to hear the music coming out of it: evidently, as a moment later they see through the open door, the pianist, with the choral assistance of some rather tight young Englishman leaning on the piano is singing some English comic song.
The Young Man at the Piano:

> Oh, poor Mary Ann
> When she got to the top
> Her heart went flipperty-flop
> As the wheel began to stop
> The man in the moon began to laugh
> Oh Mary began to squeal
> She lost her situation
> Through the great—big—wheel—[87]

Barban: (to Nicole—makes one of his rare excursions into humour) It's the same with Italian—I'll say the meanings are different. A hundred miles over there is Livorno. Now Livorno is a word—but Leghorn will always be first a hen—or a hat—

Nicole laughs, but now as most of the Englishmen take up the chorus again, one fellow, not singing at all, just accompanies the song with pointing gestures and rolling eyes intended to be funny, she slowly becomes aware, though Barban cannot be, of the diabolically apt coincidence of the words and stops still, listening.
They sing:

> Oh poor Mary Ann
> When she got to the top
> Her heart went flipperty-flop
> As the wheel began to stop

Cut to a flashback of the Ferris Wheel with Nicole in it.

> The man in the moon began to laugh
> Oh Mary began to squeal

On the screen we see Nicole laughing crazily in the Ferris Wheel: the flashback is silent while the song goes on: the shot dissolves into the night sky, with the moon dominant: the camera comes back to Nicole standing quite still, on the deck, listening, the moonlight falls upon her face, and we see how extraordinarily different is her reaction to this than we might have expected—clearly we feel again that she is cured or must be all but delivered from her ravagement, for her reaction, judging from her face, quite unhysterically is simply that of overwhelming sorrow for what she has done to Dick.

They sing:

> She lost her situation
> Through the great—big—WHEEL!

Nicole: (suddenly) I've got to find Dick.

Nicole abruptly leaves Barban and the camera follows her as she hurries off, searching for Dick. As she peers here and there, we see, beyond the mast, the lovely night, hear the soft pounding of the engine. Two bells strike. The rugby football horseplay has ceased. The engine becomes louder and more dominant. Nicole even begins to run toward the bow, where a wind strikes her and she slows, suddenly we are reminded of something else: that this is a reversal of the Ferris Wheel scene itself, when Dick went to look for her, for meantime we have seen that Dick is still standing where we have seen him before, but perhaps now seriously contemplating suicide—right forward in the V of the bow. As Nicole approaches we see beyond Dick the sea surging up and sinking almost up to the hawseholes, perhaps hear it gurgling in the hawseholes, for though it is a fine night, a headwind produces a long slow slight pitching of the vessel. (Lowry, pp. 417-18)

35

Nicole tells Dick that she has been worried about him. Dick grabs her suddenly by the wrist and says that if he is ruined, she is ruined too. Nicole, tears streaming down her face, is ready at this time to drown herself with him.

Dick suddenly lets her go and, sighing, turns his back to her. Barban arrives on the scene, and they all return to the party, where Nicole and Barban dance to a jazz version of "Carry Me Back to Old Virginny"[88] *while Dick goes on drinking. Nicole is amazed when Barban suggests she might tell Dick to change his behaviour. Lowry instructs: "Cut, as if through a hot break in the music, to a rocket slithering up the sky with a magnificent gathering whish, bursting into a thousand stars: the bursting rocket illumines garishly the faces of Dick and Barban on the waterfront at Cannes. Barban has Dick [. . .] by the arm. [. . .] Nicole is ahead of them waiting by the car"* (Lowry, p. 421). *Dick is in no condition to drive, so it is decided that Barban will drive everyone home to the Villa Diana.* (See Lowry, pp. 418-21 and Fitzgerald, 3, v.)

Cut to the car with Barban getting into the driving seat, Nicole already beside him in the front, and from the point of view of Dick who, weaving considerably, is preparing to get into the back: almost simultaneously with the cut another rocket rips up the sky, from nearer at hand, causing Dick to inhibit his stride from entering the car, and totter into a place where he can see the bursting rocket better, looking up into the sky with drunken ironic wonder: suddenly the detritus and ashes, but not ridiculously, rather tragically, begin to fall over Dick.

(The secondary value of this, after the purely cinematic, is that it illustrates the Bergsonian concept of one fundamental process of life itself, here in dramatic operation, that a movement that is beginning to make itself in one direction, has to unmake itself in the other: it has a tertiary value, as tragic irony, in the last scene of all.)

Cut to Nicole and Barban in the front seat of the car, looking at each other. Dick stumbles into the car, drops heavily into the back seat, immediately falling half asleep, his arm resting on the hamper there, we can assume of champagne and caviar. Barban leans over past Nicole and closes the door. Again they look at each other, silently, for a moment. Cut in, from the scene in the funicular, the moment where Barban presented Nicole with the rose. Then back, as Barban starts the engine, puts on the headlights and they drive away: we see Barban for a brief further moment at the wheel, then as the camera falls on Dick alone in the back seat, we hear the sound of the piano piece, Beiderbecke's *In the Dark*, as we dissolve to Nicole, walking down the garden of the Villa Diana.[89]

The principal difference that we notice in Nicole, as we see her move down through the garden this time, is that though she seems as interested in flowers as ever, her hands are no longer neurotically restless, albeit she plucks a blossom or two off. She approaches Dick's workroom, from which now this piano piece, *In the Dark*, that we have been hearing already, seems to be emerging. It is late afternoon, just before sunset of the next day.

Dick is now revealed in his workroom, as through Nicole's eyes. He is not working, however, but sitting listening intently to a piano record of this *In the Dark*, playing with a fairly soft needle, on the gramophone. This gramophone is Nicole's old large-horned one she had in the sanatorium, which we saw in the first Villa Diana sequence here in the corner, but which he has now brought to the centre of the room and placed on a table. Nicole stands on the threshold and Dick does not see her at first. He is staring at nothing, he clenches his fists and leans forward in an attitude of torment and despair, then he gazes at the gramophone and the record. Nicole's eyes pass from Dick to the room, wander round it: we see much the same books as before, with the monumental names on the desk, with the same air of uncompletion, evidence of the same kind of eternal work in progress. In one corner too we see his old megaphone, crushed and dented now. Nicole's eyes come back to the gramophone. Perhaps we ourselves were "reminded" of this workroom in the Sanatorium Zurichsee itself. But now, due to the dominant position of this gramophone, in an indistinct, ghostly, yet much more definite fashion, we are reminded by the workroom of that little summer house at Zurichsee in those very early days: Nicole evidently has the same idea, for it fades into that for a moment through her eyes, and returns to itself as she starts forward.

Dick now becomes aware of her and straightens up, lifting his chin, and rises, though the despair does not leave his eyes.

Nicole, moved again with pity for Dick, or because again she has a hint of what he has suffered at her hands, goes to him with deep compassion, putting her arm round his shoulders and drawing her head against his.

Nicole: Ah—don't be sad! (she starts to take off the needle of the gramophone, the tune having seemed to come to an end, but Dick pushes her away coldly, preventing her hand from touching the gramophone)

Dick: That isn't the end—it only seems to be. Now it goes in reverse.

Nicole looks at him a moment, confused, and moves away a little.

The record starts again. This strange record Dick is playing on the gramophone, and which we have heard snatches of before in the film, is really two piano pieces composed by Beiderbecke, both very short, with a moment's pause in the middle. It is recorded by Decca, played by Jess Tracy, No. 18119A. The first half, called *In the Dark*, is recognizable as a kind of reversal of the same composer's *In a Mist*

"Tender Is the Night"   227

that we have heard Abe playing. The second part, called *Flashes*, is in turn a reversal of *In the Dark*. Since we are dramaturgically focussed upon an actual reversal in the drama, the effect of this background piano music, apart from its sadness, is to suggest a kind of eternalization of what is happening, however little we hear of it. The vast majority of people who do not know why they are moved, and do not care at the moment, cannot fail to be taken by the continual repeated plaintive little question in the melody, the always dying fall of the answer, resolved by the strangely classical ending. (Lowry, pp. 421–24)

36

Dick's demeanour remains cold, and Nicole finds her own pity rapidly cooling as a result. Dick tells Nicole he can no longer do anything for her; he is now trying only to save himself. His profession, he continues cruelly, sometimes throws him into contact with questionable company, and a weeping Nicole calls him a coward who wants to blame her for his own failures. She accuses him of offending everyone they meet, of taking advantage of her wealth, of being unsuccessful, of being an object of pity even for the McKiscos. Dick tells her that she cannot fight him with what he calls the empty receptacles of her own expiated sins, and Nicole retorts that she does not need to fight him, that she does not need him anymore at all. (See Lowry, pp. 424–27 and Fitzgerald, 3, vi, ix.)

The first part of the record now comes to an end again in the record's middle. In the moment of silence Dick and Nicole confront each other; then, sobbing coolly, Nicole turns and goes out. The record begins again on its second half, as it does so Dick goes in the direction of the shelf where we see his telescope lying beside the dented and useless megaphone. For a moment, with an air of finality, he leans forward, resting his forehead on the shelf. There, behind some of the detritus of his useless lares and penates, he now finds a drink, either hidden at some earlier escape, or placed there tactfully this morning. He drinks from it reflectively, then finishes it. Then he takes the telescope, and looks out at the place where Nicole had stood at the beginning of the film. He takes in this emptiness, then squares his shoulders, adjusts the telescope and looks out to sea: nothing there either, though the sea is angry-looking out at the horizon, with running white horses, cathedral-window rays of light slanting through some seaward clouds give the effect of molten glass. He swings his telescope up toward the constellated Greek Phoenician walls, the tower with the horns, the bell that at this moment tolls, the great gate, then up toward the evening shadows on the road toward the station. The Isotta is coming down it, doubtless bearing Baby. Then he looks out to sea again. Suddenly, below along the cliffs, the seagulls begin to pass. Dick moves out of his workhouse looking toward the beach, his shadow falls on the garden.

All this little while the second half of the record has been going on: now suddenly as we dissolve to Nicole, we hear the fragment at the beginning of the *Japanese Sandman*, the bit that Nicole likes; Nicole inside the house is still crying, now in front of the double photograph on the piano—the one we know—of Dick in uniform and herself as a girl. It is of course the same room with the French windows where Abe had once sat at the black piano, now closed, as if in mourning for him, a feeling heightened by the strains of *In the Dark*, that now is clearly audible from the garden again.

Suddenly Dick's photograph blurs as through her tears, then the photo turns into that of Barban in uniform.

Barban himself, the camera now reveals, is there at this moment, standing on a stair, above her, filling his pipe and looking at her tenderly, in spite of anything he may say. (Lowry, pp. 427-28)

37

Nicole and Barban are very tender with each other, and while they are talking, Baby arrives at the Villa.

The next day in Cannes Dick and Nicole get haircuts and shampoos in adjoining rooms of a hair salon, as is their habit. A headline from a newspaper lying on a bench draws attention to the Tour de France. Baby arrives and tells Nicole she wants to have the whole affair with Dick settled immediately. Dick overhears them and tells Baby that he and Nicole will meet with her in a nearby café. (See Lowry, pp. 428-30 and Fitzgerald, 3, viii, xi.)

Cut to Dick and Nicole walking down the avenue toward the sidewalk Café des Allies. At a little distance beside it, and almost precisely where it had been parked the other night, the Isotta is standing. We may assume that what has happened is that all three of them have come down to Cannes that afternoon with sundry necessary errands to be done, some while before, having had an abortive conversation about the situation that left Baby impatient; they separated, but made some arrangement to meet later. Since Baby left them either something has occurred in Baby's plans to make it seem imperative, or her impatience itself makes her want a show-down immediately: Dick, suspecting what the business is all about, wants it over too.

Nicole with her hair half cut, Dick with his half shave, bedraggled and tragic, half glowering at one another, at the same time pathetic, are something like punished children: apparently at one moment it almost occurs to both of them to join hands, then they think better of it. But if anguish can be expressed by people's backs—and finally what we see of them, since they are going away from us literally, and it is the last time we see them together alone, is mostly that—their backs express anguish. And meantime, somehow, as we follow them, we feel none of Nicole's inevitable and necessary hardness, none of Dick's opportunism. We don't have any feeling even of the more obvious side of Dick's abnegation, such as it is, we sense only their real love for one another, and that they are ill-starred lovers, we feel even that what they have to do is dictated by love at bottom, quite without benefit of psychology, so that we have the suspicion for a moment that the sacrifice extends ambiguously to Nicole too, who is less obeying Dick, than being the "little Miss Nicole who understands," who does not want to ruin him, that in her hardness lies a success of which Dick approves: as they approach the café the Mediterranean is to be seen on their right, across the promenade.

Under a table umbrella at the Café des Allies Baby is waiting. The café is deserted at Baby's end, but at the other end, all this while, a band is softly playing: I kiss your little hand, Madame. A waiter hovers near at their approach. Baby has something or other before her with a straw in it. (Lowry, pp. 430-32)

38

Baby tells Dick that Nicole no longer loves him, that she is completely well and does not need him any more. Nicole says to Dick that he no longer cares for her, that their life was never the same after Rosemary; Baby adds that Dick cannot stop treating Nicole like a patient. A bum suddenly interrupts them; Dick recognizes him as the one who had accosted them in Paris: "It is the bum, of the night of Abe's farewell party, and there is a quick, silent flashback as if through Dick's mind to that point in the cabaret scene with Abe where he accosted them at the bar, held just long enough for us to recognize him, as the bum's voice, together with the other Americans, makes a counterpoint to what the others are saying—this flashback, in a more immediate sense, giving the impression of cause and effect overlapping for the moment. The orchestra also begin tuning up" (Lowry, p. 433). *The bum seems to remember Dick and shows him a cartoon that he had shown him earlier—a caricature of millions of Americans disembarking from liners and carrying bags of gold. The bum is dispatched by a waiter, and before Baby can continue her diatribe, Dick says that he and Nicole will arrange matters themselves. At that moment the café orchestra breaks into a song with the word "father" in it, and Dick moves to stop them. Nicole, preventing him from doing so, asks if she is to go through the rest of her life flinching at that word.* (See Lowry, pp. 432-35 and Fitzgerald, 3, xi, vii.)

Dick, made all at once to look humiliated by this, gazes at Nicole, looking at her for a long moment, then bows, and walks away. We notice the Mediterranean again on the right beyond the promenade: it is rather rough.

The Vocalist:

> Thank ze *moon*light,
> Thank ze *June* night,
> Thank ze *stars* in heaven above—

Nicole: (suddenly, mutedly, as if about to start after Dick) Dick—oh, he's going in the wrong direction—

Baby: We should have let him confine himself to his bicycle excursions.

But now, as if in comment on Baby's remark, we see that coming in the opposite direction to the way Dick is going, which is away from us, a lone cyclist is approaching, preceded by his shadow, then three together simultaneously, out of the direction of the westering sun; there is an increasing commotion that nearly drowns the music—indeed Dick did not have to ask them, the musicians finish their number hastily and stop to look themselves, as does everyone else, a commotion which presently comes to a serpentine head on the promenade and a group, presently a crowd, of people, spring from hidden siestas, line the curbstone. Now boys sprint past on bicycles, automobiles jammed with elaborate be-tasseled sportsmen slide up the street, horns are tooted to announce the approach of the race, and unsuspected cooks in undershirts appear at restaurant doors, all this while the camera has been slowly moving up on Dick, away from Nicole, in the opposite direction to the cyclists: a troupe of fifty racers swarm after the first, strung out over two hundred yards, a few smiling and self-conscious, a few obviously exhausted, most of them indifferent and weary, in striped dirty shirts, legs caked with dust and sweat, faces expressionless, eyes heavy and endlessly tired.

We are now at Dick's shoulder again, as he glances from time to time at the bicyclists. At about the moment the camera reaches him the bum catches him up.

The Bum: (panting) Say, don't you remember me?

Dick: (still walking) Yeah. I remember you. I come from Tombstone, Nova Scotia—87th Division.

The Bum: Boy, you didn't look any too happy with them dames. Say, Buddy, you did me a good turn that night in Montmartre, I'm telling you, and I'm not the sort of feller who forgets a pal, let alone a fellow American, and if you're short—(he feels in his pocket as if to produce, perhaps, even a dollar, produces a bundle of what we can surmise are French postcards)—this is the real stuff! (as Dick tries to refuse them) Naw—keep 'em, kid, they're the real McCoy. Glad to do a favour for a pal—I got 'em in Marseilles—going back there again to do a little panhandling, when I'm through with this—(catching sight of some more Americans and giving Dick a parting salacious grin) Got everything here, Buddies! *Times*! *Herald*! Real French—

While this has been going on, the bicycle marathon has been passing them along the promenade, the cyclists passing look continually more exhausted, indifferent and wan: after that a retinue of small boys have passed, a few defiant stragglers, and lastly, at this moment, a light truck carrying the dupes of accident and defeat goes by.

As Dick stands there with his postcards, it is as if this were his final payment for everything; he laughs rather wanly at the postcards. An excited crowd of people are still pressing along the sidewalk in the same direction. Dick doesn't want the postcards but doesn't know what to do with them. On a sudden inspiration he puts them in the jacket pocket of a jostling, obviously important, British whiskerando in the uniform of a Brigadier General.

Cut to another coiffeur's. In fact, the proprietor has been watching the race outside and goes in with Dick. It is a smaller coiffeur for men.

The Barber: (eyeing Dick) Oh, la la!

Dick: (watching his half-shaved face in the mirror as the barber puts the apron round him; in the mirror we also see a few more super stragglers, accidents; and the sea, on the other side of the promenade) Je fais un tour de grand duc des coiffeurs.

Dick's half shaved face gazes back at him from the mirror while the barber is stropping his razor, (a moment that in itself is not without a certain threat of yet further torture) and whether it is this spectacle of his own visage or the thought of the whiskerando outside that suggests it, his face turns in the mirror into that of the chief engineer of the *Diderot* with its splendid handlebar moustache, half of it shaved off to annoy Commandant Gregoire: cut to a few more stragglers, seen sideways by Dick, riding past the coiffeur's, bent over their handlebars, and fading into a quick shot of the handlebar theme in the new Antibes Bar, which is immediately followed by a shot of the sailor, seen through the skylight of the firemen's foc's'le of the *Diderot*, pedalling with his fists on either side of his face, as if riding the handlebars of an imaginary moustache-bicycle, in parody of the chief engineer: we come back to Dick laughing to himself in the barber's chair, though his own face now returns to the mirror it regards us, a preparate blob of soap upon it, with a huge sadness like that of a tragic clown.

Dick: (in a tone amounting to some obscure decision) Puis-je avoir un journal de Marseilles, René.

René hands him the *Journal* and we look at the front page over Dick's shoulder. It has pictures of the bicycle race. Then, as with Dick's hands, we turn to a page called En Rade—the equivalent of our "I Cover the Waterfront" section. Here, under a part that mentions briefly the names of a few freighters of different nationalities in port at Marseilles, what they are loading, and where going, there is a brief comment that turns into English: Commandant Aidonopaulos, of the Greek cargo ship *Aristotle*, and a frequent visitor to our shores within the last years, is in harbour again after a stormy voyage from Cyprus. This time the vessel is loading wine for the French West Indies, and cherries-in-brine and old marble for the United States. The *Aristotle* is bound for Tarragona, Spain, Algiers, and destined for Norfolk, Virginia, in the United States. Commandant Aidonopaulos said that in the aftermath of her wars, despite heroic efforts, Greece is still tragically in need, and must employ all the ships she has to—

Cut to Dick, shaved and brushed, in a phone booth.

Dick: (phoning) Marseilles, bien . . . Est-il le Consulat grec? . . . Oui . . . Est-ce-que le Commandant Aidonopaulos est là? Oui . . . Parle Anglais? . . . They told me . . . Yes. Is Commandant Aidonopaulos . . . (so far we have simply seen Dick speaking into the phone, now, or a little before this, as he goes on speaking with his head inclined upwards, it is as if he were looking out at the flowing Times Building news again, distantly, but seen clearly through the window of the booth, on which, timed simultaneously with what he says, is appearing:

CHARLES LINDBERGH TOOK OFF IN HIS PLANE THE SPIRIT

OF ST LOUIS IN A DARING ATTEMPT TO FLY THE ATLANTIC ALONE . . . BALTIMORE MARYLAND: SENATOR WILLIAMS OF BOISE IDAHO TODAY COMPLETED A TRIP ON THE FREIGHTER ROBERT LINCOLN AS SUPER CARGO . . . CANTON CHINA . . . IDEOLOGICAL DIFFERENCES MAY . . . OSWEGO NEW BRUNSWICK . . . which is followed by the hallucinatory battle between the Ego, the Id and the Superego, with Ego holding the ground as it fades, just before Dick says, c'est urgent.)

Dick: (who has not of course stopped talking) Merci, cinq, Ruelle de la Demie-Lune . . . Oui. Dites donc—s'il vous plaît, qu'un ami—yes, a very good friend of his, the Commandant of the French ship *Diderot*, Commandant Gregoire, has told me to look him up . . . Oui, Monsieur—merci—parce que c'est très urgent—

Cut to Dick and Captain Aidonopaulos in a restaurant in Marseilles, high above the harbour and looking far out over it. They are almost as high up as the figure of Notre Dame de la Garde that stands watch aloft for the city below, and the golden image gleams in the last rays of the sun. Aidonopaulos, wearing his uniform, is a splendid, bearded, Homeric looking Greek, slightly taller than Dick, although he appears a kindly fellow. They rise from their wine and stand looking out over the sea where the ships of many nations lie like toys, tilted at various angles in the roadstead. There are lowering clouds in the sunset, occasional faint thunder and lightning. In what music there is, otherwise majestic, or suggesting pure longing for the sea, there sounds an imperceptible unsentimental hint of *Carry Me Back to Old Virginny*. This hint, though slightly ironic, does not detract from what one obtains from this scene which, posing a strong contrast with part of the beginning of the next scene on the beach, is an indefinable sense of something persistently heroic in man's destiny, of the eternal involvement of men pitted against the darkness and the deep.

Dick: Well, naturally I will, I was asking you a favour, Captain.

Aid: I will see to it that it is refunded, if necessary by myself—it's merely a matter of formality with our government that we should not appear to sign you on here in Marseilles, Doctor. (laughing) There are other formalities too on board, in every country. Should we have needed new blankets here and it be freezing, the steward will have them sealed in his locker amidships until such time as it is too hot to breathe. But I think you will have an interesting voyage on our old ship. There she is—Ah, there is the *Aristotelis* now (we see a ship moving far away and below) warping in there a little, tomorrow she goes to the coal tips and Friday we are off.

Dick: I hope it was not too much to ask.

Aid: Nothing could be too much to ask for a friend of Gregoire's. We were apprentices together once, on a Finnish sailing ship. We were wrecked at the Horn. Three days we clung to that wooden ash chute, and I am a very poor swimmer; he saved my life, that Breton.

Dick: Well, now you're going to save mine.

Aid:—In return for your saving ours. Let us hope it won't quite come to that . . . (chuckles) But we shall run into the Equinox . . . So—(he rises) Here is to your country, Doctor,—to America.

Dick: And here is to Greece! (They drink)

Aid: (reminiscently, for a moment) But of course you will be homeward bound, while all of us poor devils will be outward bound. (He fills Dick's glass, they sit down, with reminiscent purpose, in the manner of sailors) There's a story of the English poet John Masefield, who was once wrecked at the Horn, and perhaps this will tell you how I felt that time with Gregoire. For three days and three nights he wore his jack-knife in his cap—

Dick: (but there is something youthful in his face) Why did he do that?

Aid: To catch the lightning—

Cut through a flash of lightning and banging of thunder, to a steep dark moving shot of the cliffs, of the French coast between Marseilles and Antibes, brightening into day, with the sea crashing on the rocks. The camera is travelling along the cliffs, following the foaming sea margin for a while, finds the towers and walls of Antibes at a distance, comes immediately to the beach at Antibes.

It is a clear, beautiful, slightly windy day with the sea a bit choppy, and many people on the beach including Lanier and Topsy, who, the nurse near, are playing in the surf. The camera moves up to them and we see that Lanier is crying a little, though in an almost adult and restrained fashion, while Topsy is as stoically uncrying as Nicole once was as a child.

Lanier: Je ne suis pas ce que je suis, car si je suis ce que je suis—I don't know *why* Dick won't let us see him off.

The Nurse: (with a French accent) Go and play, children. Your father has much to think about now he must go to America.

Topsy: (pushing Lanier) Cry baby. See, I'm not crying. Daddy told me—

Lanier: Aw, you're too young to be unhappy.

Lanier plunges savagely into the surf after this last statement and we cut to Nicole and Baby before their dressing tent, with Barban near, in bathing trunks, lying on his stomach in the sand, facing away from the sea. Nicole and Baby are half facing the sea, half toward Gausse's and the cliffs.

Baby: Dick's still there.

Nicole: I saw him.

Baby: I think he might have the delicacy to go!

Nicole: (slowly) This is his place—in a way, he discovered it. You know that. Old Gausse always says he owes everything to Dick.

We are looking momentarily again at what Gausse does owe to Dick, in fact quite a lot: the Hotel des Etrangers refurbished and overflowing with "society," and its human outworks, the beach populated, the whole adorned with signs Buvez Dr. Popsicoola pour votre santé, or advertisements for the Antipolis Cabaret, avec les jolies "Black Bottom Girls," etc., but, sympathetically, it is a working proposition. Then the camera comes back to Nicole and the others.

Baby: He's moved up higher on the terrace. Anyhow, there are so many people now he doesn't *have* to see us.

Barban, vaguely disgusted with Baby's cynicism, scornfully scoops up a handful of sand, slowly lets it trickle through his fingers as Nicole speaks.

Nicole: Dick was a good husband to me for six years. All that time I never suffered a minute's pain because of him, and he always did his best never to let anything hurt me.

The camera now follows the direction of Nicole's eyes and locates Dick on a high cliff above the beach in the sun and wind of the beautiful morning. High up behind him are the castellated battlemented towers of the old Grecian town. From a distance, though he looks metallic at first against the sky, he is still, despite his late dissipations, a fine figure of a man; but now the camera moves up on him we see that while this is so, how much older he looks. Even so at close range he looks still finer. Wearing the sports clothes with the seaman's or fisherman's jersey we have seen him in at the beginning, he has about him the adventurous air of an archetypical American, as he gazes round at the town, and it is with the air of a pioneer that he surveys the sea beyond, as if whatever it represents of the unconscious to him were an as yet untraversed prairie. And whether he is a little ahead of the day in this next respect does not matter as, with this air too, he raises his flask and drinks, symbolically, the health of the beach. As he raises the flask, through Dick's eyes we look down at the beach below with its crowds and umbrellas; then we see it as it was before, clean and empty in the sun, the old group on the beach—Nicole, Abe, Tommy and Dick himself, projected from himself, raking the beach, the others all laughing with him—it was no good, really, even then, but it seems so—then we come back to the present beach. At this point Dick catches sight of Lanier and Topsy and turns, looking up at the Villa Diana, and the camera moves up to it, following the dear familiar outlines of his home, where we see his gardener again, as before, but this time honing his scythe.

Cut back to Dick, standing on the cliff, then down to the beach once more as his eyes rove across the crowd until they fasten on Nicole.

Suddenly the scene is repeated from Nicole's standpoint. She sees two people standing against the sky. On the sound track while the figures are held:

Dick: I love you, Nicole.

Nicole: You love me! I don't ask you to love me always like this, but I ask you to remember. Somewhere inside me there'll always be the person I am tonight . . .

Cut to Nicole, as the other Nicole beside Dick fades.

Nicole: (rising) I'm going to him.

Barban: (pulling her down firmly) Better let well alone.

We see Dick once more from Nicole's standpoint, alone against the sky. He is still looking down at Nicole, holding her eyes even at this distance for a long moment, then he turns away. As he does so the screen begins to darken, and cutting across the pathos there is a tremendous savage and protracted roar from a ship's siren.[90]

Simultaneously Dick, preceded by a sailor with a sea-bag slung over his shoulder, is seen walking up a steep tilted gangway amidships of a freighter lying alongside the wharf under the coal tips, the freighter's bow in huge close up photographed from below so that the perpendicular dividing line of her bow is nearly the height of the screen to the right, and the ship so foreshortened that her funnel and most of her mainmast are visible. It is twilight, the freighter is sombre under arc lamps and her sidelights and mastlights glow sinisterly. On her bow is plainly and immediately visible, in Greek characters, her name: ΑΡΙΣΤΟΤΕΛΗΣ: this changes into ARISTOTLE, then back into Greek characters. Immediately the gangway is drawn in: sailors are seen casting off ropes as the siren dies away, only its echoes reverberating around the harbour.

Lap dissolve to the *Aristotle* steaming outward bound—as the overlapping echoes of the siren die we are aware of the ship's engine, like a bass accompaniment to the rhythm and tune, very faintly at first, of *Frère Jacques*.[91]

Cut to a shot of the sailors in silhouette, the port watch coiling down ropes on the stern: right astern, leaning over the rail, is the shadowy figure of Dick, watching the water churned by the propellors, unearthly in the moonlight. *Frère Jacques* now increasingly becomes a deep triumphant cacophony, polyphony, in the background, expressive of the film itself, becoming more and more "free" yet more and more subsumed in the clash and crash and reiterated emphasis of the engine. The camera leaves Dick and follows the wake toward the moon and the horizon.

Cut to a shot of Nicole's hands holding the Marseilles *Journal de Commerce*. Barban's hands come in beside hers. During this the sounds of *Frère Jacques* and the ship's engine do not cease. In the paper we read: *S.S. Aristote* (grec)—A Toulon, pour Norfolk, Virginie, Etats Unis: this immediately becomes *S.S. Aristotle* (Greek) in Toulon, for Norfolk, Virginia, United States. Instantly Toulon, while the rest is held, changes to: in Barcelona, Spain: in Barcelona to in Tarragona, Spain, then the whole reads: *S.S. Aristotle* (Greek)—in Tarragona, Spain, for Algiers, and Norfolk Virginia, United States—

While *Frère Jacques* becomes more furious, dissolve to a flagstaff at twilight on the breakwater in Antibes: the gale warning is run up by a man in oilskins: waves and spray break over the jetty: then all we see is the storm-tossed flag against the tempestuous sky.

Cut to Nicole, Barban, Baby, the McKiscos, standing at the parapet of the Villa Diana in the same stormy twilight: the sea roars beneath, it is briefly evident that they have all become friendly, though no one speaks. The wind whips their clothes and hair. Far below the lighthouse swings its beam across the wild Mediterranean and the night.

Dissolve, *Frère Jacques* and the ship's engine growing louder, to the *S.S. Aristotle* herself; the camera comes along a narrow alleyway with a steward to the dispensary, above the galleries of the engine room: the door is on the hook, Dick is bandaging the arm of a fireman, covered in coal dust, the ship is pitching and rolling severely and it is hard for them to keep their place. It is just after dark.

The Fireman: (in Greek) Thank you, Doctor. Well, down the little hell again. (rolls a cigarette)

A Steward: (knocks, then enters. in English) Excuse, Doctor. The Captain—

Dick: (putting away his instruments) Anything serious?

The Steward: (smiling) Serious! The Captain asking you to join him with apéritif.

This amuses them; Dick lights the fireman's cigarette.

Cut to the bridge of the *Aristotle*: the man at the wheel, Aidonopaulos, and the fourth mate on duty. The skipper's room gives on the bridge from aft. From the wireless operator's cabin comes the spurting hammering sound of the wireless and occasionally we hear the racing of the propellor. The bridge, like that of the *Diderot*, is glassed in. What we see through the glass is the forepart of the ship lifting and swaying in a rising equinoctial storm. There is a sound of the wind whining and screaming. Dick joins the men on the bridge where they are all standing, followed by the chief officer.

Aid: Ah, Dick—here's an interesting sight. We've got a third light up there on the masthead. (On the rolling and pitching mast we make out another light, through the bridge window. in Greek) How many did you say you saw, quartermaster?

The Man at the Wheel: (in Greek) There're three or four, sir. It's hard to make out.

Aid: (in English, to Dick) It's an albatross. The mother—frightened of the storm. She's got her young up there to protect them—very rarely they come in from the Atlantic if the weather's bad enough. It's the mother's beak makes that third light.

Dick: I seem to remember—

The Chief Officer: (in English, laughing) Just what I always said, Doctor, nature was a menace to navigation.

Dick is visibly moved at the sight of the birds and it is as if *Frère Jacques* with the engines were for a moment pronouncing the fellowship of every living thing.

Cut to the ship's bell: as on the *Diderot*, it comes toward us and is struck by hand.

Cut to the wireless operator's room: he is furiously tapping, sending or receiving messages.

Cut to the Captain's cabin with Dick and Aidonopaulos at chess. The ship is now rolling so violently that the cabin table is tied down with ropes. The chessmen are of those type that are set in little holes so they do not scatter at each lurch. The only thing that does not obey the law of slide and counterslide motion in the room is a bottle of liquor which reposes in a sea boot by the Captain's side—he pours them both a drink and replaces the bottle.

Dick: Giocomo Piano opening.

Suddenly the spurting hammering noise of the wireless reaches a climax.

Aid: Pawn to king's four. (There is a knock at the door. Aidonopaulos, in Greek) Come in.

The wireless operator enters, hands Aidonopaulos a message.

Aid: (gets up, looking grave, to Dick in English) I'll have to change our course a bit—(Dick fractionally ponders his chess move)

Cut back to Nicole's and Barban's hands holding the *Journal de Commerce*: we read: *S.S. Aristote* (grec)—de Marseilles, pour Virginie, Etats Unis. Then the French words before that turn into: Overdue in Algiers: *S.S. Aristotle* . . .

Cut to a confused gale of hammering and static in the dark wireless operator's cabin on board the *Aristotle*. The operator is sending out distress signals. The cabin door has been broken but the S.O.S. signals go on.

Cut to a closeup of a bulkhead, it begins to leak a little—it is exactly like the image of the dam against the flood—seamen try to stop the leak.

Cut back to the drawing room at Antibes with Abe's black, closed piano: Nicole and Barban are listening to the new radio: there is a world conveyed in their look but they say nothing, Barban puts his hand over hers but they do not speak.

From the radio: (while beneath the voice the S.O.S. signals do not cease) This is L.M.N.O. Gibraltar. The Greek Freighter *Aristotle*, bound for Norfolk Virginia in the United States is reported in distress off the Balearics and sending out S.O.S. signals tonight. Nearest to the scene is the British Blue Funnel cargo vessel, *Telemachus*. But ships of four flags are reported hastening to the stricken vessel ... the Italian oil tanker *Alicante*, and another Greek freighter, the *Dimitrios N. Bogliazides*, which ...

Cut back to the *S.S. Aristotle*: a confused shot of the wireless operator hammering away at the keys, then a confused scene of sailors, mostly in souwesters and oilskins, unleashing a lifeboat—one lifeboat is patently smashed and the sea breaks over the scene to starboard. Cut to the bulkhead, it gives way and the flood pours in: cut to the Captain shouting in Greek through a megaphone.

Aid: (in Greek) Abandon ship! Married men with families first! We have only two lifeboats! Keep calm—the wireless operator will continue to send messages as long as possible—we are in a sea-lane—

Cut to a rocket going up.

Cut to Dick, half engulfed in a wave, kneeling to an unconscious sailor in the scuppers. He picks him up, carries him over his shoulder to where the lifeboats are half-lowered on one side; the sailor at the lifeboat's windlass helps him and they drop the unconscious sailor into the lifeboat. Cut to the funnel: the steam whistle: it sounds the Abandon ship signal—cut to the engines: *Frère Jacques*: (the ship, headed into the storm, is barely in forward motion, but they are trying to keep steerage way on her as long as possible) then the chief engineer below the fiddley, standing in the prison-like galley of the engine room.

The Chief: (in Greek) Abandon ship!

A few firemen appear down below. Cut to some firemen coming up the ladder, the chief engineer half way down, shouting; no one is in a panic but the noise is appalling.

Cut to Dick, staggering on to the bridge to find Aidonopaulos at the wheel himself, bleeding badly from one wrist. As Dick reaches him, Aidonopaulos lets the wheel spin idly, with an exclamation, showing the ship has become uncontrollable from this source. Forward, a derrick is tearing itself loose, but the lights, including that provided by the mother albatross and her little brood, are still burning.

Aid: Are you married? (Dick, who has coolly managed to preserve some equipment with him, does not reply, begins to examine and swiftly bind up Aidonopaulos' wrist) Come on, man, no heroics now—my orders were married men first. My position is different. I'm bound to stay here.

Dick: (working over his wrist) You're liable to bleed to death, Captain. Let's deal with one thought at a time.

Cut to the wireless operator's cabin—the noise is terrific, as he goes on sending out S.O.S. signals to the end. Water washes around his feet.

Cut to the engines: *Frère Jacques*: *Frère Jacques*: in the stokehold a negro who has heroically been raking out the fires hurls a slicebar across the deck in a cloud of rising steam.

Cut to a lifeboat, filled with sailors, they seem yelling for the others to jump, lifted on the crest of a high wave, while the tireless noise from the wireless operator's cabin goes on. Then we see another lifeboat, lifted suddenly into overwhelming darkness.

Cut to the demolished bulkhead, the flood is in complete possession.

Cut to the bridge: Dick and Captain Aidonopaulos look at the hopeless scene forward where the derrick has now broken loose.

Now the noise from the wireless cabin ceases; we see that forward, on the masthead, the lights are still on, and the bird is still there with her young. Behind Dick and the Captain the Captain's cabin and the bridge is taken up with the few figures, presumably unmarried, left on the ship: these are a tattooed negro fireman smoking a cigarette, a Greek trimmer covered with coal dust, two seamen, one very young boy with a cross around his neck, the lamptrimmer, the wireless operator, and a bearded carpenter; they are wearing lifebelts. Aidonopaulos retrieves a bottle from his sea boot and passes it round.

Aid: (in Greek) God bless you all. You know what to do, men. They have a good chance. (He gestures towards the dreadful sea, referring to the seamen in the lifeboats.)

The Negro: (in Greek, to the boy, smiling) Don't be afraid. It is nothing.

Aid: (to Dick, in English) We have a good chance, my boy. Four ships have our position . . . I've seen worse.

Dick: (with a strange look of exultance) My curiosity is inexhaustible.

Cut to a paralysing shot of the scene from the bridge, the vessel in anguish shipping sea after sea of white drifting fire, after each crash of sea the spume smoking mast-high across the eyes of the frightened birds, the mother's beak of protective love still in the masthead light, which has still not gone out.

Aid: (murmurs to Dick, in English) Our lamptrimmer trimmed his lights well.

Dick: Nicole . . .

Dissolve to the sinking ship: ΑΡΙΣΤΟΤΕΛΗΣ in Greek characters, is seen upon a lifebelt, only the light on the masthead where the birds are is visible, as the ship, with a cracking sound of ruination, begins to sink under them: the next moment we see people, among them Dick and the Captain, struggling as drowning men; where possible they seem trying to help one another. Then the masthead light becomes the evening star, as we dissolve to a hugely long shot of wreckage on the sea at twilight in a great calm. The camera travels over this together with a curving small wave until it reaches a beach. The wave, the wash, breaks on the beach, but the beach, seen to be that of Antibes, is empty in the calm twilight. And *Frère Jacques* has not ceased, mysteriously still continues, but is becoming now more and more that faint yet steady pulsation heard at the opening of the picture.

While the evening star is still visible, we begin, borne by the camera, to be carried gradually upwards, at first toward the old castellan gated city of Antibes, with the white Alps beyond. The camera pauses an instant by a sign on which we see ΑΝΤΙΠΟΤΙΣ only, then we move upwards to the tower and the gates. The ancient gates open, and through them dimly pass two figures: they are Nicole and Barban, indistinct but recognisable, beyond them a silhouette of dark trees tossing against the twilight sky, the white Alps in the far distance.

The screen darkens, and we become conscious of the night again as the camera moves beyond the city and higher and upwards toward the Alps and the starry heavens, so that the sensation we have is of chiasmus, the reverse of the beginning, as if we were leaving the earth and returning to the sky, at the same time into the origin of that faint wordless yet deep bass rhythm still expressed by the throbbing of *Frère Jacques*.

A bright, sailing moon now appears, is dominant an instant, disappears behind curdling clouds, is left behind and below as at this point we begin to be borne straight upwards into the night sky and the stars, that source bearing and direction of so much of human wisdom—but eternal reminder also that our being and will are elsewhere—where Perseus and Orion are ever fixed, but which too is continually evolving, which even at this moment in the cinema is living in Homeric days, if we like, and long before: which is past and future at once, heresy and divine symbol, and the resolution of the film symbolically in terms less of happiness or unhappiness, than of our human hope or love or fear, or reverence for God. There is a half silence, through which this faint echo of *Frère Jacques* persists, but it is as if the ship's engine had become now again the rhythm of the universe itself, even of love itself, half heard, but still pulsating, vibrant and rhythmic in the theatre, like "something that binds the dead to the living and the living to the unborn," so that we feel that, should our world have ended, or end, it would still go on.

Suddenly the shot of the night sky and the stars blazing with which the picture opened is repeated, or reestablishes itself, and the music does two things; all at once it rises to a dissonant scream, a paean of dreadful pain: then, as all the planes upon which the film has progressed are resolved, and while the stars themselves remain on the screen, it strides forth in triumphant harmony. (Lowry, pp. 435–55)

Notes

1 Concerning "how to write ARISTOTLE, OEDIPUS TYRANNUS and ANTIPOLIS in Greek capitals," Lowry wrote his school-teacher friend Downie Kirk in March 1950: "I want them visually in Greek capital letters first for dramatic effect." He was interested in this regard not only in a possible cinema audience, but also in the reader of the literary manuscript: "it would make a large difference in the presentation if at least I can make the Greek capitals look right" (*Selected Letters of Malcolm Lowry*, ed. Harvey Breit and Margerie Bonner Lowry [Philadelphia and New York: J. B. Lippincott, 1965], pp. 194, 195. Hereafter referred to as *Selected Letters*).

2 Lowry to Downie Kirk again: "what I want is the wording of an hotel advertisement by a railroad in the Riviera, its ironic appeal is to Americans (in the work) so that I have to break it down in parts into *bad* English, but meantime it is better for me to know what it would be in *good* French" (*Selected Letters*, p. 194).

3 "[T]here is nothing on the other shore of the Mediterranean that awakens in me the memory of heroic days as does this." (French writer Guy de Maupassant's description of Antibes, as quoted by Lowry in his *Notes on a Screenplay for F. Scott Fitzgerald's Tender Is the Night*, ed. Matthew J. Bruccoli [Bloomfield Hills, MI., Columbia, SC: Bruccoli Clark, 1976], p. 7. Hereafter referred to as *Notes*.)

4 George Gershwin (1898-1937), great American composer and pianist and creator of such standards of American music as "Rhapsody in Blue" and "An American in Paris." Although often associated with the Jazz Age, Gershwin in fact made only superficial use of jazz devices and did not play an important part in the development of jazz. "Somebody Loves Me" dates from 1924 and had already found its way into a number of motion pictures by the time Lowry was writing his screenplay.

5 Composed by Lee Roberts and J. Will Callahan in 1917, "Smiles" was

written as a cheerful song for soldiers and civilians during the First World War. It became extremely popular in vaudeville, dance halls, and restaurants and was released in numerous recordings.

6 Composed by Raymond Egan and Richard Whiting in 1920, "The Japanese Sandman" was made popular in vaudeville and was included in the 1939 film *Rose of Washington Square*.

7 Leon Bismarck (Bix) Beiderbecke (1903-31), American jazz cornetist, pianist, and composer of great subtlety and finesse. Although in his lifetime he was appreciated by only a handful of musicians and fans, he acquired the status of a legend over the years and was probably the first white musician to be admired and imitated by black jazzmen. He died in 1931 of alcohol-related causes. "In a Mist," along with "Flashes" and "In the Dark," which are heard later in the screenplay, was part of a suite for piano composed by Beiderbecke.

8 Baker's novel *Young Man With a Horn*, inspired by, but not based on Beiderbecke's life, was made into a Hollywood film of the same name in 1950.

9 Willard Robison (1894-1968), American pianist, vocalist, bandleader, and composer, who flourished during the 1920s and 1930s. Lowry wrongly refers to him as Willard Robinson in *Dark as the Grave Wherein My Friend Is Laid*, p. 210 (Penguin), p. 197 (General).

10 Friedrich Wilhelm Murnau (1888-1931) was one of the greatest directors of the German silent cinema. *Sunrise* (1927) was Murnau's first American film and deals with the loss and redemption of love. It opens with a title that describes the film as "the song of two humans. This story of a Man and his Wife is of nowhere and everywhere, you might hear it anywhere and at any time. For everywhere, the sun rises and sets—in the city's turmoil or under the open sky on the farm, life is much the same, sometimes bitter, sometimes sweet, tears and laughter, sin and forgiveness."

11 "Au Claire de la lune," traditional folk song dating from the eighteenth century.

12 The poem quoted here and elsewhere throughout the scene is Keats' "Ode to a Nightingale." "It is difficult to believe," Lowry writes, "that Fitzgerald's novel has existed for sixteen years without anyone having called attention to the source of its title [...]. For it is one of the few truly great titles, a stroke of genius by itself that one would like Fitzgerald to get credit for, yet only in some such way as this can it assume its true significance among the few others that are Dantean inscriptions over the gates of hell, heaven and purgatory" (*Notes*, pp. 60, 71). Noting that the Scribner's edition of *Tender Is the Night* has Fitzgerald's epigraph, with a citation, from Keats' "Ode to a Nightingale," Matthew Bruccoli suggested in 1976 that the Lowrys would have used "either the 1948 Grey Walls edition or the 1945 Viking Portable edition—both of which omitted

the epigraph" (*Notes*, p. 83). As we point out in our Introduction, they used the Viking Portable edition (*The Portable F. Scott Fitzgerald*).

13 Serge Sergeyevich Prokofiev (1891-1953), noted Russian classical composer, also contributed brilliant musical scores to Eisenstein's *Alexander Nevsky* (1938), the director's first sound film, and *Ivan the Terrible* (1943-46). *Peter Grimes* is a 1945 English opera by Benjamin Britten.

14 *Othello*, Act I, sc. ii, 11.1-4:

> Though in the trade of war I have slain men,
> Yet do I hold it very stuff o' the conscience
> To do no contrived murder: I lack iniquity
> Sometimes to do me service.

It is indeed, as Abe points out, Iago and not Othello who speaks these lines.

15 Popular American song written in 1920 by Malvin and John Schonberger. "Whispering" became rapidly popular and sold over a million copies in the early 1920s, and it was included in a number of films of the 1940s and 1950s.

16 Jazz piece recorded in New York in 1927 with Joe Venuti on violin and Eddie Lang on guitar.

17 Allusion to Giuseppe (Joe) Venuti (1899-1978), jazz violinist and frequent musical partner of guitarist Eddie Lang from 1925 until Lang's death in 1933, and Claude Debussy (1862-1918), French composer and one of the principal figures in the evolution of music between Wagner and the middle of the twentieth century.

18 *Seven Chances* is a 1925 film by Keaton. *Intolerance* is the 1916 film of the great American director, D. W. Griffith. Keaton's own *Three Ages* (1923) in fact parodied *Intolerance*.

19 "Re Dick, Rosemary, taxi scene. Dimly apparent also, though we have slightly altered Fitzgerald here, should be what one takes to be his true meaning, (just as valid in this version of ours, if not more so) in introducing 'Daddy's Girl' at all, and then throwing Dick into this ironic paternal juxtaposition with the actress playing it who is in love with him. If this is just a coincidence, it is a coincidence of *destiny*, morally speaking, part of Dick's punishment for having, as we shall see, been a 'deserter,' to himself. [. . .] It is as though Dick is destined to have his original mistake thrown in his face in various forms until he has atoned for it, and the longer he puts it off, the further back he will have to go" (Lowry, *Notes*, pp. 7-8).

20 Born Reginald Leigh Daymore (1891-1967) in England, Denny starred in numerous silent and early sound comedy-adventure films, usually portraying a vigorous man of action. *California Straight Ahead* is from 1925.

21 Alexander Ivanovich Kuprin (1870–1938) was a leading Russian novelist and story writer of the early twentieth century who emigrated to France after the Revolution. *The Pit* (1908–15), his longest work, was intended as an exposé of the evils of prostitution. Kuprin's first success, however, had come in 1905 with the publication of his novel entitled, coincidentally enough, *The Duel*.

22 Famous clowns of the era. The Fratellinis were a family of circus clowns, the most famous of whom were the three Fratellini brothers, François, Paul, and Albert. In the mind of the French public, they raised clowning to the level of an art, and by 1923, the Fratellinis had become the darlings of the Parisian intellectuals. Unfortunately, their only visit to London was a flop. Grock (1880–1959) was the stage name of Charles Adrien Wettach, born in Switzerland and for many years a much-loved star of the British music-hall, the supreme clown of his generation. He played in London almost continuously up to 1924, after which he returned to the continent.

23 Eddie Lang (Salvatore Massaro, 1904–33) was a jazz guitarist and the first to make an international name as a jazz soloist. He also played and recorded with violinist Joe Venuti, with whom he had played in his school orchestra in Philadelphia. Jean Baptiste (Django) Reinhardt (1910–53) was a Belgian gypsy and a splendid guitarist, whose beautiful technique was all the more wondrous for his having had two fingers of his left hand seriously disfigured in a fire. Reinhardt brought a unique style to jazz in which the gypsy qualities of his music were so pronounced that he is denied the jazz label by many fans. Nonetheless, he is felt by many to be the first overseas musician to influence jazz music in America. "Sweet Georgia Brown" is an American popular song composed in 1925 and actually recorded by Reinhardt in 1937.

24 Maurice Chevalier (1888–1972), French entertainer who gained an international reputation in the Paris music halls of the 1920s before turning to movies later in his life.

25 The café names are "borrowed from Fitzgerald's 'Babylon Revisited,' a story about *after* the crash. [. . .] We leave them here tentatively for the effect we want to produce would be similar, and while our net borrowing is minimal, Fitzgerald's *original* intention here was undoubtedly Babylonian but with the accent on damnation and spiritual emptiness, rather than psychical, as in the story" (Lowry, *Notes*, p. 8). In Fitzgerald's short story, as in Lowry, the "two great mouths" of the cafés yawn; and there are *cocottes* (as also described by Lowry in the next long paragraph) "prowling singly or in pairs."

26 There have been many songs by this name, the most famous being published in 1925 and made popular in the 1929 film, *Innocents in Paris*, starring Maurice Chevalier.

27 Composed by Gus Kahn and Isham Jones in 1924, "I'll See You in My Dreams" later provided the title for, and was used prominently in, the 1951 film biography of Kahn.
28 Classical piece written by the French composer Maurice Ravel in 1928.
29 Traditional Irish folk song.
30 Fritz Lang (1890-1976), director of such German films as *Destiny* (1921), *Metropolis* (1926), and *M* (1932), in which the actor Peter Lorre made his name. Lang also worked in Hollywood, where he created such films as *Fury* (1936) and *You Only Live Once* (1937) and even directed several Westerns.
31 In his notes to the screenplay, Lowry defends his use of the automobile accident to replace the incest motif in Fitzgerald's story. The change, he argues, "is made possible by Fitzgerald himself. He made the incest motif only really important in one place. True, it goes on echoing dolorously in our minds throughout the book but that is not because he has dealt with it adequately but simply because it is so shocking that we don't forget it, even if he almost does. In the film the primary cause of Nicole's insanity has to be at the same level of the action as the rest, be welded in it, and part of it, and solved within it, and an important part of the film's resolution. This is where the car motif comes in. And what we lose on the swings, so to speak, we make up on the Isotta and the Ferris Wheel" (*Notes*, p. 12).
32 Allusion to the 1919 German expressionistic film, *The Cabinet of Dr. Caligari*, renowned for its visual experiments and excessive, striking and fantastical images.
33 Dick's remark about the apple tree, Lowry writes in his notes, provides a hint of the extent of his emotional involvement with Nicole: "even were he almost totally impersonal he would feel a certain sense of loss at this point, something like that of an author correcting the last proofs of a book, or a painter parting with his painting" (*Notes*, p. 13).
34 "What Dick should be doing, in fine, even is still doing and still half thinks he is doing—and indeed would have done but for a stroke of fate in the face of which he is not strong enough—is to prepare Nicole for a Barban that does not yet 'exist'; what he succeeds in doing is not only almost entirely ruining her for himself, and in herself, but for the real Barban when he arrives on the scene" (Lowry, *Notes*, pp. 13-14).
35 Lowry had his own psychoanalytical reading of the song: "Who is this Japanese Sandman who can do all these magical things, for he surely must be some sort of magician, even if he gets paid for it? [. . .] He may be death, he may be destiny, he may be night, he may even live in America, while at the same time managing to remain mysteriously a Japanese Sandman, but he cannot be all these things at once at this present moment without being one thing which is surely—ah!—some kind of

psychoanalyst. And so the Japanese Sandman is Dick too. The only trouble is this: Nicole will give him silver all right, and he will give her gold. But the gold happens unfortunately to be of a kind still susceptible to the mutations of alchemy and so will inevitably turn back into the obscure amalgam of the night whence it came" (*Notes*, p. 22).

36 After Nicole tells Dick about her plans, Dick mumbles three words to himself in German before telling her that he is leaving the clinic. Lowry comments in his notes: "The first two words are the psychological cousins-German to Nicole's temporary forgetting, *Fehllandung*, 'bungling of acts,' *vergreifen*, 'the automatic execution of purposive acts in wrong situations': Dick is thinking ironically of his own behaviour here; the third word, *Ubertragung*, means 'transference,' we don't want—and indeed it would be fatal—to know exactly what he means here" (*Notes*, p. 22).

37 In his notes Lowry further explains his use of Gluck's *Orféo*: "to the thirty percent or so of the millions of opera lovers [. . .] it will prove a considerable moment. Yet another dimension can be added by those rarer ones whose imagination will allow Eurydice's company in Tartarus to include, in addition to such energetic characters as Ixion and Sisyphus, such charmers as Electra [. . .]. While those who do not get the point at all will have heard some supernaturally good music in exactly the right place by someone they have thought was on your payroll, whereas in fact not even Petrillo could charm the old wizard of the glass harmonica into the musician's union" (*Notes*, pp. 23-24).

38 The Knights Templar, founded c.1119-20 by French knights, was the first and most notable of the military religious orders of the Middle Ages.

39 In his notes, Lowry comments further on Dick's inability to resist: "We may sympathise with Dick finally for giving in but it scarcely offers an explanation if Dick is really at bottom sincere about his job. What is actually the trouble is something perhaps even more tragic still. Dick himself is divided; divided unconsciously about his vocation and beginning to doubt his fitness for it, and even the nature of the vocation itself, he therefore does not look, unconsciously, to its tenets of responsibility to represent his higher self to him [. . .] so that at the critical point he becomes at the mercy of his human instincts and desires" (*Notes*, pp. 25-26).

40 "[Dick] for his part, must surely be subject now to a temptation that by this time puts all the others in the shade for it stems from his reason, apart from the fact of his being in love with her. Have not things gone too far already? must be the substance of Dick's mute self-questioning: if Nicole was in no condition to survive what she might have interpreted as a tragedy before, how much less will she be now? Therefore, are not their destinies for better or worse, interwoven anyhow?" (Lowry, *Notes*, pp. 26-27).

41 1946 film directed by Roberto Rossellini.
42 Georg Kaiser (1878-1945) was a German dramatist and a major exponent of expressionism. *Von Morgens bis Mitternachts* is perhaps his best-known play and was first seen in 1917. It is the sombre story of a bank clerk whose bid for freedom from the futility of modern civilization leads to suicide. It was translated into English as *From Morn to Midnight* and produced for the first time in English in 1920. Also in 1920, director Karl Heinz Martin turned it into a German Expressionist film.
43 In his notes, Lowry reminds us that Dick is marrying Nicole while Dohmler is away in Berlin and while Gregorovious is too busy in Dohmler's absence to put up any opposition: "Whether simply leaving this understood, because to go into it would have revealed Dick as an artful dodger, was a grave flaw in the novel is beside the point in the film where, not only do we have the excuse that the memory rarely *dramatises* those moments in life where one has been actually mean, however it may be tormented by them, but we are actively presented with—not merely told there was—a *fait accompli*" (*Notes*, p. 27).
44 "The important points to be made here are: (1) that they have been truly, simply happy together, as lovers. (2) Dick's domination over Nicole, and his constant watchfulness over her in the ups and downs of her illness, for her illness is arrested exactly at the point where she should have freed herself from Dick, i.e., the transference should have been terminated. (3) the economic element" (Lowry, *Notes*, pp. 27-28).
45 One of the first French weekly illustrateds, founded in 1863 by Marcelin. It had its most flourishing period during the late nineteenth century with a staff that included brilliant artists and writers but no professional journalists. It continued, though less influentially, into the twentieth century.
46 In his notes, Lowry suggests that Dick has already decided not to buy the clinic: "But if he declines Baby's offer of the clinic, he is buying up paradoxically the greatest opportunity of his life by making the greatest sacrifice, a sacrifice of which he will say nothing to Nicole. At the same time—we may suppose—he will take her to Zurich and then absent himself for a long period of time during which we at least may believe that a miracle may happen. But if he not only makes his dramatic decision but acts upon it in minute and unselfish particulars during the miserable and undramatic future he will become a heroic figure. And he will have made in far bitterer terms and by another kind of causality, the sacrifice he failed to make earlier and which has precipitated the whole drama" (*Notes*, pp. 32-33).
47 A comedy about egocentricity and medical ethics by Shaw (1856-1950), first presented in New York in 1915 and revived in 1927.

48 *S.S. Tenacity*, a play by Vildrac, presented in London and New York in 1920.
49 Lowry to Downie Kirk: "How, roughly, should one translate "Daddy's Girl," as the name for a film, into French? (Fillette de Papa? Poule de Papa? . . .) It should be ironic, if possible. It appears as an advertisement (much as *Las Manos de Orlac* does in the *Volcano*)" (*Selected Letters*, p. 195).
50 Theodor Friedrich Emil Jannings (1884-1950) was a renowned German character actor of the silent era. He was widely acclaimed in his prime as the world's greatest film actor, though his acting was more in the theatrical than the screen tradition. *Le Dernier Rire* is a 1924 German film directed by F. W. Murnau. The original title is *Der Letzte Mann*, literally, *The Last Man*, but it was translated into English as *The Last Laugh*, hence perhaps Lowry's choice of title here, although the film was also known in French as *Le Dernier des Hommes*.
51 In classical mythology, Perseus, a king of Mycenae and Tiryns, was the rescuer of Andromeda, who had been chained to a rock in order to placate a sea-monster. In return for slaying the monster and saving the maiden, Perseus had been offered the hand of Andromeda in marriage by her father, Cepheus. Unfortunately, unknown to Perseus, Cepheus had also promised Andromeda to his brother, Phineus. In the battle that ensued between the two suitors and their followers, Perseus tore Medusa's head—which he had cut off in a previous adventure and was now carrying around with him—from its pouch and held it high, turning his adversaries into stone. Perseus then took Andromeda home with him to Argolis, where she bore him many children.
52 "The sign at the toll bridge reads:

> STOP! PAY TOLL!
> HALT! ZOLL ZU BEZAHLEN!
> HALTE PEAGE A ACQUITTER!
> FERMATI! PEDAGGIO PAGARE!"
> (Lowry, *Notes*, p. 33)

53 The extended New York section below bears affinities to Lowry's novella *Lunar Caustic* (begun by Lowry in New York in 1934 and published posthumously in 1963) and to the New York sequence in Chapter Nine of *Under the Volcano* (1947).
54 *Moana—A Romance of the Golden Age* is a 1925 American documentary about life in the South Seas, directed by Robert Flaherty.

Mare Nostrum is a 1926 film directed by Rex Ingram (1892-1950), an Irish-born director of the silent era who came to America in 1911 and who, among other things, discovered Rudolph Valentino. In the film, a Spanish sea captain has his ship attacked by a German submarine during the First World War. He dies heroically during the altercation, fighting to the end and going down with his ship.

Georg Wilhelm Pabst (1885-1967) was born in Bohemia and directed both silent and sound films in Germany, France, and Austria. *Secrets of a Soul* (*Geheimnisse einer Seele*) was made in 1926.

The Flesh and the Devil is a 1927 American film directed by Clarence Brown. In it, Gilbert plays an Austrian aristocrat who, as a result of his affair with Garbo, is forced to kill her husband in a duel and flee the country. Garbo plays a temptress, constantly luring Gilbert into trouble; she eventually drowns while attempting to stop another duel between Gilbert and her second husband.

Hit the Deck is a 1927 musical comedy based on Hubert Osborne's play *Shore Leave* and made into a film in 1930.

The Hairy Ape, written by American playwright Eugene O'Neill (1888-1953) and first presented in 1922, is an expressionistic study of an American labourer's search for the meaning of his existence.

A 1927 review of Faragoh's play *Pinwheel* in the New York weekly *The Nation* read thus: "The whole bag of tricks—expressionistic, impressionistic, constructivistic, and what not—is opened at once. The spirits of Pantomime, Ballet, Parody, Satire, and Jazz are invoked, singly or together, and all consent to lend their aid. The result is an usually impudent and noisy carnival, something always surprising enough to keep the spectator wondering what will come next."

A Bill of Divorcement, written by English dramatist and novelist Clemence Dane (Winifred Ashton, 1888-1965) in 1921, deals sympathetically with the problem of divorce on the grounds of insanity.

Karel Capek was a Czechoslovakian playwright. His play, *R.U.R.* (*Rostrum's Universal Robots*) was first produced in 1923.

55 Ragtime classic written by Shelton Brooks in 1917 and popularized in vaudeville. It appeared in several motion pictures during the 1930s and 1940s.

56 American popular song originating in 1909 with the Whiffenpoof Society, a glee club at Yale University. It was popularized by singer Rudy Vallee in 1936 and featured in the 1944 Hollywood film *Winged Victory* before being revived again in 1950 by Fred Waring and his Pennsylvanians.

57 Traditional Mexican folk song.

58 Popular Ukrainian Christmas carol, written in 1936.

59 Traditional English Christmas carol.

60 Lowry had himself been a patient at Bellevue in 1935. For a fictional account, see *Lunar Caustic*.

61 *The Dial* was an American literary magazine dating back to 1840. In 1916 it moved to New York, where Lowry's friend Conrad Aiken served as one

of its editors for a time. It published works by Yeats, Eliot, Lawrence, and many others. It ceased publication in 1929 but appeared again in 1959.

The Smart Set (1890-1930) was a monthly magazine founded as a journal for New York society, by whose members it was for the most part written. It grew to become a literary journal, and although its circulation was far greater, it retained many of the traits of the average little magazine. Among the authors published in the magazine were O. Henry, Mencken, Joyce, and, after the First World War, F. Scott Fitzgerald.

Life was the third of a trio of American humorous magazines founded in close succession: *Puck* in 1877, *Judge* in 1881, *Life* in 1883. All three are now dead as humour magazines. Among its many causes and crusades—many of them rather eccentric—was its opposition to the marriage of American girls to foreign fortune-hunters. In 1936, the magazine passed into the hands of *Time*, which wanted only its name.

Judge was a comic weekly founded in 1881 and an organ for the Republican Party in the U.S. in opposition to *Puck* and the Democrats during the first decade of the twentieth century. It ceased publication in 1939.

Literary Digest was founded in New York in 1890. It was a highly successful magazine blending current events and humour and was absorbed by *Time* in 1938.

62 Allusion to Douglas Fairbanks, Sr. (1883-1939), famous Hollywood actor memorable for his popular swashbuckling adventure films of the 1920s.

63 Lowry includes this quotation from Sophocles' *Antigone* in the first of the three epigraphs to *Under the Volcano*.

64 Reference to Nicola Sacco and Bartolomeo Vanzetti, Italian-born self-confessed anarchists of the 1920s who were accused of murdering a paymaster and a guard at a shoe factory in South Braintree, Massachusetts. Although the evidence against them was not conclusive, they were sentenced to death in 1921. The public protest stemmed from the belief of many that the two men had been convicted for their radical views rather than for the crime. Sacco and Vanzetti were executed in 1927 after a commission appointed to review the case upheld the previous conviction.

65 1925 American play spoofing the horror genre. It was made into a Hollywood film starring, among others, Bela Lugosi in 1931.

66 American popular song composed by Irving Caesar and Vincent Youmans in 1924 and introduced in the 1925 musical *No, No, Nanette*, which was renamed after the song itself in 1950.

67 1927 biblical spectacular. One of the most famous films of Cecil B. de Mille (1881-1959), the great Hollywood mogul.

68 Landmark 1925 film made by the great Russian director, Sergei Mikhailovich Eisenstein (1898-1948).

69 Toller (1893-1939) was a German poet and dramatist and one of the best

and most mature exponents of expressionism. *Hoppla, Wir Leben!*, written in 1927, was first produced in London in 1929.

70 Donald Mitchell Oenslager (1902-75), American scene designer who studied in Europe and later contributed to the creation of a new age of stagecraft in the U.S., leaving a mark on American contemporary theatre.

71 In his notes, Lowry provides extensive comments on his New York section. A few examples: "as we once went into Nicole's mind, so now we go into the divided mind of the world of which America is the symbol and coefficient, and possible saviour" (*Notes*, p. 35); "the object is to imply life's hope, its terror, its humour, its beauty, the eternal horror of the world, the goodness of the earth, a fountain plays—and it is the goodness of America" (pp. 35-36); "Who is mean enough to say flying the Atlantic wasn't a courageous act? We all admire it—even Dick. So did Fitzgerald—he is very explicit on the turning point represented by Lindbergh. It is the mass frenetic reaction that is so odd—it is not odd at all. We *make* it odd, by contrast. Lindbergh is the archetypical individual American" (p. 37); "All we say is, that if an Id of America exists, the Great White Way and beneath it is a magnificent symbol of it. And what better expression of the American ego—by extension of the world—than the *Times* Building news? Does not that *Times* Building News literally represent the world to that Id of the unconscious Broadway—for its 'good'?" (p. 40).

72 *The Chocolate Soldier* was a musical version of George Bernard Shaw's comedy *Arms and the Man*.

73 American dramatist Elmer Rice (1892-1967) was the first to employ the flashback technique of the cinema on the American stage. *The Adding Machine* (1923) was an expressionistic fantasy satirizing the growing regimentation of modern man in the machine age through the life and death of a bookkeeper, Mr. Zero.

74 The tune being sung here is "Hallelujah," a sailors' chorus introduced in the 1927 musical *Hit the Deck* and repeated in the 1930 film adaptation.

75 "In the event that you wish to consider the *Diderot* sequence as cut to the bone and simply as a suggestion of itself, an old sailor could demonstrate to you how it is possible to convey all the beauty and monotony and nostalgia of the sea in a comparatively few minutes, without ever using a ship, and with a minimum of expense: a more than Long Voyage Home, in short: props needed:

    A. Many seabirds to be found off the California coast.
    B. A ship's engine.
    C. A ship's bell.
    D. Genius on the part of the recording technician and cameraman.
    E. Ditto the director and producer.

F. Charity in regard to the idea which we assure you can work more than triumphantly.
—and all this without going 10 miles from the waterfront at San Pedro" (Lowry, *Notes*, pp. 43-44).

76 The following sea-voyage section evokes passages from Lowry's short story "Through the Panama" (1960, 1961) and other of Lowry's works, including *Ultramarine* (1933). It was with reference to this section and the preceding (New York) sequence that Lowry spoke of a "poetic and visual and aural *drang*" in his filmscript.

77 Lowry called the "ubiquitous and somnolent bell-ringing brother, or Frère Jacques [...] the result of twenty years' search for an onomatopoeia for a ship's engine" (*Notes*, p. 44). Lowry used this same effect in other of his works, such as "Through the Panama," "Present Estate of Pompeii," and "The Forest Path to the Spring."

78 Eric von Stroheim (1885-1957), American director and actor, born in Vienna. His films include *Foolish Wives* (1921), *Merry-Go-Round* (1923), and *Merry Widow* (1925). Lowry's reference here is confusing, since von Stroheim's one attempt to direct in France (*La Dame Blanche*) was frustrated by the outbreak of the Second World War. His contribution to films after the war was limited to writing and acting.

79 1932 Hollywood film directed by Howard Hawks and loosely based on the career of gangster Al Capone. Raft (1895-1980) gave a memorable performance in the film as one of Scarface's lieutenants.

80 For Lowry's prose rendering of the scene in Keats' house, see his short story "Strange Comfort Afforded by the Profession" (1953, 1961).

81 Lowry discusses the "tender is the night" allusion, here and elsewhere in the script, in his notes: "Fitzgerald's readers might have responded all the more, had it been sounded more explicitly, to the chord of high seriousness he strikes at the outset with his title: in fact it might have made the trivial seem less trivial, and enclosed much else in its dark echoing wing. Yet I daresay you could get fifty more or less intelligent adaptations of this book without the real significance on the 'night' within it having even been entertained and no concession to the title beyond the vague feeling that it was a pretty good one. Yet it comes close to being its whole meaning and the night to being its real hero" (*Notes*, p. 62). See our note 12 above.

82 1927 American documentary by Merian Cooper and Ernest Schoedsack telling how a tribesman of Siam protects his family from the dangers of the jungle. The film originally ended with a stampede of elephants.

83 Noel Coward (1899-1973), noted English playwright. *The Vortex* (1924) is a study of post-First World War decadence and was Coward's first real success on the stage.

84 Popular American song composed by Irving King in 1925. Adapted from a Canadian folk song.
85 "In the following scene, not to save our English feelings, which thrive upon it, from harsh American wit, which for that matter bears an eerie resemblance to British wit at its best, but lest our otherwise fair-minded, revered Fitzgerald show himself an irrational Anglophobe, somewhat to the detriment of his art, and even the box office, some modifications more or less confined to the *punctum indifferens* have been made testifying to certain other more winning aspects of the British national character. [. . .] The degeneracy should be balanced, fragmentarily, by a sheer youthful ebulliency and exuberance that even Americans would find hard to match" (Lowry, *Notes*, p. 71).
86 "We have the impression, possibly erroneous, that this might be the only business joke in movies that was not a gag, if so a remarkable thing considering the number of businessmen in the audience, and even in the business" (Lowry, *Notes*, p. 72).
87 "The song about Mary Ann and the Ferris Wheel was sung for us, out of the blue, on New Year's Eve, by one of our neighbours, a Guernsey fisherman of 75, who had come to visit us while we were revising the scene. He did not know what we were writing about. The song was probably written about 1890, is English, forgotten, if ever remembered, and even if ever published, which is doubtful, can be no longer copyright" (Lowry, *Notes*, p. 72).
88 Composed by James A. Bland in 1878, this song became a favourite with minstrel troupes and was adopted as the official song for the state of Virginia in 1940.
89 Lowry comments in his notes regarding the scenes that follow: "It has been said that Shakespeare had no tragedy or comedy in a pure form: he works in a genre that is something in between, a fusion, 'a genre more responsive to the truth of life, in which horrors and enchantments are fused.' It seems at once that this quality is something that Fitzgerald—in the juxtaposition of these scenes as elsewhere—had in common with the old bird" (*Notes*, p. 72).
90 In his extensive comments on this last scene involving the shipwreck, Lowry says in his notes: "We venture to suggest that there is such a thing as real fate, and its machinations cannot be explained away in terms of any one consistency, though we might assume, as Eastern thought does, and Fitzgerald himself often does, a consistent system where we can understand it, of 'punishments and rewards,' indeed, of justice" (*Notes*, p. 74).
91 In the final sea-voyage sequence that follows, Lowry again evokes details from "Through the Panama."

Index

Abdul the Damned, 11
Adding Machine, The, 167, 253n
Adventure in Morocco, An, 11
African Queen, The, 22
Agee, James, 22
Aiken, Conrad, 9, 14, 251n
Alexander Nevsky, 12, 245n
"American in Paris, An," 243n
American Tragedy, An, 28
Antigone, 6, 31, 162, 252n
Aristotle, 88, 159
Arms and the Man, 253n
"Au Claire de la Lune," 61, 129, 180, 244n

"Babylon Revisited," 246n
Bach, Johann Sebastian, 62
Baker, Dorothy, 57, 244n
Baker's Wife, The, 13
Battleship Potemkin, 7, 165
Beau Geste, 223
Beiderbecke, Leon Bismarck (Bix), 31, 57, 70, 164, 165, 213, 225, 226, 244n
Bergson, Henri, 24, 225
Bête Humaine, La, 13
Bill of Divorcement, A, 147, 166, 167, 251n
Binns, Ronald, 37
Birney, Earle, 12, 13
Birney, Esther, 13
"Bixology," 70
Bland, James A., 255n
"Bolero," 82
Bosch, Hieronymus, 206
"Bravest Boat, The," 17
Breughel, Pieter, 156
Britten, Benjamin, 245n
Broken Blossoms, 19
Brooks, Shelton, 251n
Brown, Clarence, 251n
Bruccoli, Matthew J., 244n
Buddha, 35
Burra, Ed, 9

Ça Qua Ça Gaze, 75
Cabinet of Dr. Caligari, The, 4, 99, 247n
Caesar, Irving, 252n
Calder-Marshall, Ara, 9
Calder-Marshall, Arthur, 9
California Straight Ahead, 75, 245n
Callahan, J. Will, 243n
Cambridge, 8
Cambridge Film Guild (film society), 7, 8, 13
Cambridge Poetry, 9
Canadian Broadcasting Corporation, 11

Cape, Jonathon, 12
Capek, Karel, 147, 164, 251n
Capone, Al, 254n
Carlotta, Empress of Mexico, 161, 162
"Carol of the Bells, The," 155
"Carry Me Back to Old Virginny," 225, 233
Cerillo, Juan, 30
Chang!, 218
Chaplin, Charlie, 15, 21
Chevalier, Maurice, 78, 129, 246n
Chocolate Soldier, The, 167, 253n
Citizen Kane, 19, 34
Colman, Ronald, 223
Conrad, Joseph, 175, 187, 189, 192
Cooke, Alistair, 15
Coolidge, Calvin, 148, 156, 161
Cooper, Merian, 254n
Coward, Noel, 221, 254n
Crime and Punishment, 13
Cyprus is an Island, 13

Dali, Salvador, 95
Dame Blanche, La, 254n
Dane, Clemence (Winifred Ashton), 251n
Dante, 37, 206, 244n
Dark as the Grave Wherein My Friend is Laid, 12, 17, 18, 26, 32, 34, 244n
"Darktown Strutter's Ball, The," 151, 152, 165
Davenport, John, 9
Debussy, Claude, 69, 70, 245n
de Maupassant, Guy, 49, 50, 52, 64, 243n
de Mille, Cecil B., 165, 252n
Denny, Reginald (Reginald Leigh Daymore), 75, 245n
Dernier Rire, Le (*The Last Laugh*), 130, 250n
Destiny, 4, 247n
Dial, The, 159, 251n

Diderot, Denis, 70, 129, 170, 208
Doctor's Dilemma, The, 31, 130, 147
Don Quixote, 76, 79
Donat, Robert, 9
Dovjenkho, Alexander, 11
Dreiser, Theodore, 23, 28
Drifters, 11
Duel, The, 246n
Duvivier, Julien, 11
Dynasts, The, 23

Egan, Raymond, 244n
Eisenstein, Sergei Mikhailovich, 3, 7, 10, 11, 12, 23, 30, 31, 165, 245n, 252n
Eisler, Hanns, 11
Elektra, 130
"Elephant and Colosseum," 36
Eliot, T.S., 252n
End of St. Petersburg, The, 5, 7, 11
English Sporting and Dramatic News, 112, 113
Erskine, Albert, 15, 19, 24, 26, 33
España en Llamas, 10
Experiment, 8

Fairbanks, Douglas, Sr., 160, 252n
Falk, David, 33
Fall of the House of Usher, The, 13
Fantasia of the Unconcious, 179
Faragoh, F.E., 251n
Fejos, Paul, 7
Feyder, Jacques, 11
"Fierce Raged the Tempest O'er the Deep," 165
Fitzgerald, F. Scott, 6, 15, 17, 18, 19, 21, 25, 26, 27, 28, 29, 31, 51, 52, 59, 113, 175, 208, 244n, 245n, 246n, 247n, 252n, 253n, 254n, 255n
Flaherty, Robert, 147, 250n
"Flashes," 227, 244n
Flesh and the Devil, The, 147, 251n
Foolish Wives, 254n
"Forest Path to the Spring, The," 17,

32, 254n
Fosse aux Filles, La, 75, 78, 129
Fox, Stanley, 13
Fratellinis (François, Paul and Albert), 76, 78, 129, 246n
"Frère Jacques," 32, 36, 48, 52, 86, 132, 144, 152, 157, 158, 172, 173, 174, 178, 179, 180, 181, 183, 185, 187, 190, 192, 193, 194, 195, 196, 208, 236, 237, 238, 239, 240, 241, 242, 254n
Freud, Sigmund, 65, 136, 159, 162, 164, 180, 192, 215
Frontier, 11
Fury, 247n

Gabrial, Jan, 9, 10
Garbo, Greta, 147, 184, 251n
George V (King), 149, 153
Gershwin, George, 49, 57, 243n
Ghost That Never Returns, The, 11
"Ghostkeeper," 37
Gilbert, John, 147, 251n
Gluck, Christoph Willibald, 32, 106, 248n
"God Rest Ye Merry Gentleman," 155
Goethe, Johann Wolfgang von, 175
"Going Places," 69, 70
Gorilla, The, 164
Grace, Sherrill, 37
Granta, 8
Greed, 13
Grierson, John, 8, 9, 11
Griffith, D.W., 3, 4, 19, 245n
Grock (Charles Adrien Wettach), 76, 78, 246n
Grune, Karl, 4, 8, 11

Hairy Ape, The, 147, 166, 251n
"Hallelujah," 253n
Hardy, Thomas, 23
Hawkes, Howard, 254n
Hemingway, Ernest, 10
Henry, O., 252n

Hit the Deck, 147, 167, 168, 251n, 253n
Hollywood, 4, 5, 6, 8, 9, 10, 12, 14, 15, 16, 17, 18, 19, 22, 23, 24, 25, 26, 29, 31, 34, 37, 244n, 247n, 251n, 252n, 254n
Homer, 49, 63, 233, 242
Hoover, Mary, 9
Hoppla, Wir Leben!, 166, 253n
Huston, John, 15, 22

"I'll See You in My Dreams," 80, 247n
"In a Mist," 31, 57, 65, 69, 70, 87, 149, 150, 153, 159, 164, 165, 195, 213, 226, 244n
In Ballast to the White Sea, 5
"In the Dark," 165, 213, 225, 226, 227, 228, 244n
Ingram, Rex, 147, 166, 250n
Innocents in Paris, 246n
Intolerance, 7, 33, 73, 245n
Isherwood, Christopher, 20, 21, 22, 23, 24, 26, 28
Isn't Life Wonderful?, 19
Italian Straw Hat, The, 13
Ivan the Terrible, 245n

Jackson, Charles, 12
James, William, 92, 143
Janet, Pierre, 192
Jannings, Emil, 130, 250n
"Japanese Sandman, The," 56, 78, 104, 105, 163, 213, 244n, 247n
Jennings, Humphrey, 8
Joan of Arc. See Passion of Joan of Arc, The
Jones, Isham, 247n
Journal de Commerce, 237, 238
Joyce, James, 7, 34, 158, 252n
Judge, 159, 252n
Jung, Carl Gustav, 6, 173

Kahn, Gus, 247n
Kaiser, Georg, 117, 166, 249n

Kai-sheck, Chiang, 156, 161, 162
Kapek, Karel. *See Capek, Karel*
Keaton, Buster, 73, 245n
Keats, John, 36, 60, 63, 202, 203, 204, 244n, 254n
"Kerry Dancers, The," 83, 133
Killorin, Joseph, 9
King, Irving, 255n
King Lear, 6, 34
King of Kings, 165
Kirk, Downie, 32, 243n, 250n
Krauss, Werner, 4
Kuprin, Alexander Ivanovich, 75, 78, 129, 246n

Lang, Eddie (Salvatore Massaro), 77, 164, 245n, 246n
Lang, Fritz, 3, 4, 19, 87, 247n
Last Laugh, The, 4, 13, 130, 250n
Last Moment, The, 7
Lawrence, D.H., 179, 252n
Legg, Stuart, 8, 9
Letzte Mann, Der, 250n
Leyda, Jay, 7, 22
Life, 15, 95, 159, 252n
Lindbergh, Charles, 161, 167, 168, 188, 232, 253n
Lion Has Wings, The, 11
Literary Digest, 159, 252n
LLoyd, Harold, 7
London, Jack, 186
Lord Jim, 187, 192
Lorre, Peter, 4, 247n
Lost Weekend, The, 12, 25
Loti, Pierre, 186
Loves of Jeanne Ney, The, 13
Lowry, Russell, 7
Lowry, Stuart, 17, 23
Lugosi, Bela, 252n
Lunar Caustic, 36, 250n, 251n
Lye, Len, 8, 11

M, 13, 247n

Macbeth, 119, 147, 166
Mankiewitz, Joseph, 15, 23, 24, 25
Manos de Orlac, Las, 33, 250n
"Mañanitas, Las," 154, 155
Mare Nostrum, 147, 166, 204, 250n
Markle, Fletcher, 13, 20, 25
Markson, David, 27
Martin, Karl Heinz, 249n
Masefield, John, 234
Matson, Harold, 12, 15, 23, 25, 26, 29
Maximilian, Emperor of Mexico, 161
Melville, Herman, 18, 22, 189, 192
Mencken, H.L., 252n
Merry-Go-Round, 254n
Merry Widow, 254n
MGM (Metro-Goldwyn-Mayer), 13, 14, 15, 17, 20, 24, 25, 26
Metropolis, 247n
Milland, Ray, 25
Mix, Tom, 7
Moana—A Romance of the Golden Age, 147, 250n
Moby Dick, 171, 179, 186, 189, 192
Moffat, Ivan, 26
Murnau, Friedrich Wilhelm, 4, 8, 13, 19, 31, 60, 75, 244n, 250n
Mussolini, Benito, 197, 198, 206
Mystery Street, 23

Nation, The, 251n
National Film Board of Canada, 9, 10, 11
Nietzsche, Friedrich, 171
Night Mail, 13
No, No, Nanette, 252n
Noxon, Gerald, 4, 7, 8, 9, 10, 11, 12, 13, 14, 15, 19, 25, 26

October Ferry to Gabriola, 17, 32, 33, 34
"Ode to a Nightingale," 244n
Odyssey, The, 63, 64
Oedipus Rex, 130, 161
Oenslager, Donald Mitchell, 166,

253n
O'Neill, Eugene, 166, 251n
Orféo, 32, 106, 248n
Osborne, Hubert, 251n
Othello, 67, 245n

Pabst, Georg Wilhelm, 147, 162, 164, 251n
Paisan, 116
Paris en Fleures, 75, 78, 129, 130
Passion of Joan of Arc, The, 13
Peary, Robert Edwin, 136, 159, 160
Peer Gynt, 6
Perkins, Maxwell, 13
Peter Grimes, 65, 245n
Pinwheel, 147, 251n
Pit, The, 75, 78, 246n
"Play in Your Own Backyard," 101
"Port Swettenham," 8
Portable F. Scott Fitzgerald, The, 17, 244n, 245n
"Present Estate of Pompeii," 32, 254n
Prokofiev, Serge Sergeyevitch, 65, 245n
Proust, Marcel, 90
Puccini, Giacomo, 21
Puck, 252n
Pudovkin, Vsevolod, 3, 5, 7, 10

Que Viva Mexico!, 31

Raft, George, 200, 254n
Rashomon, 33
Ravel, Maurice, 247n
Redes, 11
Redgrave, Michael, 9
Reinhardt, Jean Baptiste (Django), 77, 246n
Renoir, Jean, 11
"Rhapsody in Blue," 243n
Rice, Elmer, 167, 253n
Richardson, Dorothy, 7
River, The, 10

Roberts, Lee, 243n
Robertson, George, 13
Robison, Willard, 57, 244n
Room, Alexander, 11
Rose of Washington Square, 244n
Rossellini, Roberto, 12, 249n
R.U.R. (Rostrum's Universal Robots), 147, 164, 251n

Sacco, Nicola, 161, 163, 252n
Scarface, 200
Schary, Doré, 15
Schoedsack, Ernst, 254n
Schonberger, John, 245n
Schonberger, Malvin, 245n
Schopenhauer, Arthur, 173
Secrets of a Soul (Geheimnisse einer Seele), 147, 162, 164, 251n
Selznick, David, 26, 27
Sennett, Mack, 7
Seven Chances, 73, 245n
Severn, Joseph, 203
Shaftesbury Avenue Pavilion Cinema, 8
Shakespeare, William, 6, 34, 119, 148, 255n
Shaw, George Bernard, 31, 130, 249n, 253n
Shelley, Percy Bysshe, 204, 222
Shore Leave, 251n
"Show Me the Way to Go Home," 221
Singleton, Penny, 10
Smart Set, The, 159, 252n
"Smiles," 56, 105, 135, 136, 137, 138, 140, 190, 243n
"Somebody Loves Me," 49, 243n
Song of Ceylon, The, 13
Sonnenaufgang (see also *Sunrise*), 8
Sophocles, 35, 130, 161, 252n
Spender, Stephen, 30
S.S. Tenacity, 130, 250n
Stalin, Joseph, 155, 173
Storm Over Asia, 10

Strand, Paul, 11
"Strange Comfort Afforded by the Profession," 36, 254n
Strauss, Richard, 130
Street, The, 8, 11
Student of Prague, 4
Sunrise, 8, 13, 31, 60, 244n. See also *Sonnenaufgang*
"Sur le Pont d'Avignon," 132
"Sweet Georgia Brown," 77, 246n

Taylor, Frank, 14, 15, 17, 18, 19, 20, 21, 22, 23, 24, 25, 26, 28, 29, 32, 37, 38
"Tea for Two," 164
ten Holder, Clemens, 3, 4, 36
Tender is the Night (by F. Scott Fitzgerald), 12, 17, 18, 19, 22, 25, 26, 27, 28, 34, 175, 244n
Thomas, Dylan, 21
Three Ages, 245n
"Through the Panama," 32, 37, 254n, 255n
Thunder Over Mexico, 31
Time, 97, 252n
Timon of Athens, 34, 35
Toller, Ernst, 166, 252n
Tracy, Jess, 227
Trelawny, Edward John, 204
Twentieth Century-Fox, 23, 24, 26
Typhoon, 187

Ufa (Universum Film Aktien Gesellschaft), 4
Ultramarine, 8, 31, 254n
Ulysses, 7, 34
Un du 22iéme, 11
Under the Volcano, 3, 4, 5, 6, 7, 8, 9, 10, 11, 12, 13, 14, 17, 19, 20, 22, 23, 25, 26, 27, 29, 30, 31, 32, 33, 34, 35, 36, 37, 38, 47, 250n, 252n

"Valentine," 79
Valentino, Rudolph, 250n
Vallee, Rudy, 251n
Van Sickle, Vernon, 13
Vancouver Film Society, 4, 12, 20
Vanzetti, Bartolomeo, 161, 163, 252n
Veidt, Conrad, 4
Veille d'Armes, 13
Venuti, Giuseppe (Joe), 11, 69, 70, 164, 245n, 246n
Vie Parisienne, La, 119
Vildrac, Charles, 250n
Von Morgens bis Mitternachts (From Morn to Midnight), 117, 166, 249n
von Stroheim, Eric, 198, 254n
Vortex, The, 221, 254n
Voyage du Cachalot, 186
"Voyage That Never Ends, The," 36, 37, 38

Wagner, Richard, 245n
Waring, Fred, 251n
Welles, Orson, 3, 14, 34
"Whiffenpoof Song, The," 153, 199
"Whispering," 68, 198, 199, 245n
Whiting, Richard, 244n
Wiene, Robert, 4
Wilder, Billy, 12
Winged Victory, 251n
Winters, Shelley, 21
Wright, Basil, 8

Yeats, William Butler, 252n
You Only Live Once, 247n
Youmans, Vincent, 252n
Young Man with a Horn, 57, 244n

Zwingli, Ulrich, 145